DK EYEWITNESS TRAVEL

Philadelphia

& The Pennsylvania Dutch Country

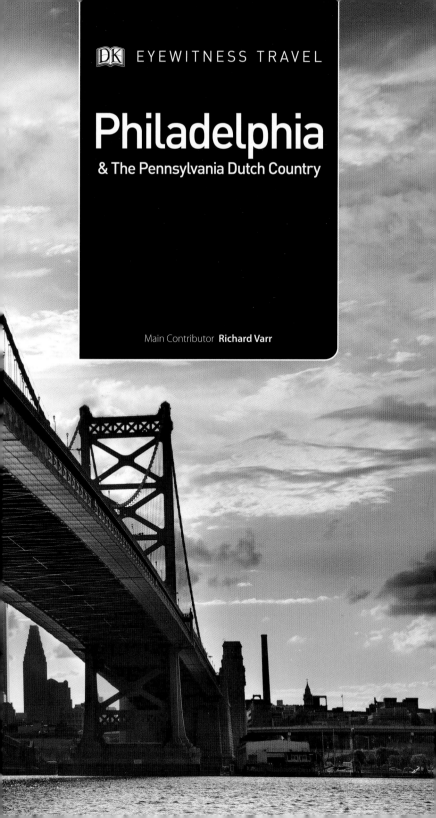

DK EYEWITNESS TRAVEL

Philadelphia
& The Pennsylvania Dutch Country

Main Contributor **Richard Varr**

Penguin Random House

Managing Editor Aruna Ghose
Art Editor Benu Joshi
Editors Ankita Awasthi, Bhavna Seth Ranjan
Designers Mathew Kurien, Divya Saxena, Shruti Singhi
Senior Cartographer Uma Bhattacharya
Cartographic Researcher Suresh Kumar
Picture Researcher Taiyaba Khatoon
DTP Coordinator Shailesh Sharma
DTP Designer Vinod Harish

Main Contributor Richard Varr

Photographer Demetrio Carrasco

Illustrators
Arun Pottirayil, T. Gautam Trivedi, Mark Warner

Printed and bound in Malaysia

First American Edition 2005
17 18 19 20 10 9 8 7 6 5 4 3 2 1

Published in the United States by
DK Publishing, 345 Hudson Street,
New York, New York 10014

Reprinted with revisions 2007, 2009, 2011, 2013, 2015, 2017

Copyright © 2005, 2017 Dorling Kindersley Limited, London
A Penguin Random House Company

Published in the UK by Dorling Kindersley Limited.

A catalog record for this book is available from the Library of Congress.

ISSN: 1542-1554
ISBN: 978-1-46546-130-8

MIX
Paper from responsible sources
FSC
www.fsc.org **FSC™ C018179**

Imposing statue of President Washington at Washington Square

Introducing Philadelphia and the Pennsylvania Dutch Country

A colorful fresco outside Market Street entrance, Philadelphia

The information in this DK Eyewitness Travel Guide is checked regularly.
Every effort has been made to ensure that this book is as up-to-date as possible at the time of going to press. Some details, however, such as telephone numbers, opening hours, prices, gallery hanging arrangements and travel information are liable to change. The publishers cannot accept responsibility for any consequences arising from the use of this book, nor for any material on third party websites, and cannot guarantee that any website address in this book will be a suitable source of travel information. We value the views and suggestions of our readers very highly. Please write to: Publisher, DK Eyewitness Travel Guides, Dorling Kindersley, 80 Strand, London, WC2R 0RL, UK, or email: travelguides@dk.com.

◀ **Title page** Ben Franklin Bridge against the skyline of Philadelphia at sunset   **Front cover image** Philadelphia City Hall, USA
Back cover image Ben Franklin Bridge and the Philadelphia skyline reflected in the Delaware River

Contents

Philadelphia Area by Area

Townhouses in a tree-lined street, Philadelphia

The 18th-century Independence Hall

Travelers' Needs

Survival Guide

HOW TO USE THIS GUIDE

This travel guide helps you get the most from your visit to Philadelphia. It provides detailed practical information and expert recommendations. *Introducing Philadelphia* maps the city and the region, sets it in its historical and cultural context, and describes events through the entire year. *Philadelphia at a Glance* is an overview of the city's main attractions. The main sightseeing section of the book is *Philadelphia Area by Area*, which covers all the important sights, with photographs, maps, and illustrations. *Farther Afield* suggests sights just outside the city core, while *Beyond Philadelphia* describes Dutch Country and historic Gettysburg, among other areas. Information about hotels, restaurants, shopping, entertainment, and sports is found in *Travelers' Needs*. The *Survival Guide* has practical advice on everything from using Philadelphia's medical services and transport system to public telephones and post offices.

Finding Your Way Around the Sightseeing Section

Each of the four sightseeing areas in Philadelphia is color-coded for easy reference. Every chapter opens with an introduction to the area of the city it covers, describing its history and character, and has a Street-by-Street map illustrating an interesting part of that area. Finding your way around the chapter is made simple by the numbering system used throughout. Sights outside Philadelphia have a regional map.

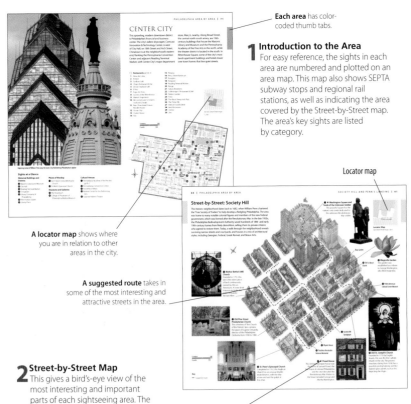

Each area has color-coded thumb tabs.

1 Introduction to the Area
For easy reference, the sights in each area are numbered and plotted on an area map. This map also shows SEPTA subway stops and regional rail stations, as well as indicating the area covered by the Street-by-Street map. The area's key sights are listed by category.

Locator map

A locator map shows where you are in relation to other areas in the city.

A suggested route takes in some of the most interesting and attractive streets in the area.

2 Street-by-Street Map
This gives a bird's-eye view of the most interesting and important parts of each sightseeing area. The numbering of the sights ties in with the preceding area map and with the fuller descriptions of the entries on the pages that follow.

Stars indicate the sights that no visitor should miss.

Philadelphia Area Map

The colored areas shown on this map *(see inside front cover)* are the four main sightseeing districts used in this guide. Each area is covered in detail in *Philadelphia Area by Area (see pp38–111)*, as are sights located outside the city center and the walks. These areas are also highlighted on other maps throughout the book. In *Philadelphia at a Glance (see pp26–33)*, for example, they help locate the top sights.

Numbers refer to each sight's position on the area map and its place in the chapter.

Practical information provides everything you need to know to visit each sight. Map references pinpoint the sight's location on the *Street Finder maps (see pp190–97)*.

3 Detailed Information

All the important sights in Philadelphia are described individually. They are listed in order, following the numbering on the area map at the start of the section. Practical information includes telephone numbers, opening hours, and map reference. The key to the symbols used is on the back flap.

The visitors' checklist provides all the practical information needed to plan your visit.

Story boxes provide information about historical or cultural topics relating to the sights.

4 Philadelphia's Major Sights

These are given two or more full pages in the sightseeing area where they are found. Historic buildings are dissected to reveal their interiors; color-coded floor plans in museums and galleries help you find important exhibits.

Stars recommend the features that no visitor should miss.

INTRODUCING PHILADELPHIA
AND THE PENNSYLVANIA DUTCH COUNTRY

GREAT DAYS IN PHILADELPHIA

You could easily spend a few weeks enjoying all the historic sights and attractions in Philadelphia, not to mention separate excursions to the Pennsylvania Dutch Country and Gettysburg. Most visitors, however, only have a few days and will want to make the most of their time. Outlined here are ideas for four separate days of sightseeing and enjoyment – three of them in Philadelphia and one in the Pennsylvania Dutch Country. They include suggestions on what to see, where to eat, and what to do for entertainment. Of course, the suggestions are just that, and can be modified to suit your requirements. The prices are indicative of the cost of transport and admission (if any) for two adults or a family of four.

Interior of Congress Hall, adjacent to Independence Hall

Historic Philadelphia

Two adults allow at least $120

- **Tour Independence Hall and National Constitution Center**
- **Lunch at Bourse Building**
- **Tour historic Old City**
- **Watch the Lights of Liberty Show**

Morning
It is best to arrive at the **Independence Visitor Center** *(see p47)* when it opens at 8:30am to pick up your free, timed tickets to **Independence Hall** *(see pp44–5)*. The earlier you arrive, the better the chances of being admitted quickly. Note that tickets are usually gone by noon. Once you have your tickets, the day can be planned accordingly. Visitors are first guided through the **Liberty Bell Center** *(see p46)*, and should spend the remainder of the morning visiting the **National Constitution Center** *(see pp50–51)*. Stop for lunch at the upscale food court in **The Bourse** *(see p143)* in Independence Mall East.

Afternoon
Start off by visiting the **Christ Church Burial Ground** *(see p48)*, where Benjamin Franklin is buried. Allow 15 to 30 minutes here, and then go on to take a half-hour tour of the **Betsy Ross House** *(see p54)*. Visit the Colonial portrait gallery at the **Second Bank of the United States** *(see p49)* and pass by the imposing façades of the **First Bank of the United States** *(see p55)* and the **Philadelphia Merchants' Exchange** *(see p56)*. The **City Tavern** *(see p57)* is a good place to stop for some refreshment.

In the evening, take in the one-hour **Lights of Liberty Show** *(see p187)*, the premier night-time 3D experience. It features spectacular images flashed onto historic buildings, taking visitors on a starlit journey through Independence National Historical Park. Reservations required.

A Shopping Day

Two adults allow at least $80

- **Browse boutiques along Rittenhouse Row**
- **Lunch at Rittenhouse Square**
- **Visit King of Prussia Mall**

Morning
Start by browsing through the elegant boutiques on **Rittenhouse Row** *(see p156)*, which has such high-fashion names as and Ann Taylor. Also visit the nearby **Shops at Liberty Place** *(see p156)*. As noon approaches, check out the specialty shops at the **Bellevue Building** *(see p156)*

Mural at Italian Market, famous for specialty foods and eateries

and then have a quick bite at the building's upbeat food court. For restaurants with outdoor seating, head toward **Rittenhouse Square** *(see p80)*. **Devon Seafood Grill**, **Smith & Wollensky**, and **Parc** are good choices *(see p149)*.

Afternoon
Visit **Fashion Outlets Philadelphia** mall *(see p156)* for some more shopping. Do not miss the nearby **Reading Terminal Market** *(see p75)*, and if you have time left over, head to the **Italian Market** *(see p101)* for coffee and Italian pastries. End your spree by taking a SEPTA bus to visit the colossal **King of Prussia Mall** *(see p156)*.

The Franklin Institute in the Parkway Museums District

A Family Day

Family of four allow at least $240

- **Visit a museum around Logan Square**
- **Walk along Penn's Landing**
- **Take the RiverLink ferry**
- **Visit the Adventure Aquarium**

Morning
Visit one of the four museums along the Benjamin Franklin Parkway – **the Franklin Institute** *(see p87)*, the **Academy of Natural Sciences** *(see p87)*, the **Barnes Foundation** *(see pp88–9)*, or the **Philadelphia Museum of Art** *(see pp92–5)*. Break for lunch at one of the museum cafeterias before

heading to the interactive **Please Touch Museum** *(see p170)* for children up to the age of seven.

Afternoon
After lunch, head over to **Penn's Landing** *(see p68)* and visit the **Independence Seaport Museum** *(see pp66–7)*. Alternatively, take the RiverLink Ferry to the **Camden Waterfront** *(see p103)*. The ferry runs from May through September. Make it a point to head to the **Adventure Aquarium** *(see p173)*, as the kids will love the aquatic life there. In the warmer months, the **Ghost Tour of Philadelphia** *(see p187)* is a great option for an evening activity. In winter, ice-skate on one of the city's many rinks such as the **Blue Cross RiverRink** *(see pp168–9)*.

Pennsylvania Dutch Country

Family of four allow at least $230

- **Tour Landis Valley Museum**
- **Have an Amish-style lunch**
- **Visit the Amish Experience**
- **Hop on board the Strasburg Railroad**

Morning
Arrive at **Lancaster Central Market** *(see p116)* by 8am to eat a hearty country breakfast. Only a few minutes' away is the **Rock Ford Plantation**

The Blacksmith Shop at the Landis Valley Museum

(see p116). Go on to the **Landis Valley Museum** *(see pp118–19)* off Route 272 and spend some time exploring this living history village that provides an insight into the region's early farming communities. Head east on Route 340 through Bird-in-Hand and stop for a family-style lunch at the **Plain and Fancy Farm Restaurant** *(see p153)*, next to the **Amish Experience** *(see p120)*.

Afternoon
Visit the Amish Experience and wander through the Country Homestead, a typical Amish home. Then watch the multimedia cultural presentation, *Jacob's Choice*, at the Amish Experience Theater. Spend the second part of the afternoon at Kitchen Kettle Village in **Intercourse** *(see p120)*, shopping for crafts and jarred foods. During the summer months, you can extend the day by hopping onto the 7pm train on the **Strasburg Railroad** *(see p121)* for the last ride through miles of farmland.

Tourists shopping for art and antiques in Lancaster

2 Days in Philadelphia

- Walk through atmospheric Independence National Historic Park
- Admire the panoramic views from the top of the tower at City Hall
- Immerse yourself in art at the Philadelphia Museum of Art

Day 1
Morning Start with a free guided tour of **Independence National Historical Park** *(pp42–3)*, which has some of the city's oldest buildings, including the **Liberty Bell Center** *(pp46–7)*. Then branch out into other parts of the Old City, stop at **Christ Church** *(p54)*, and walk down the cobbled **Elfreth's Alley** *(p54)*. Next, head to the **National Constitution Center** *(pp50–51)*.

Afternoon Take a stroll through leafy **Society Hill** *(pp60–61)*, pausing for reflection at its beautiful churches, such as **Mother Bethel** *(p62)*, before reaching the Delaware River at **Penn's Landing** *(p68)*. The main attraction here is the **Independence Seaport Museum** *(pp66–7)*, which boasts a wealth of maritime history.

Day 2
Morning Head straight for **City Hall** *(p74–5)* and enjoy splendid 360-degree views of the city from the viewing deck in the tower. Afterwards, admire some of the renowned works of art on display at the **Pennsylvania Academy of the Fine Arts** *(pp76–7)*, America's oldest art museum. Next, visit the photogenic **Reading Terminal Market** *(p75)* for a snack.

Afternoon Pick up the trail for the **Parkway Museums District** *(pp84–5)* with a look around grand **Logan Square** *(p86)*. At the far end of the Parkway, you can emulate Sylvester Stallone by jogging up the "Rocky steps" to the **Philadelphia Museum of Art** *(pp92–5)* which is full of exquisite works from around the world. End the day by relaxing in the expansive natural surroundings of **Fairmount Park** *(p99)*.

Betsy Ross House, one of the most visited historic sites in Philadelphia

3 Days in Philadelphia

- Travel back in time with a stroll along Elfreth's Alley
- Admire sculptures at the Rodin Museum
- Meander along the banks of the Delaware River to Penn's Landing

Day 1
Morning Bask in the city's history in quaint **Elfreth's Alley** *(p54)*, said to be the nation's oldest continuously inhabited street. Pay your respects to luminaries buried at **Christ Church** *(p48)* and the creator of the first American flag at the **Betsy Ross House** *(p54)*. Complete the morning by touring the austere **Independence National Historical Park** *(pp42–3)*, **Independence Hall** *(pp44–5)*, and the **Liberty Bell Center** *(pp46–7)*.

Afternoon Sign an interactive version of America's constitution at the **National Constitution Center** *(pp50–51)*, before

heading down Market Street to **City Hall** *(p74–5)*, where you can admire the Mayor's Reception Room. Later visit the **Pennsylvania Academy of the Fine Arts** *(pp76–7)* that houses works by Homer, Eakins, and Hassam.

Day 2
Morning Start the day by sipping coffee under the Swann Memorial Fountain in **Logan Square** *(p86)* and then visit the nearby **Franklin Institute** *(p87)*, with its wealth of scientific and technological exhibits. At the far end of the Parkway, don't miss treasures such as van Gogh's *Sunflowers* and stunning Asian sculpture at the **Philadelphia Museum of Art** *(pp76–7)*. Unwind with a picnic in lush **Fairmount Park** *(p99)*, which borders the Schuylkill River.

Afternoon Refreshed, take in the bold sculptures at the **Rodin Museum** *(p90)*, then cross the road to **The Barnes Foundation** *(p88–9)*, where you will find paintings by the likes of Renoir, Cézanne and Matisse. End the afternoon by catching the last of the action at **Reading Terminal Market** *(p75)* and grabbing some inexpensive treats to eat.

Day 3
Morning Begin with an early walk through Race Street Pier park to **Penn's Landing** *(p68)* on the banks of the Delaware River. Explore vessels such as Submarine *Becuna* and Cruiser *Olympia*, part of **Independence Seaport Museum** *(pp66–7)*. Spend some time relaxing at either the **Rose** or **Magnolia Garden** *(p64)*.

The Independence National Historical Park in the neighborhood of Old City

For practical information on travelling around Philadelphia, see pp186-87

Afternoon If it's a fine day, **Philadelphia Zoo** *(p100)* offers a vast collection of creatures to admire. The interesting **University of Pennsylvania Museum of Archaeology and Anthropology** *(p101)* provides backup in inclement weather. Take transport out to attractive colonial **Germantown** *(p98)*, with its appealing architecture.

5 Days in Philadelphia

- Learn about USA's fight for freedom at the National Constitution Center
- Witness the life of the Amish in Pennsylvania Dutch Country
- Picture the carnage of the Civil War in the countryside around Gettysburg

Day 1
Morning Marvel at the creative genius on display at the **Philadelphia Museum of Art** *(pp92–5)*, where one of the star exhibits is a re-creation of a cloister from a medieval French abbey. Farther down the Parkway, admire the ingenuity behind the inventions displayed at the **Franklin Institute** *(p87)*. Take a lunch break in the impressive surroundings of **Logan Square** *(p86)*.

Afternoon Continue with a visit to **City Hall** *(pp74–5)* and see the imposing interiors of some of the official chambers. Feast your eyes on wonderful art, such as Vincent Desiderio's triptych Pantocrator, at the **Pennsylvania Academy of the Fine Arts** *(pp76–7)*. After a call at the Gothic Revival **St Mark's Episcopal Church** *(p80)*, end the day at classy **Rittenhouse Square** *(p80)*, famous for its fine dining.

Day 2
Morning Book a free tour of **Independence National Historic Park** *(pp42–3)*, to see where some important events in the United States' inception happened. Call by the burial ground at **Christ Church** *(p48)*, final resting place of Benjamin Franklin, before visiting the historic **Betsy Ross**

The scenic Fairmount Park, part of Philadelphia's greenbelt

House *(p54)*. Later, pass through **Elfreth's Alley** *(p54)*, with its row of early 18th-century houses.

Evening Visit the **Independence Seaport Museum** *(pp66–7)*, which boasts much seafaring paraphernalia. Then explore the rest of **Penn's Landing** *(p68)*, the renovated southern end of Philadelphia's port, and walk through **Society Hill** *(pp60–61)*, home to many fine restaurants.

Day 3
Morning The absorbing **National Constitution Center** *(pp50–51)* provides an instructive insight into early American history. Next, visit the equally informative **African American Museum** *(p53)* nearby. From there it's only a few blocks to the lively **Chinatown** *(p78)*.

Afternoon Get serious with The Thinker, who sits ponderously in the grounds of the delightful **Rodin Museum** *(p90)*. Move on to **the Barnes Foundation** *(p88–9)*, housing a superb collection of Impressionist and Postimpressionist paintings. Get some fresh air in **Fairmount Park** *(p99)* or visit **Eastern State Penitentiary** *(p91)*, one time home of Al Capone.

Day 4
Morning Grab some breakfast in colourful **Reading Terminal Market** *(p75)* before heading to the enjoyable **Philadelphia Zoo** *(p100)* or the impressive **University of Pennsylvania Museum of Archaeology and Anthropology** *(p101)*. Drive up to **Germantown** *(p98)* for lunch on one of its colonial streets.

Afternoon Carry on along US-30 into the heart of Pennsylvania Dutch Country. Stop at authentic farms in villages with names such as **Paradise** *(p121)*, **Bird-in-Hand** *(p120)*, and **Intercourse** *(p120)*. Also visit the county town of **Lancaster** *(p116)* and the frozen-in-time **Landis Valley Museum** complex *(pp118–19)*.

Day 5
Morning Divide the morning between **Harrisburg** *(p126)*, home of the Pennsylvania State Capitol and the National Civil War Museum, and nearby **Hershey** *(p126)*. Famed for the eponymous chocolate, you can choose between several fun, kid-friendly activities and theme parks.

Afternoon End your tour in **Gettysburg** *(pp122–5)*, scene of the Civil War's most famous battle. Get your history right at the superb Visitor Center Museum, before taking a guided or self-guided car tour of the **National Military Park** *(pp124–5)*.

The ornate Friendship Gate at the entrance to Chinatown

Putting Philadelphia on the Map

Located in the northeast region of the United States, Philadelphia sits on the southeastern edge of Pennsylvania along the Delaware River, which separates Pennsylvania from New Jersey. Founded by William Penn in the late 17th century, Philadelphia is now the nation's fifth-largest city and the second largest on the East Coast. More than 1.5 million people live within the city's 135-sq-mile (350-sq-km) area.

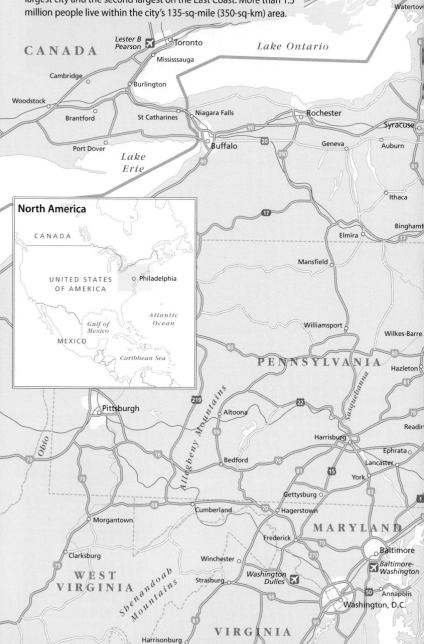

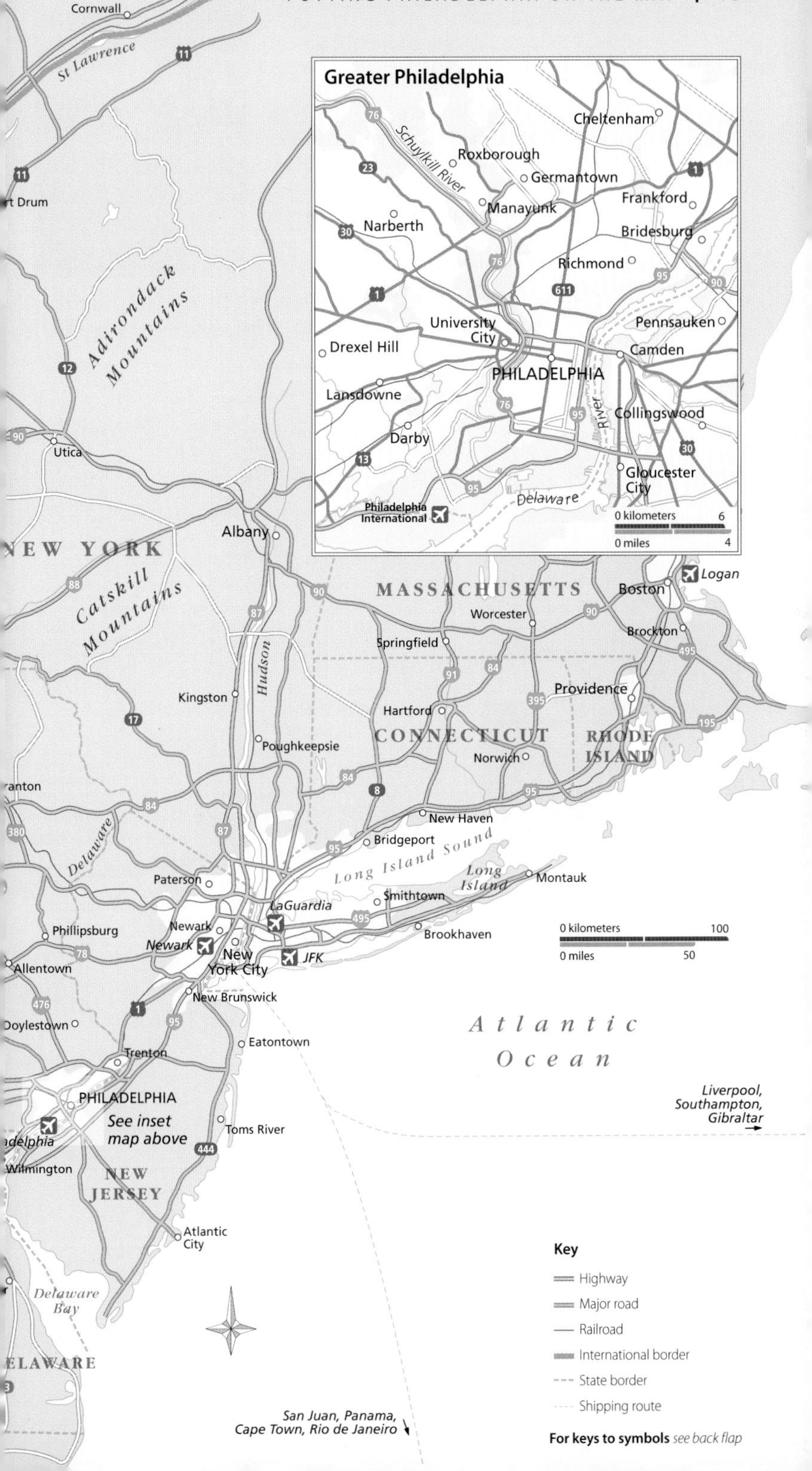

Cornwall

St Lawrence

11

11

rt Drum

Adirondack Mountains

12

90

Utica

Greater Philadelphia

76

Schuylkill River

23

Roxborough

Germantown

Manayunk

30

Narberth

1

611

University City

Drexel Hill

Lansdowne

76

Darby

13

95

Philadelphia International

Cheltenham

Frankford

1

Bridesburg

Richmond

95

90

Pennsauken

PHILADELPHIA

Camden

Collingswood

River

30

Gloucester City

Delaware

0 kilometers 6

0 miles 4

NEW YORK

Catskill Mountains

88

Albany

37

Hudson

Kingston

17

Poughkeepsie

MASSACHUSETTS

90

Worcester

Springfield

91

84

Hartford

CONNECTICUT

Norwich

8

Boston

Logan

90

Brockton

495

395

Providence

195

RHODE ISLAND

195

ranton

Delaware

84

87

95

Paterson

LaGuardia

Newark

Newark

New York City

JFK

Phillipsburg

78

Allentown

476

Doylestown

95

1

Trenton

380

New Brunswick

Eatontown

New Haven

Bridgeport

Long Island Sound

Smithtown

Long Island

495

Brookhaven

Montauk

65

0 kilometers 100

0 miles 50

A t l a n t i c

O c e a n

Liverpool, Southampton, Gibraltar →

PHILADELPHIA

See inset map above

delphia

Wilmington

NEW JERSEY

Toms River

444

Atlantic City

Delaware Bay

ELAWARE

San Juan, Panama, Cape Town, Rio de Janeiro ↘

Key

━━ Highway

━━ Major road

─── Railroad

▬▬ International border

--- State border

····· Shipping route

For keys to symbols *see back flap*

Central Philadelphia

Flanked by the Delaware and Schuylkill rivers, central Philadelphia comprises several distinct neighborhoods, which together span more than three centuries of development. Much of the modern-day layout is based on city founder William Penn's original grid pattern – a crisscross of streets with five green squares. Four of these squares remain as pleasant, shaded parks today. The fifth, Penn's original Center Square, contains City Hall. The oldest districts are Old City and Society Hill.

Central Philadelphia
Center City *(see pp70–81)* skyscrapers can be seen along the Schuylkill River.

Statue of George Washington at The Oval
A prominent equestrian statue pays tribute to America's founding father and first president against the backdrop of the imposing temple-like façade of the Philadelphia Museum of Art *(see pp92–5)*.

Rittenhouse Square
One of William Penn's original five squares, this Center City park *(see p80)* is popular with downtown workers and residents. Extravagant high-rise buildings and upscale restaurants surround the square.

For keys to symbols *see back flap*

Key

☐ Star sight

Old City Hall
Located next to Independence Hall *(see pp44–5)* in the heart of Old City, where a new nation was born in 1776, Philadelphia's Old City Hall was home to the US Supreme Court from 1791 to 1800.

Penn's Landing
This waterfront area hosts summer festivals and is home to the city's tall ships, the submarine *Becuna* and the USS *Olympia*. Also located here is the Independence Seaport Museum *(see pp66–7)*.

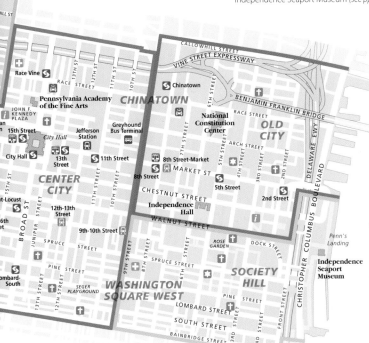

THE HISTORY OF PHILADELPHIA

William Penn first landed in the New World in 1682. Armed with a land charter, he founded a colony based on religious freedom that just a century later would give birth to a new nation. Penn named the new city Philadelphia, derived from Greek words meaning "City of Brotherly Love."

Before William Penn's arrival, the Delaware River basin and the Schuylkill River watershed were inhabited by Algonquian-speaking Native Americans known as Lenni-Lenape. They were mostly peaceful hunters and gatherers, and many lived along the Delaware River and its tributaries. They were named "Delawares" for that reason by the first European settlers.

First European Explorers and Settlers

Chartered by the Dutch East India Company, Englishman Henry Hudson's ship, the *Half Moon*, sailed into Delaware Bay in 1609 and claimed it for Holland. Dutch navigators followed shortly after: Captain Cornelius Hendricksen sailed up the Delaware in 1616 to where it meets the Schuylkill River; and in 1623, Cornelius Jacobsen explored the region further, leading to the establishment of a number of trading posts, including one on the Schuylkill in 1633.

The first settlement in what is now Pennsylvania, however, did not occur until 1643, when Swedish Lutheran settlers – who had first settled in Wilmington,

Delaware, in 1638 – established their capital of New Sweden on Tinicum Island, near present-day Philadelphia. Eight years later, the Dutch, whose previous colonial efforts had been directed elsewhere, seized control and annexed the region as part of the Dutch Colony. From 1655 to 1664, the Dutch controlled the area until the English captured the Dutch colonies, calling them New York, after the Duke of York.

The Founding of Pennsylvania and Philadelphia

The son of a wealthy British admiral, William Penn was born in 1644. While attending Oxford University, Penn joined the Religious Society of Friends, the Quakers, a group who worshiped, without dogma or clergy, silently, in unadorned meetinghouses. The faith was based on pacifism and equality. Expelled from university, Penn was later harassed and even imprisoned for his devotion to Quakerism. However, his wealth and social position allowed him to retain influence in the king's court.

1609 Explorer Henry Hudson sails into Delaware Bay

Henry Hudson, English navigator

1638 Swedish Lutheran settlers arrive in Wilmington, Delaware

1644 Birth of William Penn

1664 England takes control of the Dutch colonies

1600	1615	1630	1645	1660	1675

1616 Dutch Captain Cornelius Hendricksen sails up the Delaware to the Schuylkill River

1623 Dutchman Cornelius Jacobsen explores the region further

1643 Swedes establish capital on Tinicum Island near present-day Philadelphia

1655 Dutch seize control of New Sweden

◀ Detail from *Penn's Treaty with the Indians* by Edward Hicks, 1830–1840

William Penn receiving the Charter for Pennsylvania from King Charles II of England

The Charter for Pennsylvania was founded in 1681 as a result of a debt owed by King Charles II to Penn's father. The king repaid the £16,000 debt by granting the younger Penn land between Maryland and New York. In October 1682, Penn's ship, the *Welcome*, landed at New Castle in Delaware with many Quaker passengers. A few days later, Penn sailed up the Delaware to the capital of his new colony: Philadelphia.

As a Quaker, Penn espoused nonviolence, and one of his first initiatives was to reach an agreement with the Delawares, thus forming treaties and enduring friendships with the Native Americans. The new colony also promised religious freedom, and was seen as a "Holy Experiment." More settlers followed, including both English and Dutch Quakers, German Mennonites, and the Amish, who settled in what is now called Pennsylvania Dutch Country.

Penn and surveyor Thomas Holmes designed Philadelphia in a grid pattern between the Delaware and Schuylkill Rivers. Their plan included five public spaces, as Penn and Holmes wanted to create a "green countrie towne." These tree-lined areas – Washington, Rittenhouse, Logan, and Franklin Squares – still remain today. City Hall now occupies the original "Center Square" at the junction of Market and Broad Streets.

Colonial Expansion

At the beginning of the 18th century, Philadelphia was already witnessing rapid growth. Penn had left Philadelphia in 1684

Detail from *Peaceable Kingdom* by Edward Hicks (1780–1849), painted in 1826

1683 Penn signs treaty with Delawares	**1684** Penn leaves Philadelphia and returns to England	**1699** Penn returns to Philadelphia	**1701** Penn grants charter to City of Philadelphia	**1718** Death of Penn in England
1680	**1690**	**1700**	**1710**	
	1682 Penn arrives in Pennsylvania and establishes Philadelphia			
Gloria Dei Church **1677** Swedes establish Gloria Dei church			**1701** Penn leaves America for good and returns to England	**1710** Christ Church built at 2nd Street

but returned in 1699 to find the population at more than 7,000. In October 1701, he granted a charter to the City of Philadelphia and left for England, never to return. As a port city, Philadelphia soon became an important center of commerce, with imports of sugar, rum, and molasses from the Caribbean. As trade flourished, so did manufacturing and shipbuilding. An increase in the number of homes led to a burgeoning community of craftsmen. The city also boasted a paper mill, furnaces, distilleries, tanneries, and a glass factory. One of its most famous residents, Benjamin Franklin (see p55), arrived from Boston in 1723. His achievements as a scientist, inventor, printer, publisher, and statesman turned Philadelphia into a cultural center. In 1751, along with physician Thomas Bond, Franklin founded Pennsylvania Hospital, America's first public hospital.

Franklin, famous Philadelphia resident

The mid-1700s saw a clash between pacifist Quaker beliefs and the need to establish defenses for the colony. Pennsylvania was part of the British Empire and was involved in skirmishes against the French over land in North America. The conflicts climaxed with the French and Indian War, fought between the French and the British from 1754 to 1763, where a 21-year-old native of Virginia named George Washington received his first command. Britain was

eventually victorious, but the war's end signaled a turning point for colonists, who now craved independence from Britain.

New Nation Takes Shape

On July 4 1776, independence from Britain was declared in Philadelphia, and in 1789 George Washington was elected the first president of the fledgling nation. The city remained the political heart of the country for a decade, serving as the capital from 1790 until 1800. During this time, America's first bank was chartered in 1791 to unify the nation's currency and to pay off war debts. The US Mint was established the following year.

In 1793, Philadelphia suffered a yellow fever epidemic, resulting in a large loss of life. Despite this, immigrants continued to flock to the city, increasing its population to nearly 70,000 by 1800, making it America's largest city at the time.

Yellow fever epidemic in Philadelphia, 1793

1723 Benjamin Franklin arrives from Boston

1743 Franklin founds American Philosophical Society

1754 Start of the French and Indian War

1763 French and Indian War ends

1720   1730   1740   1750   1760

1724 Carpenters' Company founded

Journal published by Franklin in 1741

1751 Pennsylvania Hospital founded

Pennsylvania Hospital

Colonial Philadelphia and the American Revolution

The years leading up to, including, and after the American Revolutionary War are arguably the most important years of the history of Philadelphia. Rebellion against British rule began as early as 1765 with opposition to taxation without representation in Congress. A decade later, the colonists elected Washington to lead their army – the Continental Army – in the war for independence. In 1776, the Declaration of Independence was signed in Philadelphia, though by 1777 the city was again occupied by British forces. Freedom was gained in 1781, and Britain at last recognized the colonies' independence with the 1783 Treaty of Paris. Five years later, the US Constitution *(see pp50–51)* was ratified at Independence Hall, Philadelphia.

George Washington
The Second Continental Congress elected Washington to lead the Continental Army against the British in 1775.

Drafting the Declaration
Thomas Jefferson wrote the first draft of the Declaration of Independence. Leaders of 13 North American colonies later ratified it at Independence Hall.

Declaration of Independence (1776)
Delegates of the Continental Congress ratified the Declaration of Independence on July 4, 1776. This 1817 John Trumbull painting shows the presentation of the Declaration by the drafting committee. The signing of the Declaration was completed that August.

1774 First Continental Congress held

1775 Second Continental Congress in Philadelphia

1776 Signing of the Declaration of Independence

1781 British surrender at Yorktown, Virginia

Postcard depicting George Washington

1789 George Washington elected nation's first president

1775

1780

1785

1777 Continental Army retreats after losing battles at Brandywine and Germantown

1776 Washington's army crosses Delaware River and defeats hired Hessian soldiers at Trenton

1783 Signing of the Treaty of Paris

1788 US Constitution ratified

Crossing the Delaware River
Washington's army crossed the Delaware River on Christmas Day in 1776, as depicted in this 1851 Emmanuel Leutze painting. They later defeated British troops at Princeton.

The Battle of Germantown (1777)
British troops barricaded themselves behind the stone walls of Cliveden, a Germantown mansion, forcing the Continental Army to retreat.

Valley Forge, 1777–78
After losing the battles of Brandywine and Germantown in 1777, Washington's army lost over 2,500 men to exposure and disease during the winter encampment here.

Adoption of the Constitution (1787)
In 1787, delegates from all 13 original states, except Rhode Island, gathered at the Constitutional Convention in Philadelphia to draft and adopt a Constitution for the new nation.

1790 Death of Benjamin Franklin

1793 Yellow fever epidemic kills 4,000

1800 Capital moves to Washington D.C.

White House, Washington D.C.

1790

1795

1800

1791 First Bank of the US chartered

The First Bank of the United States

1790 Philadelphia becomes the nation's capital

1799 Death of George Washington

The City & Port of Philadelphia (1800), engraving with watercolor by William Russell Birch

Industrialization

By the 1830s, the city's financial and political prominence had begun to wane, as Washington D.C., due to its location midway between the north and the south, became the nation's capital. Commercial activity and trade also diminished, as it could not compete with the more accessible port of New York City. Instead, Philadelphia turned to industry and manufacturing, becoming a regional center for textiles, iron and steel, and the shipping of coal. Shipbuilding continued along the Delaware. The city kept growing, with row houses built within the city limits and in surrounding boroughs and districts, including Germantown and Chestnut Hill. These areas soon became new neighborhoods by way of the city consolidation bill of 1854, under which they were incorporated within the city limits.

Growth also brought social clashes. For instance, there were rebellions against anti-slavery movements, and Pennsylvania Hall, the meeting place of the abolitionists, was set on fire in 1838. The 1840s saw violence against Catholics and immigrants, especially the Irish, with angry mobs burning down St. Augustine's Church, across from St. George's Church, in 1844.

Post Civil War Philadelphia

The need for weapons, munitions, uniforms, and warships for the Union forces bolstered Philadelphia's economy during the Civil War years (1861–65). During the nation's centennial celebrations in 1876, the city held one of the first World Fairs and dedicated grand new buildings, some of which can be seen even today. These include Memorial Hall, a Beaux-Arts structure in Fairmount Park, and the Victorian-style Pennsylvania Academy of the

Centennial Exhibition in 1876 at Fairmount Park, one of the oldest municipal parks in America

| | *Burning of St. Augustine* | **1844** Anti-Catholic rioters burn churches | **1856** Completion of Pennsylvania Railroad to Pittsburgh | **1876** City celebrates centennial with nation's first World Fair | **1907** First underground rail line commences | **1920s** Broad Street Subway completed |

| | **1840** | | **1860** | | **1880** | | **1900** | | **192(** |

1861 Civil War begins

1854 Surrounding boroughs incorporated

1838 Anti-abolitionists burn Pennsylvania Hall

Wagons from the Civil War era

1890s Electric trolleys introduced

1929 Gre Depressic begi

1914 World War I begins

Fine Arts. Politically, however, this was a time of corruption as Republican leaders controlled city contracts and thousands of jobs. Their influence only waned in the 1930s and 40s when voter support was lost due to allegations of corruption and financial mismanagement in city government.

Streetcar on 9th Street,
Philadelphia, 1921

The Early 20th Century

The city's infrastructure was well established by the end of the 19th century. For instance, its streetcar system was run by electric power as early as the 1890s. There were further improvements in mass transit with the completion of its first underground rail line, the Market Street Subway, in 1907. Economic and industrial activity in Philadelphia remained brisk during World War I (1914–18), though it registered a dip during the Great Depression of the 1920s and 30s. World War II (1939–45) revived steel, chemical, and petroleum production, but Philadelphia gradually lost most of its manufacturing sector to other regions of the US.

Modern Philadelphia

After World War II, the city lost jobs and population to the suburbs, and then underwent political restructuring in 1951, with a new city charter that called for a stronger mayor and new city departments. It was also a time of urban preservation efforts downtown, but some neighborhoods in the city's north and west deteriorated. Racial tensions mounted in the 1960s and through the mayoral terms of Frank Rizzo and W. Wilson Goode, the city's first African-American mayor, before stabilizing in the late 1980s. In 1985, during Goode's term as mayor, the controversial bombing of the headquarters of the black radical group MOVE, resulted in the deaths of 11 persons.

Today, Philadelphia's economy is diversified. While some manufacturing units remain, corporate business has gained ground. Companies here specialize in technology, banking, pharmaceuticals, and insurance. Tourism is also key to the local economy. The city has more than 80 universities, colleges, medical schools, and world-class hospitals. In 2008, Philadelphia bolstered its global presence by hosting two Olympic trials ahead of the Beijing games. In the same year, the baseball team, Philadelphia Phillies, won the World Series. In 2015, Pope Francis visited Philadelphia. The following year, the 2016 Democratic National Convention, which nominated Hillary Clinton as the party's presidential candidate, was hosted here. The Comcast Innovation & Technology Center became Philadelphia's tallest building, at 1,121 ft (342 m) in 2017.

Celebrations at the Democratic National Convention in 2016 in Philadelphia

1941 US enters World War II

1951 New city charter provides strong mayoral leadership

Wilson Goode, Philadelphia's first African-American mayor

1976 Bicentennial celebrations in Philadelphia

1985 Bombing of MOVE head-quarters

1990s Philadelphia becomes a model for urban renewal despite a declining population

2008 Philadelphia Phillies win the World Series

2015 Pope Francis concludes his US tour with a visit to Philadelphia

2016 City hosts Democratic National Convention

2014 Historic ruling overturning the ban of same-sex marriage in Pennsylvania

1940   1960   1980   2000   2020

PHILADELPHIA AT A GLANCE

Many of Philadelphia's most popular sights are to be found in Old City, within what's called "America's most historic square mile." They include Independence Hall *(see pp44–5)* and the iconic Liberty Bell *(see p46)*. Outstanding museums, including the Pennsylvania Academy of the Fine Arts *(see pp76–7)*, the Philadelphia Museum of Art *(see pp92–5)*, and the Barnes Foundation *(see pp88–9)*, are located in the city center. More than 100 places of interest are described in the *Area by Area* and *Beyond Philadelphia* sections of this book. To help you make the most of your stay, the following six pages are a guide to the best of Philadelphia, with a selection featured below.

Philadelphia's Top Ten Sights

Independence Hall
(see pp44–5)

Liberty Bell Center
(see p46)

The Barnes Foundation
(see pp88–9)

Fairmount Park
(see p99)

Pennsylvania Academy of the Fine Arts
(see pp76–7)

Philadelphia Museum of Art
(see pp92–5)

National Constitution Center
(see pp50–51)

Reading Terminal Market
(see p75)

Penn's Landing
(see p68)

Liberty Place
(see p81)

◀ The marble sculpture Semiramis in the arched foyer of the Pennsylvania Academy of the Fine Arts

Philadelphia's Best: Museums

Philadelphia has several world-famous museums that reflect its cultural diversity, as well as its maritime and colonial past. Many are along the Benjamin Franklin Parkway, including the Franklin Institute, the Academy of Natural Sciences, and the Philadelphia Museum of Art, which is the third-largest fine arts museum in the country. The Rodin Museum near Logan Square houses the largest collection of sculptor Auguste Rodin's works outside Paris, while the University of Pennsylvania Museum of Archaeology and Anthropology, across the Schuylkill River, has an excellent collection of artifacts from civilizations past and present. In 2012, the Barnes Foundation moved to the Benjamin Franklin Parkway. The foundation has an extraordinary collection of early French-modern and Postimpressionist art *(see pp88–9)*.

Philadelphia Museum of Art
This museum houses over 300,000 objects, including a 12th-century stone portal from a French Augustinian abbey *(see pp92–5)*.

Rodin Museum
The Shade is just one of nearly 130 plaster, bronze, and marble sculptures housed in an impressive temple-like structure along the Benjamin Franklin Parkway *(see p90)*.

LOGAN SQUARE
AND THE PARKW
MUSEUMS DISTR
(See pp82–95)

The Barnes Foundation
The foundation contains one of the world's leading collections of Impressionist, Postimpressionist, and early modern art, as well as African sculpture and much more *(see pp88–9)*.

Schuylkill River

BOUL

The Franklin Institute
The Giant Walk-Through Heart is a key exhibit of this children-friendly science museum named after statesman and inventor Benjamin Franklin *(see p87)*.

20TH STREET

Academy of Natural Sciences
A favorite exhibit at Philadelphia's natural history museum is Dinosaur Hall, home to fossil constructions of the largest carnivores to ever walk the earth *(see p87)*.

Pennsylvania Academy of the Fine Arts
An ornate, arched foyer is the entrance to the country's oldest fine art school and museum. It was founded in 1805 with a collection of American paintings by artists such as Benjamin West and Impressionist Mary Cassatt (see pp76–7).

The African American Museum in Philadelphia
This museum celebrates important aspects of African-American history through permanent and changing exhibitions (see p53).

Philadelphia History Museum at the Atwater Kent
On display here are more than 100,000 objects, including Norman Rockwell's *Saturday Evening Post* covers depicting "vignettes of daily life" (see p52).

VINE STREET
EXPRESSWAY

MARKET STREET

CENTER CITY
(See pp70–81)

OLD CITY
(See pp40–57)

WALNUT STREET

6TH STREET

3RD STREET

DELAWARE EXPRESSWAY

SOCIETY HILL AND
PENN'S LANDING
(See pp58–69)

National Museum of American Jewish History
Housed in an impressive five-story building overlooking Independence Square, this museum explores over 350 years of American Jewish history (see pp48–9).

0 meters 500
0 yards 500

Independence Seaport Museum
A prominent seafaring museum, showcasing the submarine *Becuna* and the cruiser *Olympia*. This view (right) is of the interior of the submarine *Becuna* (see pp66–7).

Philadelphia's Architecture

Early architectural styles, derived from the colonists' native Britain, can still be seen in the older areas of Philadelphia. Colonial buildings incorporated simple Georgian and Palladian designs, which evolved into a bolder Federal style, with touches of Roman and Greek classical styles. The 19th century brought grander designs fueled by the Victorian era and the French-influenced Beaux-Arts style, which inspired many of the city's architectural wonders along the Benjamin Franklin Parkway. While modernist buildings crowd parts of Center City, it is the scattering of Postmodernist skyscrapers that enliven the city skyline.

Philadelphia Merchants' Exchange, an example of the Greek Revival style

Betsy Ross House, a simple Georgian-style structure

Georgian

Named after three British kings called George, this architectural style proliferated in early 18th-century Britain and soon became popular in colonial Philadelphia. Developed from the Roman Palladian style and often with columned façades, many of the early Georgian-style designs in the colonies were less elaborate than their English counterparts.

Independence Hall (see pp44–5) is a Georgian structure influenced by the style of English master architect Christopher Wren, while Christ Church (see p54) is a bold example of Georgian ecclesiastical architecture. Colonial Georgian-style homes include the Germantown White House, which was George Washington's summer retreat, and Cliveden, both in Germantown (see pp108–9). Both houses have columned

doorways and nine front windows. A more simple home is the Betsy Ross House (see p54).

Federal

In colonial America, the Georgian style quickly evolved into a more sophisticated Federal style, often with classical Greek and Roman influences. Particularly popular after the American Revolution until about 1820, this architectural style is characterized by oval and circular rooms, classical entryway detailing, rounded fanlights over doors, and Palladian windows. Also typical of this style are freestanding mansions and town houses with symmetrical brick façades and shuttered windows. Entrances are often cut from granite slabs and feature gently fluted columns. The largest and most elegant rooms of Federal houses are usually found on

the second floor. Some stately examples of such architecture are Old City Hall, Congress Hall, and the east and west wings of Independence Hall. Idyllic Fairmount Park, next to the Schuylkill River, has several mansions built with this architectural style, including Sweetbriar, Strawberry Mansion, and Lemon Hill, which has oval rooms on all three floors (see pp110–11).

Greek Revival

Philadelphia's Merchants' Exchange (see p56), with a four-columned Corinthian portico at one end and an unusual, semicircular portico at the other, testifies to the nation's infatuation with Greek Revival architecture in the 1830s. It was designed by the up-and-coming architect William Strickland, already noted for designing the steeple atop Independence Hall. He also drafted the architectural plan

Strawberry Mansion, a Federal-style house in Fairmount Park

Parlor of the Victorian-style Ebenezer Maxwell House

in many late 19th- and early 20th-century buildings. The 1876 centennial celebration in Philadelphia ushered in Fairmount Park's Memorial Hall (see p111), dotted with bronze sculptures and topped by a glass and iron dome creating a spacious atrium.

With one of the city's most splendid Corinthian porticoes, 30th Street Station (see p186) is an example of this grand style, as is the Philadelphia Museum of Art (see pp92–5). Displaying much of the same grandeur is the Free Library of Philadelphia (see p86), and the similar Family Court Building next to it, both with porticoes sheltering imposing colonnaded façades. On a smaller scale, the nearby temple-like Rodin Museum (see p90) features columns and a portico topped with a balustrade.

for another prominent Greek Revival structure, the imposing Second Bank of the United States (see p49), with sturdy stone columns on its Greek temple-like façade.

A smaller Greek Revival structure, now housing the Philadelphia History Museum at Atwater Kent (see p52), was designed by John Haviland, a contemporary of Strickland. This was the first home of the Franklin Institute (see p87), where Strickland and other architects taught the nation's first architecture classes.

Gothic Revival. For example, City Hall (see pp74–5), with its colonnades and mansard roof, is a French Second Empire design. The Academy of Music (see p78), designed by prominent 19th-century architect and Philadelphia native Napoleon LeBrun, is Italianate in style, with period gas lamps on its high-windowed façade and lavish interiors. The Italianate Revival Athenaeum also has gas lamps on its walls. The city's only authentically restored Victorian home is the Ebenezer Maxwell Mansion in Germantown (see pp108–9), which is capped with a high tower, a mansard, and gable roof design.

Detail of Philadelphia Museum of Art façade

Victorian

Ornate, Victorian-style façades were designed for Philadelphia buildings from the 1850s onwards.

Victorian-era architecture is influenced by various styles, such as Second Empire, Italianate, and

Beaux Arts

American architects trained at the École des Beaux-Arts in France brought home this Greek- and Roman-influenced style of architecture, with elaborate detailing, balustrades, and prominent columns. Due to the grandiosity and size of these structures, Beaux Arts became the favored style for court houses, government buildings, museums, and railroad terminals, and was used

Philadelphia's skyscrapers, One Liberty Place (left) and BNY Mellon Center

Postmodernist

The late 20th century witnessed a rebellion against the box-like glass and steel structures built after World War II. Thus was born the Postmodern era in architecture, which featured sleek modernism tempered by conservative and historical design. This is evident in the twin towers of Liberty Place (see p81) with their pointed apexes. Also in the same style are the top floors of Three Logan Square, while the BNY Mellon Center building is crowned with a pyramid-like dome. The latest addition to the city's skyline is the cutting-edge Comcast Innovation & Technology Center.

Colonnaded entrance of the Beaux-Arts style Philadelphia Museum of Art

Philadelphia's Best: Parks and Gardens

William Penn wanted his city to be "a green countrie towne" and included five squares in his original city grid. Today, four of these, Logan, Rittenhouse, Franklin, and Washington Squares, are pleasant areas with trees and park benches. Along the Schuylkill River on the outskirts of Center City is Fairmount Park. Its 9,200 acres (3,700 ha) of parkland and gardens make it America's largest urban park. The area has biking and walking paths along the river and one of its tributaries, Wissahickon Creek, which runs within a gorge. Fairmount Park includes the peaceful Shofuso Japanese House and Garden and restored historic houses that were once the homes of the colonial elite. Beyond Philadelphia, near the Delaware state border, are the exquisite Longwood Gardens.

Schuylkill River

Morris Arboretum of the University of Pennsylvania
Located in the Chestnut Hill neighborhood, this scenic tract of land includes ponds, greenhouses, meadows, and gardens with thousands of rare plants and "trees-of-record" *(see p99)*.

*Longwood Gardens
22 miles (35 km)*

Wissahickon Gorge
The country's only covered bridge within a major city is sited on a hiking trail in this gorge, whose forests and creek are home to over 100 bird species.

0 kilometers 2

0 miles 2

Longwood Gardens
Industrialist Pierre S. du Pont designed this extravagant horticultural wonderland filled with spectacular choreographed fountains, whimsical topiaries, conservatories with exotic plants, and meadows and gardens replete with more than 11,000 varieties of indoor and outdoor plants *(see p130)*.

Logan Square

This grand square was once used as a burial ground and pastureland. Its centerpiece is the majestic, multi-spouted Swann Memorial fountain designed by sculptor Alexander Stirling Calder *(see p86)*.

Fairmount Park

This extensive greenbelt along the Schuylkill River and Wissahickon Creek is dotted with statues and features miles of running and biking paths *(see p99)*.

Washington Square and Tomb of the Unknown Soldier

Named in honor of George Washington, the first president of the US, the centerpiece of this peaceful park is his statue, and the tomb of the unknown soldier of the Revolutionary War *(see p62)*.

Delaware River

Schuylkill River

Cooper River

Rittenhouse Square

Center City's most popular park often fills with downtown workers who lunch under the trees. Reminiscent of New York's Central Park, it is flanked by upscale restaurants *(see p80)*.

Welcome Park

Named after Penn's ship, this park was completed in 1982, three centuries after the founding of Philadelphia. Marble slabs depicting the city's original grid crisscross the park *(see p57)*.

PHILADELPHIA THROUGH THE YEAR

Moderating mid-Atlantic coastal waters often temper the effects of extreme heat and harsh cold, making Philadelphia's summers enjoyable and the winters bearable. Spring flowers and warmer temperatures breathe new life into the city, with restaurants and cafés setting up tables outdoors, while city residents head to parks and riverfronts, anticipating summer festivals and excursions to beaches and lakes. Activities continue outdoors in fall, which heralds a rush of cool air and colorful foliage to Philadelphia's forested greenbelts. After Thanksgiving, activities tend to move indoors, with a rush of Christmas shoppers to quaint boutiques and shopping malls. Sports and cultural activities are in full swing during the winter months, right through to spring.

School and college track teams compete at the Penn Relays

Spring

Cherry blossoms bloom along the Schuylkill River in early spring, as Philadelphians flock to the Schuylkill River walk to enjoy the warmer weather. April also signals the start of the Philadelphia Phillies' baseball season.

March
Philadelphia Flower Show *(early Mar)*, Pennsylvania Convention Center. Largest indoor flower show in the United States.
St. Patrick's Day Parade *(mid-Mar)*, Center City. A parade celebrating Philadelphia's strong Irish heritage.

April
Subaru Cherry Blossom Festival of Greater Philadelphia *(early Apr)*. Features performances of traditional Japanese arts and culture at various locations throughout the city.

Philadelphia Antiques & Art Show *(late Apr)*, Navy Yard, 4747 S Broad St. Dealers from across the United States gather to display their unique finds.
Philadelphia Science Festival *(late Apr)*. This nine-day, citywide festival celebrates science with people of all ages through exhibitions, lectures, and the popular science carnival
Fairmount Arts Crawl *(late Apr)*, Fairmount Area. During this festival, bars, restaurants, and shops turn into galleries with installations, exhibits, live demonstrations, music, and activities for kids.

Juggler in action

Penn Relays *(late Apr)*, Franklin Field. High school and college track stars compete in the longest uninterrupted collegiate track meet in the nation.
International Children's Festival *(early to mid-May)*, Annenberg Center for the Performing Arts. Jugglers, folk singers, puppeteers, and dancers delight young audiences.
Philadelphia Phillies Baseball *(Apr–Oct)*, Citizens Bank Park. The season starts with many home games at the 43,500-capacity park.

Blooms at the Philadelphia Flower Show, a spring-time celebration

Average Daily Hours of Sunshine

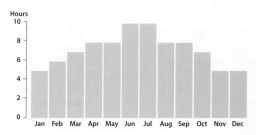

Hours
10
8
6
4
2
0

Jan Feb Mar Apr May Jun Jul Aug Sep Oct Nov Dec

Sunshine Chart
This chart shows the average daily number of hours of sunshine in Philadelphia each month. June, July, and August have long days with lots of sunshine. Spring and fall have fewer hours of sunshine, with the shortest days in winter, which can still have ample hours of bright sun on clear, cold days.

May

Broad Street Run *(early May)*, Olney to south Philadelphia. This 10-mile (16-km) run raises funds for the American Cancer Society.

Rittenhouse Row Spring Festival *(early to late May)*. This festival draws 50,000 visitors to enjoy the best of living, dining, shopping, and entertainment in this classy neighborhood.

Dad Vail Regatta *(second weekend)*, Schuylkill River at Kelly Drive. Largest collegiate regatta in the United States with more than 100 colleges and universities participating.

Devon Horse Show and Country Fair *(late May and early Jun)*, Devon Fair Grounds. Equestrian talents on display at the country's oldest and largest event of its kind.

The Mann Center *(May–Sep)*, Fairmount Park. Performances through the summer by the Philadelphia Orchestra, Philly Pops, and others.

PECO Multicultural Series at Penn's Landing *(May–Sep)*. Concerts along with ethnic events for families.

Annual Student Exhibition *(May/Jun)*, Pennsylvania Academy of the Fine Arts. This century-old tradition displays the works of award-winning students.

Philly Beer Week *(early Jun)*. Enjoy local brews, a beer tour, and beer pairing dinners in "America's Best Beer Drinking City" at this 10-day festival.

Summer

Summer ushers in a variety of festivals and live music on Penn's Landing. Fairmount Park

fills with picnickers and thousands jam roadways to the New Jersey shore. Philadelphians celebrate the nation's birth, which took place in their own city, on the Fourth of July with remembrances, concerts, parades, and a massive display of fireworks above the Philadelphia Museum of Art.

June

Bloomsday *(Jun 16)*, The Rosenbach. James Joyce fans celebrate the day on which Leopold Bloom, the protagonist of Joyce's *Ulysses*, made his "odyssey" through Dublin.

Odunde Street Festival *(mid-Jun)*, South Street. This African-American street festival marking the Yoruba New Year begins with a procession to the Schuylkill River and ends with a street fair.

Manayunk Arts Festival *(late Jun)*, Main Street. The region's largest outdoor arts and craft festival.

Canal Day *(late Jun)*, Mont Clare. Commemorate the 1823 opening of the Schuylkill Navigation System with fun runs, kids' fishing derby, kayak races, and more.

People enjoying the Varga Bar Block Party during Philly Beer Week

Fourth of July fireworks over the Philadelphia Museum of Art

July

Wawa Welcome America! *(week leading up to Jul 4)*. A week-long celebration with a concert and free events.

Fourth of July Parade *(Jul 4)*, Center City. Parade followed by fireworks.

Celebration of Freedom Ceremony *(Jul 4)*, Independence Hall. Celebrity readings of the Declaration of Independence are held at this event, followed by live music.

Equality Forum *(early to late Jul)*. Begun in the 1960s, this week-long gathering celebrates the cultural and political legacy of the gay, lesbian, bisexual, and transgender communities.

August

Philadelphia Folk Festival *(late Aug)*, Schwenksville. Music, dance, and crafts fair.

Philadelphia Eagles Football *(Aug–Dec)*, Lincoln Financial Field. The season features several home games.

Philadelphia Fringe Festival *(late Aug–early Sep)*. Citywide. Avant-garde theater.

Average Monthly Precipitation

MM
300
240
180
120
60
0

☐ Rainfall (from baseline)
☐ Snow (from baseline)

Inches
12
9
6
3
0

Jan Feb Mar Apr May Jun Jul Aug Sep Oct Nov Dec

Rainfall Chart
This chart shows the average monthly rainfall and snowfall. The heaviest rain is in July and August, with a yearly average of 41 inches. Considerable snow falls in January and February. The annual snowfall average is 21 inches.

Rowers in Lancaster County in the fall

Fall

Summer gradually gives way to cooler temperatures by mid-September, as thousands of students flock to the city's more than 80 colleges and universities. The bright reds and yellows of fall foliage begin to make an appearance by the end of September, with dramatic colors in October and early November. Football season gets into high gear, as fans head out to watch the Philadelphia Eagles. Fall also kicks off many cultural activities, signaling a new season for the city's world-class performing arts, opera, and symphony companies.

September

German-American Parade *(late Sep)*, Center City. Celebrates the city's German heritage and pays tribute to Baron Friedrich von Steuben, who was a general in the Revolutionary War.

Puerto Rican Day Parade *(last Sun)*, Center City. Celebrating Puerto Rican heritage with a festival and parade.

Campus Philly CollegeFest *(late Sep or early Oct)*. College Day concert in the Benjamin Franklin Parkway, plus various career fairs and cultural events.

October

Old City Festival *(mid-Oct)*. This annual street art festival boasts an eclectic array of art and design and samplings of food and fashion of this historic district.

Columbus Day Parade *(second Sun)*, South Broad Street. The parade honors explorer Christopher Columbus and the Italian-American community.

Philadelphia Open Studio Tours *(mid-Oct)*. Local artists throughout the city open their workshops for two weekends.

Philadelphia 76ers Basketball *(Oct–Apr)*, Wells Fargo Center. NBA basketball season begins with a number of home games.

Philadelphia Flyers Hockey *(Oct–May)*, Wells Fargo Center. The NHL hockey season kicks off with home games.

Terror Behind the Walls *(mid-Sep–early Nov)*, Eastern State Penitentiary. A "haunted" house in the former prison celebrates Halloween.

November

Philadelphia Museum of Art Craft Show *(early Nov)*, Pennsylvania Convention Center. Features handmade textiles, jewelry, household wares, and more.

Philadelphia Marathon *(third Sun)*. A 26-mile (42-km) run through the city starts and ends at the Philadelphia Museum of Art.

Thanksgiving Day Parade *(fourth Thu)*. Benjamin Franklin Parkway. The oldest such parade in the country.

Colorful floats and giant balloons at the Thanksgiving Day Parade

Average Monthly Temperature

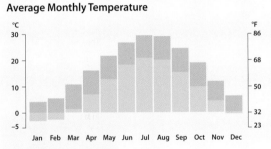

Temperature Chart
This chart shows average maximum and minimum monthly temperatures. Spring is usually mild with some brisk days. Summer is mostly comfortable, but can be hot and muggy. Fall brings clear and colder days. In winter, temperatures sometimes drop below freezing, but many days are chilly and bright.

Christmas lights at the impressive Wanamaker Building

Winter

Strings of sparkling lights illuminate streets, buildings, and trees throughout Center City and beyond, as Christmas shoppers throng the city's main shopping districts. New Year's Day brings the Mummers Day Parade, one of Philadelphia's most honored traditions, in which costumed revelers and string bands march down the street. Sports enthusiasts spend the winter months attending Philadelphia 76ers basketball and Flyers hockey games.

December

Christmas Tree Lighting *(Wed after Thanksgiving)*, City Hall. Signals the start of the holiday season.
Franklin Square Holiday Festival *(dates vary)*. This celebration includes performances by Mummers string bands, festivities, lighting events, and tax-free shopping for shoes and clothing.

Washington Crossing the Delaware River Reenactment *(Dec 25)*, Washington Crossing. Reenactment of this historic turning point in the American Revolutionary War.
New Year's Eve *(Dec 31)*, Penn's Landing. A night of celebrations with fireworks along the Delaware River.
The Nutcracker *(dates vary)*, Academy of Music. Part of Pennsylvania Ballet's season, productions of this ballet are put on before Christmas.

January

Mummers Parade *(Jan 1)*, Center City. A Philadelphia tradition, where up to 20,000 people in decorative costumes parade to the music of string bands.
Orchid Extravaganza *(mid-Jan through Mar)*, Longwood Gardens. This is a celebration of the beauty and variety of Longwood's historic orchid collection.

February

Philadelphia International Auto Show *(first week)*, Pennsylvania Convention Center. Highlights the latest in classic and luxury cars.
Chinese New Year Celebrations *(dates vary)*, Chinatown. Parades and festivities for two weeks.
Mardi Gras *(Fat Tuesday before Ash Wednesday)*, South Street. Day-long revelry and celebration.
African American History Month *(all month)*. Various events throughout the city.

Public Holidays

New Year's Day (Jan 1)
Martin Luther King Day (3rd Mon in Jan)
Presidents' Day (3rd Mon in Feb)
Memorial Day (Last Mon in May)
Independence Day (Jul 4)
Labor Day (1st Mon in Sep)
Columbus Day (2nd Mon in Oct)
Veterans Day (Nov 11)
Thanksgiving Day (4th Thu in Nov)
Christmas Day (Dec 25)

Mummers Parade, a Philadelphia New Year's Day tradition

PHILADELPHIA AREA BY AREA

Library Company, country's first lending library founded by Benjamin Franklin

Sights at a Glance

OLD CITY

The foundations of Philadelphia, and all of the United States, are rooted in the neighborhood of Old City, which includes the Liberty Bell and Independence Hall, both of which form part of Independence National Historical Park. This area was settled by city founder William Penn and his fellow Quakers in the late 17th century.

It later served as the seat of government for rebellious colonial patriots during the American Revolution in the 1770s. Today, well-preserved historical structures, buildings, and homes that date back to the 18th and 19th centuries, some still situated on narrow cobblestoned streets, stand alongside modern buildings and high-rises.

☐ **Restaurants** *pp143–5*

1 Amada
2 Aqua Malaysian & Thai Restaurant
3 Ariana Restaurant
4 Bistro 7
5 Buddakkan
6 Café Ole
7 Chloe
8 City Tavern
9 Common Wealth
10 Cuba Libre Restaurant and Rum Bar
11 DiNardo's Famous Crabs
12 El Fuego
13 Eulogy Belgian Tavern
14 Farmicia
15 Fork
16 Franklin Fountain
17 Han Dynasty
18 Jones
19 Kabul Afghan Cuisine Restaurant
20 Kisso Sushi Bar
21 La Peg
22 La Veranda Restaurant
23 Morimoto
24 Mrs. K's Coffee Shop & Café
25 Panorama
26 Race Street Café
27 Serrano-Tin Angel
28 Sonny's Cheesesteaks
29 Spasso Italian Grill
30 The Bourse
31 The Continental Restaurant and Martini Bar
32 The Plough & The Stars
33 Wedge + Fig

See also Street Finder maps 3 & 4

0 meters 500
0 yards 500

Street-by-Street: Independence National Historical Park

Known locally as Independence Mall, this urban park encompasses several well-preserved 18th-century structures associated with the American Revolution. The Declaration of Independence that heralded the birth of a new nation was written and signed in this historic area. Dominated by the tall brick tower of Independence Hall, the park includes the US Mint and several special-interest museums that explore Philadelphia's colonial and seafaring past, as well as its ethnic heritage. At least 20 of the buildings are open to the public.

Plaque commemorating Independence Hall

❼ US Mint
This mint, the oldest in the country, struck its first coins in 1793. It also mints commemorative coins such as the Eisenhower dollar.

❻ ★ National Constitution Center
This museum features interactive exhibits explaining the US Constitution. Visitors can walk among life-sized statues of the delegates who were present when this document was adopted in 1787.

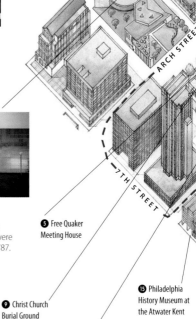

❺ Free Quaker Meeting House

⓯ Philadelphia History Museum at the Atwater Kent

❾ Christ Church Burial Ground

❹ Independence Visitor Center
Located in what is called "America's most historic square mile," the Independence Visitor Center provides visitors with practical information and a cultural and historical orientation. Timed tickets for Independence Hall are available here.

Key
— Suggested route

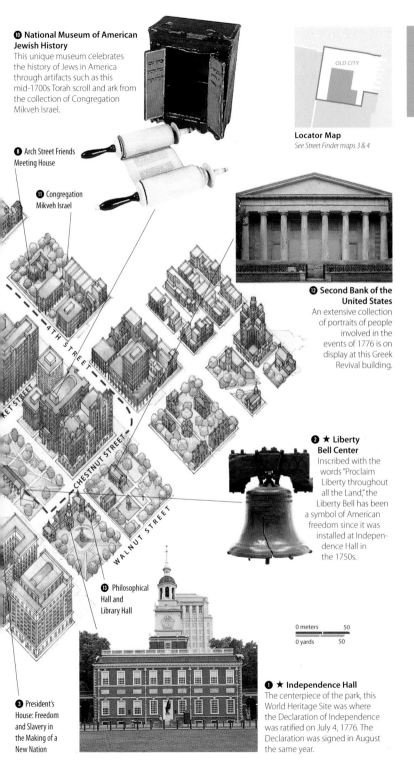

⑩ National Museum of American Jewish History
This unique museum celebrates the history of Jews in America through artifacts such as this mid-1700s Torah scroll and ark from the collection of Congregation Mikveh Israel.

Locator Map
See Street Finder maps 3 & 4

⑧ Arch Street Friends Meeting House

⑪ Congregation Mikveh Israel

⑫ Second Bank of the United States
An extensive collection of portraits of people involved in the events of 1776 is on display at this Greek Revival building.

❷ ★ Liberty Bell Center
Inscribed with the words "Proclaim Liberty throughout all the Land," the Liberty Bell has been a symbol of American freedom since it was installed at Independence Hall in the 1750s.

⑬ Philosophical Hall and Library Hall

| 0 meters | 50 |
| 0 yards | 50 |

❸ President's House: Freedom and Slavery in the Making of a New Nation

❶ ★ Independence Hall
The centerpiece of the park, this World Heritage Site was where the Declaration of Independence was ratified on July 4, 1776. The Declaration was signed in August the same year.

❶ Independence Hall

This unadorned brick building and clock tower are the most important structures in Independence Hall National Park. Earlier designated the State House of Pennsylvania, it is the site of the drafting and signing of the US Constitution and the Declaration of Independence, the document that declared America's freedom from the British Empire in 1776. Designed by master carpenter Edmund Woolley and lawyer Andrew Hamilton, Independence Hall was completed in 1753, more than two decades after construction began. Today, the meeting rooms are simply furnished, as they were in the late 1700s, and park personnel re-create history by pointing out the Windsor-style chairs from which colonial leaders debated the contents of the Declaration.

Congress Hall
Congress met in this hall from 1790 to 1800. Presidential inaugurations were also held here for George Washington and John Adams.

The Declaration of Independence

Following colonial resistance to British "taxation without representation," the first shots of rebellion rang out in 1775 at the battles of Concord and Lexington outside Boston. Within a year, a strong feeling for independence overwhelmed the colonies. Known for his powerful writing style, Thomas Jefferson, Virginia Delegate and future president, took on the task of drafting a document declaring independence. He eloquently asserted man's right to freedom and rebellion while listing colonial grievances against England's King George III. After making changes, the Continental Congress ratified the Declaration of Independence on July 4, 1776.

An original copy of the 1776 Declaration of Independence

★ **Great Essentials Exhibit**
On display here are original copies of the Declaration of Independence and the US Constitution, as well as this silver Syng inkstand, said to have been used during the signing of the documents.

★ Assembly Room
Amidst its simple desks and chairs, delegates of the Continental Congress debated and signed the new nation's Declaration of Independence in 1776. Eleven years later, the Constitution was drafted and signed here as well.

VISITORS' CHECKLIST

Practical Information
Chestnut St between 5th & 6th Sts. **Map** 4 D3. **Tel** (215) 965-2305. **Open** 9am–5pm daily. Longer hours in summer. Free, timed ticket needed from Independence Visitor Center on morning of visit. For advance reservations, call (877) 444-6777 or see ⓦ **recreation.gov** 📷 🖊 🚻 ⓦ **nps.gov/inde/**

Transport
🚇 Jefferson Station. Ⓢ 5th St. 🚌 Philly Phlash.

★ Rising Sun Chair
The chair used by George Washington during the 1787 Constitutional Convention depicts a symbolic sun rising over the new nation.

Long Gallery
Running the length of the second floor, this light-filled reception room also hosted 18th-century balls and banquets.

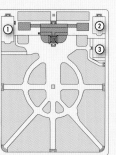

②

Independence Hall
① Congress Hall
② Old City Hall
③ Philosophical Hall

Key
▪ Illustrated Area
▫ Lawn

KEY
① **West Wing**
② **East Wing**

❷ Liberty Bell Center

Originally rung to signal Pennsylvania Assembly meetings in the State House (now Independence Hall) in the mid-18th century, the Liberty Bell is one of the world's greatest symbols of freedom, bearing the inscription "Proclaim Liberty throughout all the Land unto all the Inhabitants thereof." Famous for its irreparable crack, the 2,080-lb (940-kg) bell was moved to its current home in the Liberty Bell Center in 2003. The Center details the bell's history and significance, and how it became an icon for other freedom struggles. Clearly visible on the bell is the unsuccessful "stop drilling" repair, where, in 1846, the edges of the fracture were filed down to reduce friction and stress in an effort to slow the growth of the crack.

VISITORS' CHECKLIST

Practical Information
Market St between 5th & 6th Sts.
Map 4 D3. **Tel** (215) 965-2305.
Open 9am–5pm. ♿
🌐 nps.gov/inde

Transport
🚇 Jefferson Station.
Ⓢ 5th St. 🚌 Philly Phlash.

The Liberty Bell
The bell cracked the first time it was rung in 1753. Recast twice by Philadelphia's Pass and Stow Foundry, it was placed in the steeple of the State House (now called Independence Hall). It is said to have been first referenced as "Bell of Liberty" by 19th-century abolitionists.

Multimedia Display Gallery
This gallery displays old newspaper reports, videos, and photographs of people who have fought for liberty, such as the Dalai Lama and Nelson Mandela.

Curved wall

Entrance

Liberty Bell Center
The center is an elongated building where visitors first walk through a multimedia display gallery. This leads to the bell itself, set next to a large window with an excellent view of Independence Hall. A commemorative installation, "The President's House: Freedom and Slavery in the Making of a New Nation," is next to the Liberty Bell. This was the official residence of the President before the White House.

1752 Pennsylvania Assembly orders the bell from Whitechapel Foundry in England

1835 Termed "Bell of Liberty" by abolitionists

1841–45 Cracks again in this period

1944 Tapped during Normandy Invasion on June 6

1988 Liberty Bell Medal created

1750	1800	1850	1900	1950	2000

1776 Possibly rung on July 8 after first public reading of the Declaration of Independence

1753 It cracks when first rung, and is recast twice

1915 Tapped when transcontinental telephone service started

1976 Moved from Independence Hall to outside pavilion for country's bicentennial

2003 Bell moved to Liberty Bell Center

❸ President's House: Freedom and Slavery in the Making of a New Nation

6th & Market Sts. **Map** 4 D3.
🚇 Jefferson Station. Ⓢ 5th St.
🚌 Philly Phlash. **Open** 24 hrs a day. ♿

Focusing on the untold stories of slavery in Philadelphia, the President's House brings to light the people and events that shaped the history of the slave trade in America. The outdoor installation sits on the site where America's first president, George Washington, resided. At the time he owned nine slaves, whose stories are told here. America's second president, abolitionist John Adams, also resided here.

This outdoor installation allows guests to walk through the house's footprint and examine important artifacts. Visitors can learn about the political climate of the time by looking at exhibits that show the dynamics of the abolitionist movement in Philadelphia and the relationship between free blacks and slaves, as well as the laws signed by Washington and Adams and how they defined the American presidency.

The site's location is one of the most significant features of the attraction. The Liberty Bell, a nation's symbol of freedom, sits atop the land where the slave quarters were located. Though Philadelphia was the epicenter of the fight for freedom in the 18th century, it was still a place where not all men were free.

❹ Independence Visitor Center

6th & Market Sts. **Map** 4 D2. **Tel** (800) 537-7676. 🚇 Jefferson Station.
Ⓢ 5th St. 🚌 Philly Phlash.
Open 8:30am–6pm daily (until 7pm Memorial Day–Labor Day). **Closed** Jan 1, Thanksgiving, Dec 25. ♿ 💻 📷
Ⓦ phlvisitorcenter.com

One of the first stops for any visitor to Philadelphia should be the Independence Visitor Center. This expansive center offers information on more than 4,000 attractions in the city and the region. Apart from screening historical and orientation films, such as the short film *Independence* directed by John Huston, it has maps and brochures, touch-screen information kiosks, daily listings of events, and trip-planning services. Both National Park Service rangers and experienced City of Philadelphia tourism specialists provide assistance and advice about historical sights, attractions, shopping, and dining. A large gift shop has all manner of souvenirs themed around Philadelphia. Café Independence and Independence Mall Café offer refreshments.

Of particular interest is a rotating exhibition of original engravings of colonial Philadelphia by William Russell Birch, which were first published in 1800. Prints of these line the Market Street entrance corridor.

The Visitor Center is also the place to obtain timed-entry tickets for Independence Hall. These are available on a first-come, first-served basis.

Plain brick façade of the 18th-century Free Quaker Meeting House

❺ Free Quaker Meeting House

Arch & 5th Sts. **Map** 4 D2. **Tel** (215) 627-2667. 🚇 Jefferson Station.
Ⓢ 5th St. 🚌 Philly Phlash.
Open Jun–Aug: 11am–4pm Wed–Sun; Sep–Nov & Mar–May: 11am–4pm Sat & Sun. 📷 ♿

This simple Georgian brick building was built in 1783 for Quakers who were inspired to bear arms in the American Revolution. Bearing arms meant defying the pacifist beliefs of the order, which led to expulsion from the main Quaker community. About 200 such people called themselves the "Free Quakers" and founded their own meetinghouse. However, in the years that followed, attendance dropped to just a few dozen, and by 1834, only two Free Quakers, Betsy Ross and John Price Wetherill, still attended meetings. Shortly thereafter, the meetinghouse was permanently closed. Since then, the building has served as a school, a library, and a warehouse. Today, the building contains two benches and a window from colonial times. Also on display is Betsy Ross's five-pointed star tissue pattern, which she is said to have used to shape stars to make the colonial-era American flag. Today, the descendants of the original Free Quakers hold annual meetings here to decide how to distribute funds generated by rental of the hall and how best to invest income for charitable purposes. Actors dressed in colonial garb give lectures on the building's history, and guides demonstrate how to cut a five-pointed star in one snip.

The Independence Visitor Center in "America's most historic square mile"

❻ National Constitution Center

See pp50–51.

❼ US Mint

151 Independence Mall E, on 5th St. **Map** 4 D2. **Tel** (215) 408-0140. 🚆 Jefferson Station. 🚇 5th St. 🚌 Philly Phlash. **Open** 9am–4:30pm Mon–Fri (also Sat Memorial Day–Labor Day. 🎧 group tours by prior arrangement. 🌐 usmint.gov Federal Reserve Bank of Philadelphia: 6th & Arch Sts. **Tel** (215) 408-0112. **Open** Mar–Dec: 9:30am–4:30pm Mon–Fri (Jun–Aug: also 9am–4:30 Sat); photo ID required to enter. 🌐 philadelphiafed.org

The Philadelphia mint, the oldest in the US, produces gold bullion coins and medals, and also makes most of the coins that Americans use every day. The first US coins, minted in 1792, were copper pennies intended solely for commerce in the former colonies. Today, 24 hours a day, five days a week, hundreds of machines and operators, in a room the size of a football field, blank, anneal, count, and bag millions of dollars' worth of pennies, dimes, and quarters. The gift shop, open on a limited basis, sells commemorative coins and numismatic collectibles.

A related exhibit, Money in Motion, is on display at the **Federal Reserve Bank of Philadelphia**, which is located one block west of the US Mint. It explains US monetary policy and history with the help of interactive computer screens and impressive exhibits.

Philadelphia's oldest Quaker meetinghouse, on Arch Street

❽ Arch Street Friends Meeting House

320 Arch St, at 4th St. **Map** 4 E2. **Tel** (215) 627-0627. 🚆 Jefferson Station. 🚇 2nd St. 🚌 Philly Phlash. **Open** 11am–4pm Wed–Fri. ⛪ 10:30am Sun; 7pm Wed. 🌐 archstreetmeetinghouse.org

This brick structure is the oldest Quaker meetinghouse still in use in Philadelphia. Built in 1804, the site previously served as a Quaker burial ground and accommodated victims of the yellow fever epidemic in the 1790s. Today, the house has a central hall and two adjacent meeting rooms. The East Room features Quaker artifacts and six dioramas depicting William Penn's life as a Quaker. The West Room contains worn wooden benches and now serves as the main meeting and worship hall.

Headstone, Christ Church Burial Ground

❾ Christ Church Burial Ground

5th & Arch Sts. **Map** 4 D2. **Tel** (215) 922-1695. 🚆 Jefferson Station. 🚇 5th St. 🚌 Philly Phlash. **Open** Mar–Nov: 10am–4pm Mon–Sat, noon–4pm Sun (burial ground); 9am–5pm Mon–Sat (exc 11:30am–12:30pm Wed), 1–5pm Sun (church). 🎧 📷 🌐 christchurchphila.org

This crammed cemetery dates back to 1719, and is an expansion of Christ Church's original graveyard. More than 5,000 people are buried here, most from colonial times. The burial ground is the final resting place of Benjamin Franklin, his wife Deborah, and their daughter and son-in-law Sarah Franklin and Richard Bache. Four other signers of the Declaration of Independence – Dr. Benjamin Rush, Francis Hopkinson, George Ross, and Joseph Hewes – are also buried here. Franklin's grave is on the perimeter of the grounds, and is visible through an iron grating. Passersby toss pennies on the grave, both to show respect and to bring good luck. With headstones already deteriorating by the mid-19th century, all gravestone inscriptions were copied and published in 1864 in order to preserve records of people interred in this graveyard.

❿ National Museum of American Jewish History

101 South Independence Mall East. **Map** 4 D3. **Tel** (215) 923-3811. 🚆 Jefferson Station. 🚇 5th St. 🚌 Philly Phlash. **Open** 10am–5pm Tue–Fri, 10am–5:30pm Sat & Sun. **Closed** Mon, Jewish holidays. ♿ 🌐 nmajh.org

This is the only institution in the nation dedicated solely to the story of the American Jewish experience. The core exhibition traces the lives of American Jews from 1654 to the present, exploring how they created a new home in a free

Inspecting coins at the US Mint

land and examining how this country shaped their lives, communities, and livelihoods.

The museum includes more than 30,000 artifacts, films, and state-of-the-art technology that provide a powerful testament to what free people can accomplish for themselves and for society at large.

Exhibits devoted to everyday relationships and popular culture make the collection accessible to both Jewish and non-Jewish audiences. The *Only in America Gallery/Hall of Fame* illustrates the accomplishments of prominent American Jews.

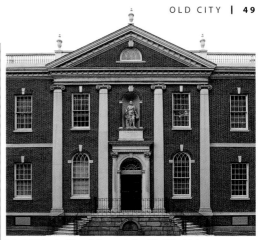

Federal-style façade of Library Hall, a reproduction of the 1789 original

⓫ Congregation Mikveh Israel

44 N 4th St. **Map** 4 E2. **Tel** (215) 922-5446. 🚇 Jefferson Station. Ⓢ 5th St. 🚌 Philly Phlash. **Open** 10am–5pm daily. ⏰ 7:30am Mon–Fri, 9am Sat, 8:30am Sun & public hols. ♿
🌐 mikvehisrael.org

Philadelphia's oldest Jewish congregation, Mikveh Israel, was founded in 1740. The congregation built its first synagogue in 1782, and moved into its current building in 1976.

Mikveh Israel's archival collection includes two pairs of Torah finials crafted by silversmith Myer Myers in 1772 and letters written by US Presidents George Washington and Abraham Lincoln. Past congregation members included colonial patriot and financier Haym Salomon; Nathan Levy, whose ship brought the Liberty Bell to America; and Rebecca Gratz, who founded educational and social institutions. The synagogue still holds a traditional service, which has remained virtually unchanged since the colonial era.

⓬ Second Bank of the United States

420 Chestnut St. **Map** 4 D3. **Tel** (215) 965-7676, (800) 537-7676. 🚇 Jefferson Station. Ⓢ 5th St. 🚌 Philly Phlash. **Open** 11am–4pm Wed–Sun.
♿ 🌐 nps.gov/inde

Built between 1819 and 1824, this is one of America's finest examples of Greek Revival architecture. Once a repository that provided credit for federal government agencies and private businesses, it now houses a collection of over 150 paintings from the late 18th and early 19th centuries. On view are portraits of colonial and federal leaders, military officers, explorers, scientists, and Founding Fathers.

Many portraits are by Charles Willson Peale (1741–1827), his brother James, and their respective children, who together form America's most distinguished family of artists. Peale began collecting portraits after the Revolutionary War. Today, more than 100 of his paintings, including likenesses of George Washington, Thomas Jefferson, and the Marquis de LaFayette, the Continental Army's French ally, are on display, as are portraits by other artists.

⓭ Philosophical Hall and Library Hall

105 S 5th St. **Map** 4 D3.
Tel (215) 440-3400. 🚇 Jefferson Station. Ⓢ 5th St. 🚌 Philly Phlash. **Open** APS Museum: mid-Apr–Dec: 10am–4pm Thu–Sun (Memorial Day–Labor Day: 10am–5pm Thu–Sun). **Closed** public hols.
🌐 apsmuseum.org

A Colonial-era "think tank," the American Philosophical Society was founded in 1743 by Benjamin Franklin to promote the study of government, nature, science, and industry. Built in 1789, the Federal-style Philosophical Hall was a meeting place for doctors, clergymen, and the Founding Fathers of the nation. Reopened in 2001 for the first time since the early 19th century, the hall today hosts art, history, and science exhibitions.

The society also owns Library Hall, once the home of the Library Company founded by Franklin in 1731. The company's vast collections served as the Library of Congress until 1800. The current building, a 1950s reconstruction of the 1789 original, stores some of the society's most precious works, including the title page of an 1859 manuscript of Darwin's *On the Origin of Species,* the journals of explorers Lewis and Clark, and Jefferson's handwritten Declaration of Independence.

Redbrick exterior of Congregation Mikveh Israel

❻ National Constitution Center

The inscription "We the People" is boldly engraved on the massive Indiana limestone façade of this sprawling center, which was opened on July 4, 2003. It interprets the US Constitution through more than 100 interactive and multimedia exhibits, including artifacts, sculptures, photographs, video, and film. Visitors can listen to President Franklin Delano Roosevelt's speeches or to actual arguments from Supreme Court cases at a replica of the Supreme Court Bench, or walk through a re-creation of the 19th-century Senate floor. The circular main hall also contains displays that illuminate the text of the Constitution and highlight the themes of liberty and freedom.

Engraved Façade
"We the People," part of the opening words of the US Constitution, engraved on the façade of the center.

F.M. Kirby Auditorium
and Theater

The US Constitution

After the Revolutionary War, delegates from the original 13 states, except Rhode Island, gathered in Philadelphia for the Constitutional Convention in 1787. It took them nearly four months to draft a document creating a strong centralized government for the new nation. Adopted on September 17, the Constitution ensures individual liberties and defines distinct powers for Congress, the president, and the federal courts, while also establishing a system of "Checks and Balances" so that no branch of government can dominate the others.

A copy of the Constitution of the United States

Grand Hall Overlook

Terrace

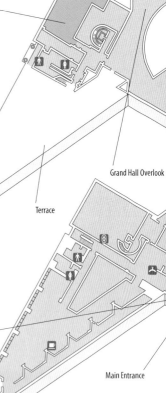

Main Entrance

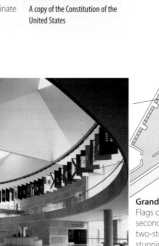

Grand Hall Lobby
Flags of US states hang from the Grand Hall's second-floor overlook, from where the lobby's two-story glass windowpanes provide a stunning view of Independence National Historical Park.

★ **"Freedom Rising"**
The circular, 350-seat Kimmel Theater features "Freedom Rising," a multimedia production that narrates the story of the US Constitution. This 17-minute show is projected on a 360-degree screen.

Second Floor

VISITORS' CHECKLIST

Practical Information
525 Arch St. **Map** 4 D2.
Tel (215) 409-6700.
Open 9:30am–5pm Mon–Sat, noon–5pm Sun. **Closed** Jan 1, Thanksgiving, Dec 25.

w constitutioncenter.org

Transport
Jefferson Station.
5th St. Philly Phlash.

Center Guide

The Grand Hall Lobby and Kimmel Theater are on the first floor. Permanent displays and interactive exhibits are situated on the second floor in the circular DeVos Hall.

★ **American National Tree**
With the "We the People" wall in the foreground, the circular American National Tree features stories of more than 100 Americans who have influenced the Constitution. Each story exemplifies tolerance, diversity, and opportunity.

Box Office

First Floor

Key

- ☐ Richard and Helen DeVos Exhibit Hall
- ☐ Kimmel Theater
- ☐ Posterity Hall
- ☐ Signers' Hall
- ☐ F.M. Kirby Auditorium and Theater
- ☐ First Public Printing of the Constitution
- ☐ Non-exhibition space

★ **Signers' Hall**
Walk among life-sized bronze statues of the 39 men who signed the Constitution (including that of Benjamin Franklin, seated in the front), and the three who dissented.

⓮ Curtis Center and Dream Garden Mosaic

601 Walnut St, at 6th St. **Map** 4 D3. **Tel** (215) 238-6450. 🚇 Jefferson Station. 🚊 5th St. 🚌 Philly Phlash. **Open** 8am–6pm Mon–Fri, 10am–1pm Sat. ♿

This 1910 Beaux-Arts building is where Cyrus Curtis oversaw his publishing empire, which included the *Ladies Home Journal* (founded 1883). His publishing company also breathed new life into the *Saturday Evening Post* after its purchase in 1897, and created popular magazines such as *American Home, Jack and Jill, Holiday*, and *Country Gentleman*.

Inside the building is the enormous *Dream Garden Mosaic*, a 49-ft x 15-ft (15-m x 4.5-m) glasswork that dominates the lobby. Designed by Maxfield Parrish, the mosaic was completed in 1916 by Louis Comfort Tiffany and Tiffany Studios. The artwork, depicting a garden with trees and streams, has more than 100,000 pieces of hand-fired Favrile glass. In 1998, Las Vegas casino owner Steve Wynn tried to buy it, but the people of Philadelphia resisted the move. Local artists and historians helped in raising $3.5 million for the Pennsylvania Academy of the Fine Arts *(see pp76–7)* to buy back the mosaic. It later underwent painstaking restoration.

Atwater Kent exterior detail

⓯ Philadelphia History Museum at the Atwater Kent

15 S 7th St. **Map** 4 D3. **Tel** (215) 685-4830. 🚇 Jefferson Station. 🚊 8th St. 🚌 Philly Phlash. **Open** 10:30am–4:30pm Tue–Sat. **Closed** Jan 1, Thanksgiving, Dec 25. 🅿 📷 **W** philadelphiahistory.org

Philadelphia's official history museum since 1938, the former Atwater Kent Museum was refurbished and rebranded (to its current name) in 2010. Its collection of 100,000 objects and images spanning over 300 years remains the museum's foundation. Designed by John Haviland in Greek Revival style and completed in 1826, this was the original home of the Franklin Institute. The nation's first architecture classes were taught here. The building was saved from demolition in 1938 when A. Atwater Kent purchased it for a museum.

A colorful walk-on map of the city covers the first-floor gallery. Past exhibitions have included furniture used by President George Washington while living in Philadelphia and Benjamin Franklin's wineglass. The museum has an expansive collection of *Saturday Evening Post* covers showing "vignettes of daily life" in America by Norman Rockwell, who created 322 images for the Philadelphia-based magazine between 1916 and 1963.

Declaration House, reconstructed in 1975 by National Park Service

⓰ Declaration House

7th & Market Sts. **Map** 4 D2. **Tel** (215) 965-7676, (800) 537-7676. 🚇 Jefferson Station. 🚊 8th St. 🚌 Philly Phlash. **Open** hours vary (usually Jul & Aug only), call to confirm.

The current brick structure of Declaration House is a 1975 reconstruction of the Georgian-style home where Thomas Jefferson drafted the Declaration of Independence *(see p44)* from June 11 to 28, 1776. He had rented two upstairs rooms from bricklayer Jacob Graff, who had built the house in 1775. Although only a few blocks from Independence Hall, the house faced a field and stable, and offered Jefferson a quieter setting to write the Declaration.

Today, along with a bust of the famous American statesman and third president, the house includes copies of Jefferson's rough drafts of the Declaration. The two rooms upstairs contain

Dream Garden Mosaic, an enormous glass artwork gracing the Curtis Center lobby

period furnishings, and include re-creations of Jefferson's bedroom and parlor, where he wrote the document.

⓱ The African American Museum in Philadelphia

701 Arch St. **Map** 4 D2. **Tel** (215) 574-0380. 🚇 Jefferson Station. Ⓢ 5th St. 🚌 Philly Phlash. **Open** 10am–5pm Thu–Sat; noon–5pm Sun; Martin Luther King Day. **Closed** Mon, public hols. 📷 ♿ 📷 ♿ 🌐 aampmuseum.org

A Smithsonian affiliate, this museum is one of several founded in Philadelphia during the nation's bicentennial year. The museum is dedicated to "collecting, preserving, and interpreting the material and intellectual culture of African Americans" in the local area and the Americas. Since opening in 1976, the collection has swelled to more than 500,000 artifacts, including photographs, documents, fine and folk art, costumes, books, periodicals, and a number of other memorabilia.

Permanent and changing exhibitions celebrate important aspects of African-American life and history, including the Civil Rights movement, and contributions in the arts, entertainment, sports, medicine, politics, religion, law, and technology. The permanent exhibit, "Audacious Freedom: African Americans in Philadelphia in 1776–1876," uses interactive displays to recount the stories and contributions made by people of African descent in Philadelphia. Previous exhibitions have showcased African woodcarvings and textile designs while interpreting the

L'Ouverture by Ulrick Jean-Pierre, African American Museum

traditions and ceremonies of several African countries. Others have focused on struggles against slavery and oppression, including the Haitian Revolution, which resulted in

Exhibit at the African American Museum

Haiti establishing the world's first black republic in 1804. The museum also organizes regular workshops and demonstrations.

⓲ St. George's United Methodist Church

235 N 4th St. **Map** 4 E2. **Tel** (215) 925-7788. 🚇 Jefferson Station. Ⓢ 5th St. 🚌 Philly Phlash. **Open** 10am–4pm Mon–Fri (summer: Wed–Fri). 📷 🌐 historicstgeorges.org

The American Methodist movement began in St. George's United Methodist Church in 1769, making it the country's oldest Methodist church in continuous use. This simple brick structure, its inside walls adorned with a muted blue tint, has not changed much since it was remodeled in 1792. Colonial-era wooden pews and floorboards remain, as do the wrought-iron candle chandeliers and candelabra, although now wired with electric lights. A two-room museum has 18th- and 19th-century artifacts, hymnals, bibles, and other important church keepsakes. They include a 1785 silver chalice from John Wesley, the founder of the movement, the original handwritten journals of Joseph Pilmoor, the first pastor of the church, and a bible from Francis Asbury, considered the father

of the American United Methodist Church.

St. Augustine's Church across the street dates back to 1801. Burned down in 1844 by anti-Catholic rioters, the current building was designed by architect Napoleon LeBrun and rebuilt in 1847.

⓳ Fireman's Hall Museum

147 N 2nd St. **Map** 4 E2. **Tel** (215) 923-1438. 🚇 Jefferson Station. Ⓢ 2nd St. 🚌 Philly Phlash. **Open** 10am–4:30pm Tue–Sat. 🌐 firemanshallmuseum.org

Housed in an old firehouse that was operational between 1902 and 1952, this unique museum narrates the history of firefighting in Philadelphia, back to colonial times. The building still contains the original brass sliding pole used for quick access to fire trucks. Several pieces of old equipment are on display, including an 1896 hook-and-ladder, a 1903 high-pressure Cannon Wagon, and a 1907 steam-powered pumper. Of special note are two well-preserved hand-pumpers – one from 1815, and the other from 1730, six years before Benjamin Franklin founded the nation's first fire department. Also on display are axes, saws, nozzles, old fire plaques indicating insured buildings, and leather fire hats from the early 19th century. A large stained-glass window memorializes fallen firefighters.

Façade of the Fireman's Hall Museum

⓴ Elfreth's Alley

N 2nd St between Arch & Race Sts.
Map 4 E2. 🛈 Elfreth's Alley Museum,
126 Elfreth's Alley, (215) 627-8680.
🚇 Jefferson Station. Ⓢ 2nd St.
🚌 Philly Phlash. **Open** noon–
5pm Fri–Sun. 🚯 🅿 🛍
🆆 elfrethsalley.org

The oldest continuously
occupied residential street
in the country, this narrow
cobblestoned lane is lined
with 33 historic homes, most
in simple Georgian style.
Named after Jeremiah Elfreth,
a blacksmith who built and
rented out some of the first
homes, the alley dates back to
1702, when it was a path used
by carts hauling goods from the
Delaware River docks. Its early
occupants were tradespeople,
artisans, and sea captains, while
the industrial boom later
brought in laborers and tailors.

The oldest homes are at 120
and 122, built between 1724
and 1728. The street's Mantua
Maker's Museum House, at 126,
has been restored to resemble
the period between 1762 and
1794, when it was owned by
sisters-in-law Mary Smith and
Sarah Milton, makers of
mantuas and dresses. The home
at 124 is now a gift shop.

Halfway down the street is
another smaller alley, Bladen
Court, which includes three
houses and a courtyard. Visitors
can take a guided or self-guided
audio tour. Twice a year, in June
and December, many Elfreth
Alley residents open their
homes for tours during Fete
Day celebrations.

Elfreth's Alley, dating to the early 18th century

Betsy Ross House, where the first
American flag was sewn

㉑ Betsy Ross House

239 Arch St. **Map** 4 E2. **Tel** (215) 686-
1252. 🚇 Jefferson Station. Ⓢ 2nd St.
🚌 Philly Phlash. **Open** Dec–Feb:
10am–5pm Tue–Sun; Mar–Nov:
10am–5pm daily. **Closed** Jan 1,
Thanksgiving, Dec 25. ♿ limited
access. 🆆 **historicphiladelphia.org/
betsy-ross-house**

One of Philadelphia's most
visited historic sites, this simple
colonial home was where
Quaker seamstress and
upholsterer Betsy Ross is said
to have sewn the first American
flag – although no official
documentation exists to prove
it. Instead, the story was handed
down through generations of
her family. Nonetheless, the
1740 row house has been
restored to around 1777, when
Ross was supposedly commissioned by George Washington
to create the "Stars and Stripes"
for the struggling new nation.
The home, with narrow
stairwells and low ceilings, is
decorated with period antiques
and reproduction pieces, but
also has a few original items
that once belonged to Ross,
including her eyeglasses, a
family Bible, and an American
Chippendale walnut chest-
on-chest.

㉒ Christ Church

2nd St above Market St. **Map** 4 E2.
Tel (215) 922-1695. 🚇 Jefferson
Station. Ⓢ 2nd St. 🚌 Philly Phlash.
Open 9am–5pm Mon–Sat; 12:30pm–
5pm Sun. **Closed** Jan & Feb: Mon &
Tue. ✝ 9am & 11am Sun, noon Wed.
🆆 oldchristchurch.org

Founded in 1695, Christ Church
was Philadelphia's only Church of
England parish for 66 years. The
existing structure, built in 1744 in
Georgian style, after Wren's
London churches, was the town's
tallest building at the time. Often
called the "Nation's Church," it
was where revolutionary leaders,
including Benjamin Franklin,
Betsy Ross, and George and
Martha Washington, once
worshiped. Plaques mark some
pews used by the colonial elite.

Inside is the baptismal font
in which William Penn was
baptized, dating from the 14th
century and donated by
London's All Hallows Church
in 1697. Bishop William White
(see p56), parish rector for 57
years, is buried in the chancel
of the church.

㉓ Franklin Court and B. Free Franklin Post Office

Between 3rd & 4th Sts and Chestnut &
Market Sts. **Map** 4 E3. **Tel** (215) 965-
2306, (800) 537-7676. 🚇 Jefferson
Station. Ⓢ 2nd St. 🚌 Philly Phlash.
Open court: 9am–dusk; post office:
9am–5pm Mon–Sat. ♿

This expansive court, which cuts
through an entire city block, is
where Benjamin Franklin's home
once stood. Although razed
in 1812, a "Ghost House" frame
depicts the exact positions of
the house and adjacent print
shop, while excavations
underneath reveal the original
foundations. The impressive

Benjamin Franklin Museum has exhibits explaining Franklin's life. On the court grounds are several former residences once owned by Franklin, which now house artifacts, replicas and demonstrations of colonial printing and bookbinding operations, and the B. Free Franklin Post Office and Museum, which has an active post office. Another building houses the restored offices of *The Aurora*, the newspaper published by Franklin's grandson, Benjamin Franklin Bache.

Classical façade of the First Bank, designed by Samuel Blodgett

Tribute to valor – the National Liberty Museum

㉔ National Liberty Museum

321 Chestnut St. **Map** 4 E3. **Tel** (215) 925-2800. 🚉 Jefferson Station. 🚇 2nd St. 🚌 Philly Phlash. **Open** 10am–5pm daily. **Closed** Jan 1, Thanksgiving, Dec 25. 🎫 (under-5s free). ♿ 🌐 libertymuseum.org

Through exhibits heralding freedom and diversity, the National Liberty Museum takes an unconventional approach to its mission of defusing violence and bigotry. The museum honors 1,000 people worldwide who have stood up against repression. On display are life-sized dioramas of South Africa's Nelson Mandela in his jail cell, and concentration camp victim Anne Frank's Amsterdam bedroom, in which she hid from the Nazis. Another display

has photographs of every rescue worker who died in the September 11, 2001 attacks. With more than 100 glass artworks, the museum is the only one in the world to use glass as a symbol for freedom, and has a two-story structure, the *Flame of Liberty*, by Dale Chihuly, as its centerpiece.

㉕ First Bank of the United States

116 S 3rd St between Chestnut & Walnut Sts. **Map** 4 E3. **Tel** (215) 965-2305. 🚉 Jefferson Station. 🚇 2nd St. 🚌 Philly Phlash. **Closed** to the public.

The dispute over building the First Bank instigated the new nation's first debate on the interpretation of the US Constitution *(see pp50–51)*,

which neither allowed nor prohibited the building of a federal bank. Alexander Hamilton, treasury secretary from 1789 to 1795, led the charge to provide the nation with a firm financial footing and a means to pay off the Revolutionary War debt. Chartered by President Washington and Congress in 1791, the bank building was completed six years later, with its classical design signifying culture and political maturity.

In 1811, Congress voted to withdraw the charter. The building was then occupied by Girard Bank through the 1920s, and finally taken over by the National Park Service in 1955. Original brick rooms and sheet-iron vault doors still remain in the building.

Benjamin Franklin

One of America's finest statesmen, Benjamin Franklin wore many hats as a printer, inventor, author, philosopher, postmaster, and diplomat. Born in Boston in 1706, Franklin moved to Philadelphia in 1723. He established the first library and fire department in the city, and upgraded its postal services. Franklin also founded the University of Pennsylvania and the Pennsylvania Hospital. In the Revolutionary War, he presided over the 1776 Constitutional Convention and helped draft the Declaration of Independence *(see p44)*.

Benjamin Franklin (1706–90)

He won favor with the French, who would come to America's aid against the British. In 1787, he signed the US Constitution, and died in Philadelphia three years later. In 2006, the city honored Franklin with a year-long celebration of his 300th birthday.

㉖ Carpenters' Hall

320 Chestnut St. **Map** 4 E3. **Tel** (215) 925-0167. 🚇 Jefferson Station. 🚇 5th St. 🚌 Philly Phlash. **Open** Jan–Feb: 10am–4pm Wed–Sun; Mar–Dec: 10am–4pm Tue–Sun. **Closed** Jan 1, Thanksgiving, Dec 25. 🌐 carpentershall.org

This two-story structure was built for the Carpenters' Company, the country's oldest trade guild, established in 1724. It played an important role in the Revolutionary War, secretly hosting the First Continental Congress in 1774.

Today, the Carpenters' Hall houses displays of original Windsor chairs, used during the Congress, and colonial-era carpenters' tools. Two rebuilt structures share the grounds – Pemberton House, named after a Quaker merchant, is now a gift shop, while the New Hall Military Museum displays weapons of the colonial army and navy. The original 1791 building housed War Department offices.

Georgian-style Carpenters' Hall, designed by Robert Smith in 1770

㉗ Dolley Todd House

4th & Walnut Sts. **Map** 4 D3. **Tel** (215) 965-7676. 🚇 Jefferson Station. 🚇 5th St. 🚌 Philly Phlash. **Open** Jun–late Aug. 📷 compulsory; free tickets from Independence Visitor Center on first-come, first-served basis. ♿

This Georgian-style home shows how Philadelphia's middle class lived in the late 1700s. What makes Dolley Todd House particularly interesting is

Reconstructed dining room of Bishop White House

its famous resident, Dolley Payne, who later married James Madison, the fourth president of the US. Built in 1775, the home was occupied by Dolley and her first husband, lawyer John Todd, both Quakers, from 1791 to 1793. Dolley lost Todd and their infant son in 1793 during the city's yellow fever epidemic. The following year, she met Madison during an arranged meeting.

Today, the three-story home has been restored to when John and Dolley Todd lived here, with furnishings that reflect subtle Quaker conservatism. Period items include replicas of Dolley's dressing table, and John Todd's first-floor law library, with more than 300 volumes.

㉘ Bishop White House

309 Walnut St. **Map** 4 E3. **Tel** (215) 965-7676. 🚇 Jefferson Station. 🚇 5th St. 🚌 Philly Phlash. 📷 compulsory; free tickets available at Independence Visitor Center on first-come, first-served basis. ♿

The residence of Bishop William White for nearly 50 years, this three-story Federal structure, built in 1786, is an excellent example of a late 18th-century upper-class Philadelphia home. Dr. White, the first Episcopal Bishop of Pennsylvania and rector of Christ Church (see p54) and St. Peter's Episcopal Church (see p63), often entertained the colonial elite here, including George Washington and Benjamin Franklin. The house

has been restored, and period and original family pieces decorate the rooms, including whale-oil lamps on the fireplace mantel and an assortment of silver pieces in the dining room. Chair placement and bookcases in Dr. White's upstairs study have been accurately reconstructed, thanks to a painting of the room commissioned after his death. An inside privy, which remains today, is indicative of the home's upper-class status.

Merchants' Exchange Building, designed in Greek Revival style

㉙ Merchants' Exchange Building

143 S 3rd St at Walnut St. **Map** 4 E3. **Tel** (215) 965-2305. 🚇 Jefferson Station. 🚇 2nd St. 🚌 Philly Phlash. **Open** 8:30am–4:30pm Mon–Fri (lobby exhibit).

The oldest stock exchange building in the country, this imposing edifice is one of Old City's finest architectural gems.

Completed in 1834, it was designed in Greek Revival style by the up-and-coming architect William Strickland, already noted for designing the new steeple atop Independence Hall *(see pp44–5)* and for his work on the Second Bank of the United States *(see p49)*. Strickland's admiration of classical Greek design is reflected by the columned Corinthian portico at one end and the unusual, semicircular portico at the other.

With the financial district shifting to Center City in the late 19th century, the building soon became neglected. The National Park Service took it over in 1952, making it a part of Independence National Historical Park. Today, the Park Service maintains offices in the building. Although the Exchange is closed to the public, visitors are permitted to enter the lobby and view a small exhibit that details the history and architecture of the Exchange.

⓺ City Tavern

138 S 2nd St between Walnut & Chestnut Sts. **Map** 4 E3. **Tel** (215) 413-1443. 🚇 Jefferson Station. 🚊 2nd St. 🚌 Philly Phlash. **Open** from 11:30am; reservations taken until 8:30pm. ♿
Ⓦ **citytavern.com**

Recalling the atmosphere of an authentic London tavern, the City Tavern also boasted the second-largest ballroom in the colonies when it first opened in 1773. However, just a

City Tavern, still a popular dining spot in Philadelphia

year later, with the Revolutionary War in the offing, the three-story building was used by members of the First Continental Congress as an unofficial gathering place. Later, in 1777, when he became the leader of the Continental Army, Washington used the tavern as his headquarters.

After the Revolutionary War, the Constitutional Convention held its closing banquet here in 1787. Frequented by the likes of George Washington, Thomas Jefferson, and other colonial notables, it was once called "the most genteel tavern in America," by John Adams, the second president of the United States.

However, by the 1790s, the City Tavern had lost its prominence and served as a merchants' exchange until 1834, when it was partially destroyed by fire. The original structure was finally demolished in 1854 to make way for new brownstone buildings.

After careful research, the National Park Service reconstructed the tavern in 1975. Today, the inn is almost identical to the original, with serving staff in period dress and colonial-style dishes on the menu. These include such delicacies as sweet potato biscuits, said to be a favorite of Jefferson, turkey pot pie based on Martha Washington's recipe, West Indies pepperpot soup, and ales brewed according to Washington's and Jefferson's original recipes.

Welcome Park, dedicated to city founder William Penn

⓻ Welcome Park

S 2nd St at Walnut St (2nd St & Sansom St Alley). **Map** 4 E3. 🚇 Jefferson Station. 🚊 2nd St. 🚌 Philly Phlash.

Named after the ship that ferried Penn and the first Quakers from England to the New World, the *Welcome*, this open city square is dedicated to the city's founder, William Penn. It was constructed in 1982 to commemorate the 300th anniversary of the founding of the colony of Pennsylvania. The centerpiece of the park is a smaller version of Penn's statue from City Hall *(see pp74–5)*. Emblazoned along the south wall of the park is a timeline of Penn's life and the events leading to the creation of the new colony. The park is located where the Slate Roof House – Penn's home and the Pennsylvania Seat of Government from 1700 to 1701 – once stood. This Postmodernist square is made of concrete crisscrossed by marble slabs, depicting the main streets of the original city grid planned by William Penn and his surveyor, Thomas Holmes.

At the park's north end sits the Thomas Bond House, named after the surgeon who, in 1751, along with Benjamin Franklin and others, founded Pennsylvania Hospital, the nation's first public hospital *(see p69)*. The restored 1769 Georgian-style home is now a bed-and-breakfast *(see p136)*.

Statue of William Penn

SOCIETY HILL AND PENN'S LANDING

William Penn first stepped ashore on the banks of the Delaware River at what is today known as Penn's Landing, the eastern edge of this neighborhood. An elongated and tree-lined promenade, Penn's Landing includes a plaza for concerts, historic ships and dinner boats along the piers, and the Independence Seaport Museum. Heading west, several walkways lead to Society Hill, a well-preserved area with churches, synagogues, and 18th-century homes. The area's southern border, South Street, contrasts with the more serene Society Hill, indulging in the excitement derived from a trendy and eclectic mix of cafés, restaurants, shops, nightclubs, and bars.

Sights at a Glance

Historical Buildings and Districts
6 Physick House
12 Powel House
14 Penn's Landing
15 New Market and Head House
16 South Street and Walkway
17 Pennsylvania Hospital

Parks and Gardens
1 Washington Square
9 Rose Garden and Magnolia Garden

Places of Worship
2 Mother Bethel AME Church
3 Old Pine Street Presbyterian Church
4 St. Peter's Episcopal Church
7 Society Hill Synagogue
8 Old St. Mary's Church
10 Old St. Joseph's Church
18 Mikveh Israel Cemetery

Museums and Galleries
5 Thaddeus Kosciuszko National Memorial
11 Polish American Cultural Center Museum
13 *Independence Seaport Museum pp66–7*

Restaurants *pp145–6*
1 Bistro Romano
2 Bistrot La Minette
3 Bridget Foy's
4 Cavanaugh's Headhouse
5 Chart House
6 Famous 4th Street Delicatessen
7 Jim's Steaks
8 La Famiglia Ristorante
9 Marrakesh
10 Moshulu
11 Pizzeria Stella
12 South Street Diner
13 South Street Souvlaki
14 Southwark
15 Tattooed Mom
16 The Twisted Tail
17 Xochitl
18 Zahav

See also Street Finder maps 3 & 4

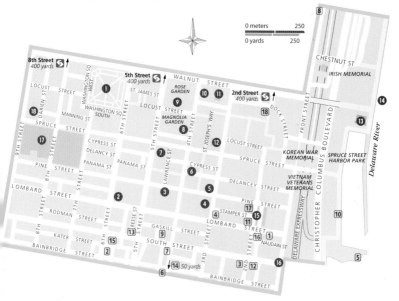

◀ Flags displayed outside homes in the Society Hill neighborhood of Philadelphia

For keys to symbols *see back flap*

Street-by-Street: Society Hill

This historic neighborhood dates back to 1682, when William Penn chartered the "Free Society of Traders" to help develop a fledgling Philadelphia. The area was home to many notable colonial figures and members of the new Federal government, which was formed after the Revolutionary War. In the late 1950s, the Philadelphia Redevelopment Authority saved hundreds of 18th- and early 19th-century homes from likely demolition, selling them to private citizens who agreed to restore them. Today, a walk through the neighborhood reveals surviving narrow streets and courtyards, and houses in a mix of architectural styles, including Georgian, Federal, Greek Revival, and Beaux Arts.

❷ **Mother Bethel AME Church**
Founded in 1794, this site is the oldest piece of land continuously owned by African Americans. A lower level museum includes the tomb of founder Richard Allen.

❸ **Old Pine Street Presbyterian Church**
The cemetery of "the Church of the Patriots" also contains the grave of Eugene Ormandy, director of the Philadelphia Orchestra from 1938 to 1980.

❹ **St. Peter's Episcopal Church**
Completed in 1761, this Anglican church has an unusual double-ended interior, with the altar at one end and the pulpit at the other.

0 meters 100
0 yards 100

Key

 Suggested route

❶ ★ Washington Square and Tomb of the Unknown Soldier
This peaceful square has the nation's only tomb dedicated to the unknown Revolutionary War soldier.

Locator Map
See Street Finder maps 3 & 4

Rose Garden

❽ Old St. Mary's Church

❾ Magnolia Garden
This garden was established as a tribute to George Washington, who liked magnolias.

⓫ Polish American Cultural Center Museum

5TH STREET

4TH STREET

SPRUCE STREET

CYPRESS ST

❼ Society Hill Synagogue

❻ Physick House

❺ Thaddeus Kosciuszko National Memorial

⓬ ★ Powel House
This restored Georgian house was the home of Samuel Powel, the last mayor of colonial Philadelphia and the city's first after the Revolutionary War. Visitors to the house included George and Martha Washington.

❿ Old St. Joseph's Church
Founded in 1733 by English Jesuits, this was the first Catholic church in the city. The present structure, dating from 1838, has a graceful curving balcony and fine stained-glass panels, such as this, depicting the Virgin.

Washington Square, one of the five original squares in Penn's grid

❶ Washington Square and Tomb of the Unknown Soldier

Walnut St between 6th & 7th Sts. **Map** 4 D3. 🚇 Jefferson Station. 🚉 5th, 8th, 9th–10th Sts. 🚌 42, Philly Phlash.

One of the five original squares in Penn's city grid, Washington Square, named after the nation's first president, is a pleasant park with benches and towering trees. This quiet space is also hallowed ground, having served as a cemetery for 90 years until the late 18th century. More than 2,000 Revolutionary War soldiers and prisoners of war were buried in massive pits here. Congressman John Adams described the pathos in a letter to his wife Abigail in 1777, writing that he spent an hour "in the Congregation of the dead" and that "I never in my whole life was affected with so much melancholy." In 1793, mass graves were again dug for victims of the city's yellow fever epidemic. Today, the park's centerpiece is the Tomb of the Unknown Soldier, with a statue of Washington, which was erected in the 1950s as a tribute to those who fought in the Revolutionary War. The tomb includes the remains of a revolutionary soldier who was buried on the site.

Washington's statue at Washington Square

❷ Mother Bethel AME Church

419 S 6th St. **Map** 4 D4. **Tel** (215) 925-0616. 🚇 Jefferson Station. 🚉 5th St. 🚌 42, Philly Phlash. **Open** 10am–3pm Mon only by appt. 🌐 **motherbethel.org**

Standing on the oldest piece of land to be continuously owned by African Americans in the US, Mother Bethel traces its roots to former slave Richard Allen (1760–1831), the first Bishop of the African Methodist Episcopal Church. Allen began preaching in 1786 at St. George's United Methodist Church *(see p53)*, where he successfully built up a black parish. He founded his own church in 1794, by buying and moving a blacksmith's shop to the current site, and using the anvil as his pulpit. The current structure was built in 1889 and still contains the original curved pews and stained-glass windows.

In 1830, the church hosted the first national convention for African Americans, and for years was a stop along the Underground Railroad, the system set up by abolitionists to transport fugitive slaves to Canada and the free states. Today, a museum in the lower level houses the tomb of Allen and his wife Sarah, along with historic church artifacts, including the original pews from the blacksmith shop.

❸ Old Pine Street Presbyterian Church

412 Pine St. **Map** 4 D4. **Tel** (215) 925-8051. 🚇 Jefferson Station. 🚉 2nd, 5th Sts. 🚌 42, Philly Phlash. 📷 10am–3pm Mon–Sat, call in advance. 🕐 10:30am Sun. 🚫 limited access. 🌐 **oldpine.org**

The only remaining colonial Presbyterian place of worship in Philadelphia today, Old Pine Street Presbyterian Church was founded in 1768. Designed in Georgian style by Robert Smith, it was later remodeled into an imposing columned Greek Revival building. George Duffield, the church's first pastor, served as chaplain to the Continental Congress of 1774, and second US President John Adams and Dr. Benjamin Rush, the "Father of American Psychiatry," were parishioners here, earning it the moniker "Church of the Patriots."

In 1777, occupying British forces used the church as a hospital and stable, also burying 100 Hessian soldiers in a mass grave outside the church wall. Today, there are more than 3,000 tombs in the surrounding cemetery, including that of Eugene Ormandy, conductor of the Philadelphia Orchestra from 1938 to 1985.

Detail of a gravestone from the Old Pine Street Presbyterian Church graveyard

Interior and altar of St. Peter's Episcopal Church

❹ St. Peter's Episcopal Church

313 Pine St. **Map** 4 D4. **Tel** (215) 925-5968. 🚇 Jefferson Station. 🚊 2nd, 5th Sts. 🚌 42, Philly Phlash. **Open** 8am–4pm Mon–Fri; 11am–3pm Sat; 1–3pm Sun. 📷 ✝ 9am, 10am & 11am Sun. 🚹 🌐 stpetersphila.org

Opened for worship in 1761, St. Peter's was founded by Society Hill Anglicans who were members of a then overcrowded Christ Church *(see p54)*, and who wanted a church closer to their homes. Christ Church and St. Peter's functioned as one parish until 1832, with Bishop White *(see p56)* serving as rector of both churches.

St. Peter's, built in Georgian style by Robert Smith, has a unique design. The placement of the wineglass pulpit and altar at opposite ends of the building, and the seats in boxed pews facing either way, give the church no definitive front or back. In 1842, well-known architect William Strickland designed the landmark tower and spire that still house bells from London's Whitechapel Foundry, which had forged the first Liberty Bell in 1753 *(see p46)*.

Buried in the graveyard are several important colonial Americans, including portrait painter Charles Willson Peale, naval hero Stephen Decatur, and George M. Dallas, vice president of the US from 1845 to 1849, after whom counties were named in Texas, Iowa, Arkansas, and Missouri.

❺ Thaddeus Kosciuszko National Memorial

301 Pine St. **Map** 4 E4. **Tel** (215) 597-9618. 🚇 Jefferson Station. 🚊 2nd St. 🚌 42, Philly Phlash. ♿ limited access. **Open** Apr–Oct: noon–4pm Sat & Sun. 🌐 nps.gov/thko

Remembered as the "Hero of Two Continents," General Thaddeus Kosciuszko fought for freedom in both his native Poland and colonial America. During the Revolutionary War, he designed and built fortifications at Saratoga and West Point that proved critical to American victories over the British troops.

After the war, Kosciuszko returned to Poland in 1784 and took part in its fight for independence from Russia, but he was wounded and imprisoned by the Russians. He was released only upon the condition that he leave Poland. He then returned to Philadelphia to recuperate from his war wounds for nine months in this Society Hill house. His upstairs room has been restored and furnished with period pieces similar to those

Physick House entrance fanlight

he owned. It also contains his medals, walking crutch, and a sable fur given to him on his release by Russia's Czar Paul I. While nursing his injuries, Kosciuszko spent most of his time reading, sketching, and receiving guests, including his close friend and then US Vice President, Thomas Jefferson.

❻ Physick House

321 S 4th St. **Map** 4 D4. **Tel** (215) 925-7866. 🚇 Jefferson Station. 🚊 2nd, 5th Sts. 🚌 42, Philly Phlash. **Open** Apr–Nov: 11am–3pm Thu–Sat (Memorial Day–Oct: also Wed), noon–3pm Sun; Mar & Dec: 11am–3pm Sat & Sun; other times by appt only. 📷 🏛 🌐 philalandmarks.org

Named after Dr. Philip Syng Physick, the "Father of American Surgery" and grandson of silversmith Philip Syng, who designed the inkwell used at the signing of the Declaration of Independence *(see p44)*, this is one of the few free-standing colonial homes that remain today. Built in 1786 by wine importer Henry Hill, this Federal-style house has what was believed to be the largest fanlight in colonial Philadelphia over its door. After acquiring the home in 1815, Physick set up his medical practice, treating such prominent patients as Dolley Madison Todd *(see p56)* and President Andrew Jackson. Physick lived there until his death in 1837, and the house has been restored to that period. Original, locally quarried Pennsylvania blue marble can be seen in the hall. Family pieces, such as a mid-18th-century oval wooden case that belonged to William Penn's grandson, a British Wagstaff grandfather clock, and original silver items are also displayed. Physick's medical instruments can be seen in an upstairs room, and include surgical tools and medicine chests with bottles.

Interior of Physick House, containing original colonial-era furnishings

❼ Society Hill Synagogue

418 Spruce St. **Map** 4 D4. **Tel** (215) 922-6590. 🚇 Jefferson Station. Ⓢ 5th St. 🚌 42, Philly Phlash. **Open** 9am–4pm Mon–Thu; call in advance. ✴ Fri night & Sat morning. 🚻 🖥 **societyhillsynagogue.org**

Originally built as a Baptist church, this impressive structure was designed by 19th-century architect Thomas Ustick Walter, who was most noted for his design of the dome and House and Senate wings of the US Capitol in Washington D.C. The original structure was built in Greek Revival style in 1830, but two decades later Walter was again commissioned to design a new Italianate façade, much of which remains today. The building was home to Baptist worshipers for more than 80 years, until a group of Romanian Jews acquired it in 1910.

By 1916, the building was known as the Great Roumanian Shul. The name, written in Yiddish, is still visible over the entrance. In 1967, it became the new home of Society Hill Synagogue, which is an active congregation rooted in the texts and practices of conservative Judaism.

❽ Old St. Mary's Church

252 S 4th St. **Map** 4 D4. **Tel** (215) 923-7930. 🚇 Jefferson Station. Ⓢ 5th St. 🚌 42, Philly Phlash. **Open** 9am–5pm Mon–Fri. 🕤 7:30am daily, plus 4:30pm Sat & 10am Sun. 🚻 🖥 **oldstmary.com**

Founded to take on parishioners from an overcrowded Old St. Joseph's Church, this redbrick church was built in 1763.

Together, the two houses of worship served the city's Catholic population as one parish until the 1820s. Old St. Mary's witnessed several significant events in the years leading up to the birth of the nation. During the American Revolutionary War, members of the Continental Congress attended services here. The first public religious commemoration of the Declaration of Independence took

Detail from Old St. Mary's Church

place here in 1779, on the third anniversary of its adoption. Following the British surrender at Yorktown in 1781, the church held a Thanksgiving service, with the flags of the conquered army laid on the altar steps. In 1810, Old St. Mary's was enlarged to its present size and became the first Catholic cathedral of the new diocese of Philadelphia. Its graveyard, dating to 1759, contains the tombs of Commodore John Barry, "Father of the American Navy," and the first to capture a British ship during the Revolutionary War; Thomas Fitzsimons, one of the signers of the Constitution; Matthew Carey, 18th-century American publisher and bookseller; and Michael Bouvier, the great-great-grandfather of first lady Jacqueline Kennedy Onassis.

Roses in full bloom in Society Hill's Rose Garden

❾ Rose Garden and Magnolia Garden

Locust St between 4th & 5th Sts. **Map** 4 D3. 🚇 Jefferson Station. Ⓢ 5th St. 🚌 42, Philly Phlash.

These two public gardens, directly across each other on Locust Street, are nestled within shaded and quiet courtyards, characteristic of Society Hill's charm. The Rose Garden stretches through the center of the entire block, all the way up to Walnut Street. It commemorates the signers of both the Declaration of Independence and the US Constitution. The funding to plant roses, which flower during spring and summer, is provided by the Daughters of the American Revolution, an organization whose members are drawn from the direct descendants of those who fought in the Revolutionary War. Inside the garden is a section of a cobblestoned street dating back to 1796.

The Magnolia Garden was established in 1959 as a tribute to George Washington, who had often expressed an interest in horticulture and, in particular, magnolia trees. Different varieties of magnolias are planted around the restful garden, whose centerpiece is a small fountain.

Italianate façade of Society Hill Synagogue

Interior of Old St. Joseph's Church with its unusual curving balcony

❿ Old St. Joseph's Church

321 Willings Alley. **Map** 4 D3. **Tel** (215) 923-1733. 🚇 Jefferson Station. 🚌 5th St. 🚐 42, Philly Phlash. **Open** 9:30am–4pm Mon–Fri (to 6:30pm Sat), 7:30am–2pm Sun. 🕛 12:05pm Mon–Sat, plus 5:30pm Sat; 7:30am, 9:30am, 11:30am & 6:30pm Sun. ♿
Ⓦ oldstjoseph.org

Located in a narrow alleyway, Old St. Joseph's was Philadelphia's first Catholic church. Reverend Joseph Greaton, an English Jesuit, founded it in 1733. In 1734, efforts were made to thwart Roman Catholic church services, but these were unsuccessful, with religious freedom for all assured by Penn's 1701 Charter of Privileges.

The old chapel was replaced by a larger building in 1757, and six years later Old St. Mary's was built a block away to handle the growing number of members. St. Joseph's current structure dates from 1838 and features a grand columned altar and a curved balcony at the sanctuary's front end. On the ceiling is the fresco, *The Exaltation of Saint Joseph into Heaven*, painted by 19th-century Italian artist Filippo Costaggini, whose work can also be seen in the US Capitol in Washington DC.

⓫ Polish American Cultural Center Museum

308 Walnut St. **Map** 4 E3. **Tel** (215) 922-1700. 🚇 Jefferson Station. 🚌 2nd, 5th Sts. 🚐 42, Philly Phlash. **Open** Jan–Apr:10am–4pm Mon–Fri; May–Dec:10am–4pm Mon–Sat. **Closed** public hols. 📷
Ⓦ polishamericancenter.org

Through portraits and memorabilia from Poland, this small museum's mission is to promote awareness and appreciation of Polish culture and history. It honors Poles who have made significant contributions to history, ranging from figures such as Nicholas Copernicus, the astronomer, and composer Frédéric Chopin, to such modern-day

Portrait of General Pulaski, Polish American Cultural Center Museum

luminaries as the late Pope John Paul II and politician and Nobel Peace Prize winner Lech Walesa. Of particular note are displays on the heroes of the American Revolutionary War, Thaddeus Kosciuszko and General Casimir Pulaski, the namesake of an annual city parade that celebrates Polish heritage. Also on display is traditional Polish folk art – festive garb, Easter eggs, decorative paper cutouts, and wooden plates.

⓬ Powel House

244 S 3rd St. **Map** 4 E4. **Tel** (215) 627-0364. 🚇 Jefferson Station. 🚌 2nd St. 🚐 42, Philly Phlash. **Open** Apr–Nov: 11am–3pm Thu–Sun (from noon Sun; Memorial Day–Oct: also Wed); Mar & Nov: Sat & Sun. 📷📷 compulsory.
Ⓦ philalandmarks.org/powelhouse

This grand Georgian home built in 1765 is an exquisite example of how the colonial elite lived. Samuel Powel, one of the wealthiest men in colonial America, was its second owner, purchasing it in 1769 when he was about to marry Elizabeth Willing. Powel was Philadelphia's last mayor before the Revolutionary War and the first after the nation's birth. He died in 1793, a victim of the city's yellow fever epidemic.

The Powels used their lavish home to entertain the country's most important citizens, such as Benjamin Franklin, George Washington, and John Adams, the second president of the US. Original features that remain today include a Pennsylvania blue marble fireplace on the first floor, the stairwell of Santo Domingo mahogany, and the cypress front door. Noteworthy furnishings include a small scale from Benjamin Franklin, original china and a sewing cabinet gifted to Mrs. Powel by the Washingtons, Gilbert Stuart portraits, and original silhouettes of Washington cut on cobalt-blue paper by Samuel Powel at a social event. Outside the house is a peaceful garden dating back to the late 1700s.

Powel House, an elegant upper-class colonial-era residence

⓭ Independence Seaport Museum

Located on Penn's Landing waterfront, the mission of this museum is to preserve US maritime history and traditions with a special focus on Delaware Bay and the Delaware River and its tributaries. Displays combine artifacts and paintings of naval encounters, along with computer games, large-scale ship models, and audiovisuals that include sounds of ship horns and accounts by sailors and shipbuilders. The museum re-creates the Benjamin Franklin Bridge as a three-story replica that spans a carpeted Delaware River. Exhibits include a replica of the bridge of the destroyer USS *Lawrence*, and of steerage compartments in which many immigrants traveled to America. There is an active boatbuilding workshop, and berthed nearby are the World War II submarine *Becuna*, commissioned in 1944, and the cruiser *Olympia*, Admiral George Dewey's flagship in the 1898 Spanish-American War.

Waterfront Museum
This expansive facility is the centerpiece of Penn's Landing.

J. Welles Henderson
Archives & Library

Submarine Becuna
This World War II vessel with torpedo launching tubes was the submarine flagship of the Southwest Pacific Fleet, which was under the command of General Douglas MacArthur.

First Floor

★ **Workshop on the Water**
Craftspeople build and restore traditional boats of the 19th century at this workshop dedicated to the skills and traditions of wooden boatbuilding and sailing in the Delaware River Valley and the New Jersey shore.

Museum Guide

The first floor houses most of the exhibits, the museum shop, and visitor information. The second floor includes the Community Gallery featuring rotating exhibits, the Olympia Gallery, What Floats Your Boat? exhibit, a concert hall, and the J. Welles Henderson Library & Archives.

Key

- ☐ Workshop on the Water
- ☐ Patriots & Pirates
- ☐ Rivers Alive & Divers of the Deep
- ☐ Rescues on the River
- ☐ Community Gallery
- ☐ Immigration
- ☐ *Titanic* Philadelphians
- ☐ What Floats Your Boat?
- ☐ Tides of Freedom
- ☐ Non-exhibition space

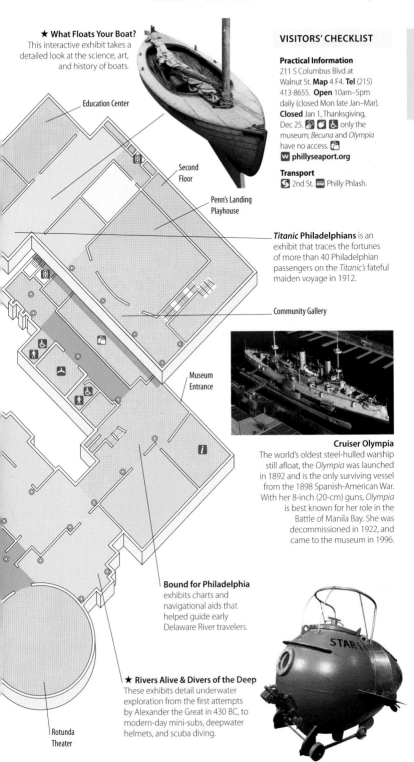

★ What Floats Your Boat?
This interactive exhibit takes a detailed look at the science, art, and history of boats.

Education Center

Second Floor

Penn's Landing Playhouse

Titanic **Philadelphians** is an exhibit that traces the fortunes of more than 40 Philadelphian passengers on the *Titanic's* fateful maiden voyage in 1912.

Community Gallery

Museum Entrance

Cruiser Olympia
The world's oldest steel-hulled warship still afloat, the *Olympia* was launched in 1892 and is the only surviving vessel from the 1898 Spanish-American War. With her 8-inch (20-cm) guns, *Olympia* is best known for her role in the Battle of Manila Bay. She was decommissioned in 1922, and came to the museum in 1996.

Bound for Philadelphia
exhibits charts and navigational aids that helped guide early Delaware River travelers.

★ Rivers Alive & Divers of the Deep
These exhibits detail underwater exploration from the first attempts by Alexander the Great in 430 BC, to modern-day mini-subs, deepwater helmets, and scuba diving.

Rotunda Theater

Small boats at Penn's Landing marina with the Benjamin Franklin Bridge in the background

❶ Penn's Landing

Western shore of the Delaware River between Market & South Sts. **Map** 4 F3. 🚆 Jefferson Station. 🚇 2nd St. 🚌 21, Philly Phlash. 🌐 **delaware riverwaterfront.com**

A popular waterfront on the Delaware River, Penn's Landing is where city founder William Penn first stepped onto his new colony in 1682 (see p20). Development of the docks began in 1967, before which it was an unappealing stretch of land. Among its attractions are grassy areas with trees, walkways, and an amphitheater for festivals and concerts are held.

Just beneath the Benjamin Franklin Bridge, the Race Street Pier (open 7am–11pm daily) is a park on the waterfront with unique architectural landscaping and spectacular views. One mile (1.6 km) north is the Independence Seaport Museum (see pp66–7) with its two historic vessels – the cruiser *Olympia* and the submarine *Becuna* – docked in a small harbor.

Several vessels are anchored here, including the 1904-built sailing ship *Moshulu* (see p146), the dinner cruise boat *Spirit of Philadelphia*, and the 1883 three-masted barkentine *Gazela*, once a Portuguese fishing boat. One mile (1.6 km) south, the newest green space here is Washington Avenue Pier, with panoramic views of the river and access to the water.

Along the Chestnut Street overpass is the impressive Irish Memorial, a bronze sculpture, which honors the more than one million people who died and the others who fled Ireland during the Great Hunger of the 1840s.

❶ New Market and Head House

2nd St between Pine & Lombard Sts. **Map** 4 E4. 🚆 Jefferson Station. 🚇 2nd St. 🚌 42, Philly Phlash.

One of the oldest in America, this covered marketplace was established in 1745. Called the "Shambles," meaning butcher shop, it was the second public marketplace in colonial Philadelphia – the first was located at the eastern end of High Street, now called Market Street. It was where vendors sold fresh produce, meat, poultry, and fish two days a week. The original New Market stretched two blocks from Pine Street to South Street and was flanked by two firehouses, known as head houses. The two firehouses once contained fire gear and apparatus for three volunteer fire companies.

Today, only the Head House at 2nd and Pine Streets remains. Built in 1805, it is thought to be the country's oldest existing firehouse. New Market was restored in the 1960s, and has since housed the farmers' market on Sundays from May to mid-December.

❶ South Street Head House District

South St. **Map** 4 E5. 🚆 Jefferson Station. 🚇 2nd St. 🚌 42, Philly Phlash.

Known as Cedar Street in colonial times, and bordering on what was then New Market and Head House Square, South Street remains a marketplace of sorts today, but with an emphasis on pop culture and counterculture. The South Street Head House District, which stretches from Front to 11th

South Street, promising revelry and an exciting atmosphere

Streets and includes some surrounding streets, is an eclectic melting pot of more than 300 shops, galleries, cafés, restaurants, bars, and more. Eateries range from pizzerias and sushi bars to vegetarian cafés and fine-dining restaurants, while shops sell everything from jewelry and fine art to funk culture items and grunge-style clothing. There are also body piercing and tattoo parlors, jazz clubs, and rocking nightclubs. The strip often overflows with younger revelers on weekend nights that usually extend into the early hours of the morning. A walkway over I-95 (also called the Delaware Expressway) links Columbus Boulevard to South Street, offering fine views of Penn's Landing, and *Battleship New Jersey* across the Delaware River.

Exterior of Pennsylvania Hospital with a statue of William Penn

⑰ Pennsylvania Hospital

800 Spruce St. **Map** 3 C4. **Tel** (215) 829-3370 (call to book a tour). 🚆 Jefferson Station. 🅂 8th St. 🚌 42, Philly Phlash. 📷 book in advance; self-guided: 9am–4pm Mon–Fri. ♿ 🌐 **pennmedicine.org**

Founded by surgeon Thomas Bond and Benjamin Franklin in 1751 to care for the "sick-poor and insane," Pennsylvania Hospital was the nation's first public hospital. The old section, the Pine Building, was built in stages. The wings are Georgian, the east wing being completed

Pennsylvania Hospital's surgical amphitheater

in 1755, and the west in 1796. The Federal-style Center House was built in 1804 and includes the Great Court, the area open for self-guided tours.

In the Great Court are the hospital's early fire pumper, purchased in 1803, and the musical planetarium clock constructed by colonial clockmaker and astronomer, David Rittenhouse in 1780.

On the second floor is a medical library founded in 1762 with a collection of more than 13,000 volumes, some dating back to the 15th century. The library, located in this room since 1807, houses the country's most complete collection of medical books published between 1750 and 1850. Under a skylight on the top floor is the nation's first surgical amphitheater, called the "dreaded circular room," which was used for operations from 1804 to 1868. Inside the Gallery Pavilion (just north of the Pine Building) is artist Benjamin West's masterpiece, *Christ Healing the Sick in the Temple*, delivered to the hospital in 1817, along with portraits of colonial physicians, including Dr. Philip Syng Physick *(see p63)* and Benjamin Rush, known for his contributions to the field of psychiatry. Outside, an 18th-century statue of William Penn stands over a peaceful courtyard overflowing with wisteria shrubbery.

⑱ Mikveh Israel Cemetery

Darien & Spruce Sts. **Map** 3 C3. **Tel** (215) 922-5446. 🚆 Jefferson Station. 🅂 8th St. 🚌 42, Philly Phlash. **Open** by appt only for visits and tours. 🌐 **mikvehisrael.org**

This burial ground, the oldest Jewish cemetery in the city and one of the oldest in America, was founded in 1740 after shipper and merchant Nathan Levy sought a place to bury one of his children according to Jewish law. Governor Thomas Penn, son of William Penn, granted land here and deemed it a Jewish graveyard. Levy, whose ship brought the Liberty Bell to Philadelphia, is also buried here. Other notables include members of the prominent Gratz family, including philanthropist Rebecca Gratz, the inspiration for the eponymous character in Sir Walter Scott's novel *Ivanhoe*; fur trader Aaron Levy, founder of Aaronsburg, Pennsylvania; rabbis of the congregation, and patriot and financier Haym Salomon. His grave is unmarked, only noted by a memorial at the entrance. Jewish soldiers of the Revolutionary War, the War of 1812, and the Civil War are also buried here. The cemetery was walled in 1751 to protect it from people "setting marks and firing shots."

Marker at Mikveh Israel Cemetery

Imposing statue of William Penn atop the iconic City Hall dotting Philadelphia's skyline

Sights at a Glance

Historical Buildings and Districts

3 Masonic Library and Museum
4 City Hall
5 Reading Terminal Market
7 Chinatown
8 Library Company of Philadelphia
13 Rittenhouse Square
15 Liberty Place

Places of Worship

2 Arch Street United Methodist Church
14 St. Mark's Episcopal Church

Museums and Galleries

12 The Rosenbach
16 College of Physicians of Philadelphia/Mütter Museum

Cultural Venues

1 *Pennsylvania Academy of the Fine Arts pp76–7*
6 Pennsylvania Convention Center
9 Academy of Music
10 Kimmel Center for the Performing Arts
11 Suzanne Roberts Theatre

CENTER CITY

This sprawling, modern downtown district is Philadelphia's financial and business center. The city's tallest skyscraper, Comcast Innovation & Technology Center, is west of City Hall, on 18th Street and Arch Street. Chinatown is at the neighborhood's eastern end, flanking the Pennsylvania Convention Center and adjacent Reading Terminal Market, with Center City's major department store, Macy's, nearby. Along Broad Street, the central north-south artery, are 19th-century buildings that house the Masonic Library and Museum and the Pennsylvania Academy of the Fine Arts in the north, while the theater district is located in the south. In Rittenhouse Square, some of the city's most lavish apartment buildings and hotels tower over town homes that line quiet streets.

☐ **Restaurants** pp146–8

1 Alma de Cuba
2 Amuse
3 Caribou Café
4 Chops Restaurant & Bar
5 Devon Seafood Grill
6 El Vez
7 Fogo de Chão
8 Lacroix at the Rittenhouse
9 Mama's Vegetarian
10 McCormick and Schmick's Seafood & Steaks
11 Nan Zhou Hand Drawn Noodle House
12 Ocean City
13 Oyster House
14 Parc
15 Penang
16 Percy Street Barbecue
17 Pumpkin
18 Rangoon
19 Reading Terminal Market
20 Rouge
21 Sakura Mandarin
22 Schleisinger's Restaurant & Deli
23 Talula's Garden
24 Tinto
25 The Black Sheep Irish Pub
26 The Prime Rib
27 Vernick Food & Drink
28 Verti Ristorante
29 Zavino
30 Zinc

See also Street Finder maps 1, 2 & 3

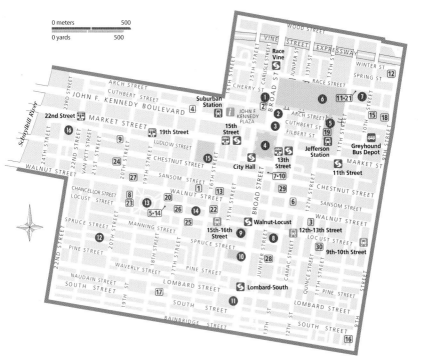

Street-by-Street: Center City

City Hall sits in the heart of Center City, where Market Street and Broad Street – the city's main east-west and north-south arteries – converge. Most of this area, dominated by 19th- and 20th-century architecture, was developed well after the American Revolutionary War. Diagonally across from City Hall is JFK Plaza, where Philadelphia's famous LOVE statue stands next to a pool and fountain, providing respite from the area's heavy commercial activity. Just a block north of City Hall are the landmark Masonic Library and Museum and the Pennsylvania Academy of the Fine Arts.

The Union League of Philadelphia on Broad Street, is a classic French Renaissance-styled building.

JFK Plaza features Robert Indiana's iconic 1960s LOVE artwork.

Dilworth Park, located on the west side of City Hall, is the city's lively new centerpiece with a lush lawn, tree groves, café dining, and a fountain that converts into an ice-skating rink in winter.

❹ ★ City Hall
A 37-ft (11-m) high statue of William Penn stands atop this Beaux-Arts building, one of the largest and most elaborate city halls in the country.

MARKET ST

JOHN

CHESTNUT STREET

SANSOM STREET

JUNIPER STREET

STREET

WALNUT STREET

| 0 meters | | 150 |
| 0 yards | | 150 |

The Wanamaker Building is designed in Beaux-Arts style with a restrained Renaissance exterior. It is built around a soaring central atrium, which houses an enormous pipe organ. The building hosts an annual holiday light-and-sound show and is home to Macy's department store.

Key

 — Suggested route

❶ ★ Pennsylvania Academy of the Fine Arts
America's oldest fine art museum was founded in 1805 by portrait artist Charles Willson Peale. Its collection spans three centuries.

Locator Map
See Street Finder maps 1, 2, & 3

❻ Pennsylvania Convention Center
Opened in 1993, the center has since undergone extensive expansion to increase the amount of space to a massive 1 million sq ft (92,900 sq m) for exhibitions, trade shows, and conventions.

❷ Arch Street United Methodist Church
This Gothic Revival church is the square's oldest structure.

❸ Masonic Library and Museum of Pennsylvania
Home to the Grand Lodge of Freemasons, the impressive interiors and architecture of this temple feature Spanish, Italian, and Egyptian influences. It is also revered for its ornate Romanesque Revival façade.

❺ ★ Reading Terminal Market
Once the largest arched-roof train shed in the world, this is now one of the best farmers' markets in the country.

❶ Pennsylvania Academy of the Fine Arts

See pp76–7.

❷ Arch Street United Methodist Church

55 N Broad St. **Map** 2 F4. **Tel** (215) 568-6250. 🚉 Suburban Station. 🚇 15th St, City Hall. 🚌 Philly Phlash. **Open** 10am–3pm Mon–Fri. ✝ 8:30am & 11am Sun. ♿ 🌐 archstreetumc.org

This Gothic Revival marble building, constructed in two sections between 1864 and 1870, is the oldest structure on William Penn's original Center Square. The church was founded in 1862 during the American Civil War and was still being built when the funeral procession of President Abraham Lincoln passed by it in 1865. It was designed by Quaker Addison Hutton, whose architectural plan called for a radical change from the unadorned and plain Quaker meetinghouses of the 18th and 19th centuries.

The original construction included the installation of a 2,322-pipe organ by J.C.B. Standbridge, Philadelphia's leading builder of organs. The organ has been restored twice, once in 1916 and again in 1959. The sanctuary's spacious atrium is detailed with a Victorian stenciling pattern and stained glass. Today, a diverse congregation from the Center City neighborhood worships at the church.

Philadelphia's Masonic Library and Museum, an architectural masterpiece

❸ Masonic Library and Museum of Pennsylvania

1 N Broad St. **Map** 2 F4. **Tel** (215) 988-1900. 🚉 Suburban Station. 🚇 15th St, City Hall. 🚌 Philly Phlash. **Closed** public hols. 🎨 📷 compulsory: 10am, 11am, 1pm, 2pm, & 3pm Tue–Sat (call to verify times). ♿ 🌐 pamasonictemple.org

An architectural jewel, dedicated as the Grand Lodge of Free and Accepted Masons of Pennsylvania in 1873, this remarkable building contains a number of ornate meeting halls in various styles. Among them, the Oriental Hall's (1896) ornamentation and coloring have been copied from the Alhambra in Granada, Spain; the Renaissance Hall (1908) follows an Italian Renaissance motif; while the Egyptian Hall (1889) takes its inspiration from the temples of Luxor, Karnak, and Philae. High arches, pinnacles, and spires form the Gothic Hall, and the cross-and-crown emblem of Sir Knights – "Under this sign you will conquer" – hangs over a replica of the Archbishop's throne in Canterbury Cathedral, England. The halls were created to honor the building trades, and much of the stone and tilework are imperceptibly faux-finished – an attestation to the skill of the men who made them. President George Washington, a Freemason, wore his Masonic apron when he laid the cornerstone of the US Capitol in Washington DC. The apron is on display, along with other Masonic rarities, in a museum on the first floor.

❹ City Hall

Broad & Market Sts. **Map** 2 F4. **Tel** (215) 686-2840. 🚉 Suburban Station. 🚇 15th St, City Hall. 🚌 38, Philly Phlash. **Open** City Hall Visitor Center: 9am–4:30pm Mon–Fri; tower & observation deck: 9:30am–4.15pm Mon–Fri (timed tickets). 🎫 City Hall interior tour (2 hrs): 12:30pm Mon–Fri; tower: every 15 mins 9:30am–4:30pm Mon–Fri. 🎨 ♿ 🌐 phila.gov

Built on Penn's original Center Square, this imposing marble, granite, and limestone landmark is the largest and perhaps the nation's most ornate city hall. The building, which took 30 years to build and was completed only in 1901, is designed in French Second Empire style with a mansard roof and prominent 548-ft (167-m) high tower. City Hall was the nation's tallest occupied building until 1909. The tower, with four clocks and a 37-ft (11-m) tall statue of Penn, was the city's highest structure until 1987 *(see box)*.

Philadelphia artist Alexander Milne Calder designed the 60,000-lb (27-tonne) statue, the largest atop any building in

City Hall with Penn's statue

No Building Higher Than William Penn's Statue

While skyscrapers sprang up across America in the 20th century, Philadelphia maintained a "gentlemen's agreement" not to build higher than 491 ft (150 m) – lower than the statue of William Penn on top of City Hall. Honoring Penn and the city's colonial heritage, the rule remained unchallenged for almost a century. But, lured by new revenues and jobs, the agreement was broken in 1987 when the 61-story One Liberty Place *(see p81)* was built. It towers over City Hall by more than 400 ft (122 m). Within just five years, several other skyscrapers followed, including Two Liberty Place, the BNY Mellon Center, Three Logan Square, and, in 2017, the city's tallest skyscraper, the Comcast Innovation & Technology Center.

Ornamental, French-influenced City Hall in the midst of Center City

the world. Calder also designed more than 250 other sculptures in the building, including the tower's bronze eagles, and the bronze figures of Native American and Swedish settlers.

Inside, rooms not to be missed include the Mayor's Reception Room, and Conversation Hall, which has statues of George Washington and other colonial notables. The City Hall Visitor Center in the East Portal gives details and tours of one of the city's most iconic buildings. An elevator takes visitors to a deck that offers spectacular city views, while interior tours include the City Council Caucus Room and explore the art, history, and architecture of the building.

Jars of preserves at Reading Terminal Market

❺ Reading Terminal Market

51 N 12th St. **Map** 3 C2. **Tel** (215) 922-2317. 🚇 Jefferson Station. Ⓢ 11th St. 🚌 Philly Phlash. **Open** 8am–6pm Mon–Sat, 9am–5pm Sun. **Closed** Jan 1, Easter, Jul 4, Memorial Day, Thanksgiving, Dec 25. ♿ 🖥 readingterminalmarket.org

Once a Center City railroad terminal and marketplace, Reading Terminal Market is now considered by many to be one of the finest farmers' markets in the United States. It was created in 1892, after two farmers' markets on this site were leveled to make space for a new train terminal. These markets were relocated beneath the new train shed. So modern was the market for its time that people came from as far off as the New Jersey shore to buy fresh Lancaster County produce. Over the years, the market gradually declined and was nearly destroyed in the 1970s. New construction routed the city's trains around the old terminal in the 1980s, and the market was refurbished in the early 1990s.

Today, the revitalized Reading Terminal Market houses more than 80 vendors, 6 days a week, selling an extensive variety of free-range meats and poultry, seafood, country vegetables, pastas, Amish specialties, and baked goods, as well as other items such as books, clothing, flowers, jewelry, crafts, unique spices, and hard-to-find specialties and ethnic foods. Several stands also offer freshly-made and prepared foods, ranging from Pennsylvania Dutch country breakfasts to soul food.

❻ Pennsylvania Convention Center

Between Market & Race Sts and 11th & 13th Sts. **Map** 2 F3. **Tel** (215) 418-4700, (800) 428-9000. 🚇 Jefferson Station. Ⓢ 11th St, 13th Sts. 🚌 38, Philly Phlash. **Open** for conventions; Head House entrance open 24 hrs. 🖥 paconvention.com

A sprawling 1 million sq ft (92,900 sq m) of meeting and exhibition space make up one of the country's most unique convention centers. The building's Grand Hall, above Reading Terminal Market, was once a bustling train terminal for the Reading Railroad. Reopened in 1994, the hall retains its Victorian features, including the majestic ceiling that had once made it the largest single-arch train shed in the world. Much of the original wooden roof and milk-glass windows remain, now casting natural light onto the terrazzo marble floor with simulated tracks where commuter trains once awaited passengers. Visitors can enter through the old railroad headhouse (now part of the Philadelphia Downtown Marriott) on the Market Street side for a peek at the Grand Hall, where a storyboard outlines its history. A second entrance on North Broad Street is part of a striking floor-to-ceiling glass façade.

Scattered throughout the multiblock complex is a collection of contemporary works of art by nearly 60 artists.

Colorful wares for sale at Reading Terminal Market

❶ Pennsylvania Academy of the Fine Arts

Founded by Colonial painter and scientist Charles Willson Peale and sculptor William Rush in 1805, the Pennsylvania Academy of the Fine Arts is America's oldest art museum and fine arts school. Its galleries display works by some of the world's best-known artists. One of them, the classical stylist Benjamin West (1738–1820), a Quaker from Pennsylvania, helped organize the British Royal Academy in 1768. Former student, the Impressionist Mary Cassatt (1844–1926), and modern abstractionist Richard Diebenkorn (1922–93), among others, share its wall space. The Academy's main building, the distinctive Historic Landmark Building, with its ornate arched foyer, is considered one of the finest examples of Victorian architecture in America. The Samuel M.V. Hamilton Building, with new galleries, reopened in 2006 as part of the museum's 200th anniversary celebrations.

Historic Landmark Building
Designed by Furness and Hewitt, the Academy's main building opened during the nation's centennial in 1876.

Historic Landmark
Building Second Floor

Sculpture Exhibit
The 1873 marble sculpture *Semiramis*, by William Wetmore Story (1819–95).

★ Walt Whitman
One of America's greatest painters, Thomas Eakins (1844–1916) taught at the academy from 1876 to 1886. This portrait of Walt Whitman celebrates the well-documented friendship between the artist and his subject. The work became Whitman's favourite among all the images produced of him.

★ The Fox Hunt
This 1893 masterpiece by naturalist painter Winslow Homer (1836–1910), considered one of the greatest American artists of the 19th century, is among the Academy's vast collections.

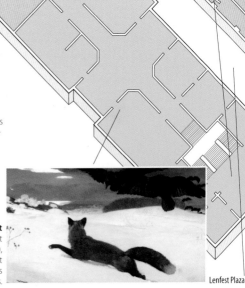

Lenfest Plaza

★ Three Wise Men Greeting Entry into Lagos
This large-scale 2008 oil-on-canvas painting,
6 ft (1.8 m) tall and almost 8 ft (2.4 m) wide,
is unique in Kehinde Wiley's oeuvre for its
subjects wearing African clothing.

VISITORS' CHECKLIST

Practical Information
118 N Broad St at Cherry St.
Map 2 F3. **Tel** (215) 972-7600.
Open 10am–5pm Tue–Fri,
11am–5pm Sat–Sun, 10am–9pm
Wed. **Closed** Mon, public hols.
🅿 🚻 1 & 2pm Wed, Fri, Sat. 📷
📱 ♿ 🅆 **pafa.org**

Transport
🚇 Suburban Station.
Ⓢ City Hall. 🚌 Philly Phlash.

Samuel M.V. Hamilton
Building Second Floor

Upper Foyer
Gallery

Samuel M.V. Hamilton
Building First Floor

Entrance

Lower Foyer Gallery

Samuel M.V. Hamilton Building
Adjacent to the Historic Landmark
Building, this newer structure doubles
the Academy's available display space,
and includes a sculpture study center and
a painting deck.

Fisher Brooks Gallery
This expansive new space on the first floor of the Samuel M.V.
Hamilton Building houses the Academy's post-World War II
collection and also holds special exhibitions.

Key

- ☐ Fisher Brooks Gallery
- ☐ Foyer Galleries
- ☐ 18th–20th-century art
- ☐ Exhibit gallery
- ☐ Tuttleman Sculpture Gallery
- ☐ Non-exhibition space

Gallery Guide

*The grand staircase of the Historic Landmark Building leads
up to the gallery level on the second floor, which displays
sculpture and 18th- to early 20th-century works, including
portraiture, Impressionist, American genre, and landscape
paintings. The Samuel M.V. Hamilton Building houses
contemporary artworks after 1945.*

Ornamental gate at the entrance of Chinatown

❼ Chinatown

North of Arch St at 10th St. **Map** 3 C1.
🚇 Jefferson Station. 🚋 11th St.
🚌 Philly Phlash.

This thriving neighborhood spans an area nearly four blocks wide and includes more than 50 restaurants, a score of grocery stores, and other shops and boutiques. Chinatown's origin dates to the 1860s, when the first Chinese laundry was established in the area. It witnessed rapid growth after World War II owing to a huge influx of immigrants.

In the US's fourth-largest Chinatown, behind those in New York, San Francisco, and Washington D.C., visitors can still find a variety of Asian fare, including traditional eel, squid, and duck dishes, and Chinese cultural gifts such as porcelain, wooden Buddhas, and dragons. The colorful Friendship Gate, with ornate dragons and Chinese art, is at 10th and Arch Streets and should not be missed.

❽ Library Company of Philadelphia

1314 Locust St. **Map** 2 F5. **Tel** (215) 546-3181. 🚇 Suburban Station. 🚋 Walnut-Locust. 🚌 21, 42.
Open 9am–4:45pm Mon–Fri.
Ⓦ librarycompany.org

Founded as the country's first lending library by Benjamin Franklin in 1731, the Library Company has the distinction of being America's oldest cultural institution. Its extraordinary collection of historic books, papers, and images – numbering more than 500,000 books, 75,000 graphics, and 160,000 manuscripts – documents American culture from the colonial era through the 19th century.

The **Historical Society of Pennsylvania**, housed on the same block as Library Company, was founded in 1824 and is one of the oldest historical societies in the US. Its stockpile has 600,000 printed items, and more than 19 million manuscripts and graphic materials from the 17th century onwards.

Dragon figurine in a Chinatown shop

🏛 Historical Society of Pennsylvania

1300 Locust St. **Tel** (215) 732-6200.
Open 12:30–5:30pm Tue & Thu, 12:30–8:30pm Wed; 10am–5:30pm Fri (last admittance at 4:45pm).
Closed public hols. 🚹 Ⓦ hsp.org

❾ Academy of Music

S Broad & Locust Sts (240 S Broad St).
Map 2 E5. **Tel** (215) 893-1999.
🚇 Suburban Station. 🚋 Walnut-Locust. 🚌 21, 42, Philly Phlash.
Open for performances. 🎟 tickets sold 1 hour before a performance & until 30 mins after the last performance begins; tickets also sold at the Kimmel Center 10am–6pm.
📅 by appt; call (215) 893-1935.
Ⓦ academyofmusic.org

Often referred to as the "Grand Old Lady of Locust Street," the Academy of Music was the city's foremost performing arts venue before the construction of the Kimmel Center in 2001. It remains the country's oldest grand opera house still in use.

Designed by Philadelphia architects Napoleon LeBrun and Gustavus Runge, the Victorian Italianate style structure took two years to build and was completed in 1857. The interior's horseshoe design offers greater visibility to the audience seated on both sides of the balconies, which are supported by Corinthian-style columns. While the façade has ornate gas lamps, the main hall still has a glittering, 5,000-lb (2,300-kg) crystal chandelier, originally with 240 gas burners and later wired for electricity. Statues representing *Poetry* and *Music* crown the proscenium arch. The former home of the Philadelphia Orchestra – which now performs in the Kimmel Center – the Academy today hosts the Pennsylvania Ballet and Opera Philadelphia (*see p164*).

The Academy of Music, home to Philadelphia's opera and ballet

The Kimmel Center's glittering, modern façade

⑩ Kimmel Center for the Performing Arts

260 S Broad St. **Map** 2 E5. **Tel** (215) 790-5800, (215) 893-1999 (tickets). 🚇 Suburban Station. 🔵 Walnut-Locust. 🚌 21, 42, Philly Phlash. **Open** 10am–6pm (box office). 🎟 compulsory: 1pm daily (free); also 10:30am Sat. 🔳 kimmelcenter.org

The centerpiece of the city's performing arts district, this modern complex includes two venues in a spacious atrium under a barrel-vaulted glass roof. The Center is named after philanthropist and businessman Sidney Kimmel, who made the single-largest private donation towards the complex.

The cello-shaped Verizon Hall, with acoustics designed specifically for the Philadelphia Orchestra, seats more than 2,500 people. The Perelman Theater seats 650 people and has a rotating stage for chamber music, dance, and theater shows.

Other highlights include an expansive lobby with a stage for separate functions, an education center for performing arts classes, and a smaller studio and theater. The center's glass-enclosed roof garden offers great city views.

The Center is the inspiration for the Philadelphia International Festival of the Arts the first three of which were held in spring in 2011, 2013, and 2016, featuring more than 100 performances across the city.

⑪ Suzanne Roberts Theatre

480 S Broad St. **Map** 3 A4. **Tel** (215) 982-0420. 🚇 Suburban Station. 🔵 Lombard-South. 🚌 21, 42. 🎟 ⬇ 🔳 philadelphiatheatre company.org

The Suzanne Roberts Theatre is home to the Philadelphia Theatre Company. The theater is named after former actress, playwright, director, and philanthropist Suzanne Roberts, who for more than 40 years, has devoted her energy and talent to the city's theater community. It is housed in a modern facility that boasts a dramatic glass façade, two-story lobby, mezzanine-level reception areas, and a 365-seat auditorium with state-of-the-art lighting and sound facilities. A second, 100-seat flexible stage is used for more intimate performances.

⑫ The Rosenbach

2008-2010 DeLancy Pl at 20th St. **Map** 2 D5. **Tel** (215) 732-1600. 🚇 Suburban Station. 🔵 Lombard-South. 🚌 21, 42. **Open** noon–5pm Tue & Fri, noon–8pm Wed & Thu, noon–6pm Sat & Sun. **Closed** Mon, public hols. 🎟 🎟 tours on the hour. 🔳 rosenbach.org

Formerly the home of Dr. Rosenbach, one of America's most prominent rare book and manuscript dealers, The Rosenbach of the Free Library of Philadelphia, an 1865 town house with a museum and research library, sits on a quiet and shaded Rittenhouse street. Dr. Abraham Simon Wolf Rosenbach (1876–1952) and his brother Philip (1863–1953) ran their company from 1926 to 1952, combining great scholarship and business acumen. Apart from books, they also bought and sold 18th- and 19th- century artifacts such as silver, furniture, sculptures, drawings, and paintings.

So precious were many of their acquisitions that the brothers kept them for their own collection, which includes nearly 40,000 rare books, manuscripts, and fine- and decorative-art objects. Some of these are displayed today, including manuscript pages of James Joyce's *Ulysses*, over 100 personal letters of George Washington, and the papers of Modernist poet Marianne Moore. In the house are the brothers' original possessions, including Chippendale furniture, gold-plated silver, and portraits by American artist Thomas Sully.

Other important items include more than 600 of Lewis Carroll's letters, original drawings and books of William Blake, and an extremely rare copy of the first edition of *Don Quixote*.

Suzanne Roberts Theatre, Avenue of the Arts

Shaded walkway and benches at Rittenhouse Square, a popular park

⓭ Rittenhouse Square

Walnut St between 18th & 19th Sts. **Map** 2 D5. 🚇 Suburban Station. 🚋 Walnut-Locust. 🚌 21, 38, 42, Philly Phlash.

One of Center City's most popular outdoor parks, on any sunny day shaded Rittenhouse Square teems with local residents and downtown workers relaxing under the trees. One of the five public areas planned by Penn in his 1682 city grid, it was originally known as Southwest Square. It was renamed in 1825 in honor of David Rittenhouse (1732–96), first director of the US Mint, astronomer, clockmaker, and a descendant of Wilhelm Rittenhouse, who established the nation's first papermill near Wissahickon Creek in 1690.

In the mid-19th century, the first house was built opposite the square, which soon became a prominent public garden. The park was given its present-day appearance in 1913 by French American Beaux-Arts architect Paul Cret, who also designed the Barnes Foundation's gallery building and the Valley Forge memorial arch. Benches line the many walkways that crisscross the park and lead to the small fountain and reflecting pool at its center. Flowers add color in spring and summer.

Since its development, the square has been a desirable address in town. Extravagant high-rise apartments and hotels, and upscale restaurants and cafés surround the square, reminiscent of a New York City park scene.

⓮ St. Mark's Episcopal Church

1625 Locust St. **Map** 2 E5. **Tel** (215) 735-1416. 🚇 Suburban Station. 🚋 Walnut-Locust. 🚌 21, 38, 42, Philly Phlash. 🕇 daily. 📷 only by appointment. 🌐 saintmarksphiladelphia.org

Founded by a local group of Anglican worshipers in 1847, St. Mark's Episcopal Church is one of the nation's best examples of Gothic Revival architecture. The parishioners raised $30,000 and hired John Notman, a prominent Philadelphia architect, to design and build a new church in the medieval designs of the 14th- and 15th-century High Gothic period. The church was opened in 1849 during the early development of the Rittenhouse Square neighborhood.

Inside is a baptistry made of inlaid Italian marble and colorful panels in a spacious sanctuary that is reminiscent of an old English church.

Not to be missed is the adjoining structure, the spectacular Lady Chapel. It was donated by Rodman Wanamaker as a memorial to his wife, who died in 1900 and is buried in the chapel's crypt. The 12 panels in this chapel have ornate carvings depicting scenes from the life of St. Mary the Virgin. Its ornate and beautiful marble altar, encased in silver, was made by Carl Krall and is one of only three such in the world. Still used for mass, it is the most well-known of St. Mark's ecclesiastical treasures. In 1937, the organ, considered to be one of the best examples of tonal construction in the nation, was dedicated to the church.

Downtown Philadelphia's Gothic-style St. Mark's Episcopal Church

⑮ Liberty Place

1625 Chestnut St. **Map** 2 E4.
Tel (215) 851-9055. 🚇 Suburban
Station. 🚇 Broad St. 🚌 Philly
Phlash. **Open** 9:30am–7pm
Mon–Sat; noon–6pm Sun. ♿
🌐 **shopsatliberty.com**

This gleaming, modern office
complex, which sprawls over a
vast area, is built on two city
blocks and anchors what were
once Philadelphia's tallest
skyscrapers. Designed by
Murphy and Jahn Associates
and built by Rouse &
Associates, the two steel
towers with sapphire-blue
glass sheathing have a
Postmodern architectural
aesthetic. Built in 1987 with
pyramidal tops and spires
reminiscent of New York's
Chrysler Building, the
945-ft (288-m) One
Liberty Place tower
was the first

structure to break the 86-year
gentlemen's agreement not to
build higher than the height of
the hat on Penn's statue on top
of City Hall *(see p74)*. The 61-story
One Liberty Place stretches
almost 100 ft (30 m) higher
than its 58-story companion
tower Two Liberty Place, which
houses luxury condominiums
("The Residences") and R2L
Restaurant, helmed by chef
Daniel Stern, located on
the 37th floor and offering
panoramic views of the city.
The mall complex that
connects the two towers
houses 60 stores that cover
the needs and fashion desires
of Center City office workers,
running the gamut from
specialty food shops, chic
boutiques, and trendy
shoe shops to more
practical outlets. A
food court has
several vendors.

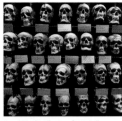

Joseph Hyrtl's collection of 139 skulls,
Mütter Museum

⑯ College of Physicians of Philadelphia/ Mütter Museum

19 S 22nd St. **Map** 1 C4. **Tel** (215) 563-
3737. 🚇 Suburban Station. 🚇 15th
St. 🚌 21, 38, 42. **Open** 10am–5pm.
Closed Jan 1, Thanksgiving, Dec 24 &
25. ♿ 🌐 **muttermuseum.org**

A nonprofit society founded in
1787 "to advance the Science
of Medicine," the College of
Physicians provides health
education to medical
professionals and the public
through the C. Everett Koop
Community Health Information
Center, the Historical Medical
Library, the Free Library, and
computerized databases.

For a visitor, the college's most
fascinating resource is the Mütter
Museum. Named after professor
of surgery Thomas Mütter,
who in 1858 donated 2,000
specimens he had used for
teaching, the museum displays
some curious and unusual items,
including preserved specimens
and wax anatomical and
pathological models. These
were used for educational
purposes in the mid-1800s,
when diseases and genetic
defects were identifiable only by
their physical manifestations.

Key exhibits include the skull
collection of Joseph Hyrtl, a 19th-
century Viennese anatomist; a
plaster cast of original "Siamese
twins" Chang and Eng, who died
in 1874; *A Stitch in Spine Saves
Nine*, which charts innovations
in spinal surgery; and the "Soap
Lady," a woman whose body
was exhumed in Philadelphia
in 1875. Memorabilia from
famous scientists and physicians
is also on display.

One Liberty Place, with Two Liberty Place behind it

LOGAN SQUARE AND PARKWAY MUSEUMS DISTRICT

Logan Square, with its multispouted Swann Memorial Fountain, is the centerpiece of Parkway Museums District, bordered by the Schuylkill River on the west and the Cathedral of Saints Peter and Paul on the east. Benjamin Franklin Parkway, often referred to as the Champs Elysées of Philadelphia, is the route for most parades held in the city. It runs through the heart of this area and is flanked by buildings with imposing architectural styles, reminiscent of the ancient temples of Greece and Rome. To the north is the Eastern State Penitentiary, a fortress-turned-museum that once housed some of the country's most notorious criminals.

Sights at a Glance

Historical Buildings and Districts

- ❷ Free Library of Philadelphia
- ❸ Logan Square
- ❾ The Oval
- ⓫ Fairmount Water Works Interpretive Center
- ⓭ Thomas Eakins House

Museums and Galleries

- ❶ *The Barnes Foundation pp88–9*
- ❺ Academy of Natural Sciences
- ❻ Moore College of Art and Design
- ❼ The Franklin Institute
- ❽ Rodin Museum
- ❿ *Philadelphia Museum of Art pp92–5*
- ⓬ Eastern State Penitentiary

Places of Worship

- ❹ Cathedral of Saints Peter and Paul

☐ Restaurants *pp148–9*

1. Bridgid's
2. Fare
3. Hickory Lane
4. Jack's Firehouse
5. London Grill
6. Luigi's Pizza Fresca
7. McCrossen's Tavern
8. Osteria
9. Pizzeria Vetri
10. Rembrandt's
11. Rose Tattoo Café
12. Sabrina's Café
13. The Belgian Café
14. The Bishop's Collar
15. Urban Farmer
16. Zorba's Tavern

0 meters 500
0 yards 500

See also Street Finder maps 1, 2 & 3

◀ Grand interior of Cathedral of Saints Peter and Paul in Philadelphia

For keys to symbols *see back flap*

Street-by-Street: Logan Square and Parkway Museums District

Central to this neighborhood is the Benjamin Franklin Parkway – a grand boulevard lined with trees and grassy areas stretching from Center City to the Philadelphia Museum of Art. Statues and sculptures around the museum add to the area's European flair. Imposing structures housing many of the city's other key museums were built along the Parkway and around Logan Square in the 19th and early 20th centuries. Today, they hold some of the world's most prized antiquities, artworks, and natural history collections. Among them are the Rodin Museum, the Franklin Institute, and the Barnes Foundation.

⑪ Fairmount Water Works Interpretive Center
Stately temple-like façades that once housed the nation's first municipal water-pumping station now serve as home to a diving, entertainment, and education center, as well as an excellent restaurant.

Statue of George Washington

⑨ The Oval
Ornate fountains and statues are the centerpieces of this traffic circle, previously named for 19th-century Philadelphia artist Thomas Eakins.

WINTER ST

⑦ ★ The Franklin Institute
A massive statue of Benjamin Franklin sits in the atrium of this popular interactive science museum. The museum highlights Franklin's discoveries in technology and also houses a planetarium and IMAX theater.

RACE ST

⑤ Academy of Natural Sciences
The oldest continuously operating natural history museum in the western hemisphere has dinosaur fossils among its more than 18 million specimens.

⑥ Moore College of Art & Design

Key

— Suggested route

❿ ★ Philadelphia Museum of Art
The country's third-largest fine art museum, sited in a landmark building, has vast collections of paintings, sculptures, and decorative arts showcasing more than 2,000 years of human creativity.

Locator Map
See Street Finder maps 1, 2, & 3

❽ ★ Rodin Museum
This small museum has more than 130 sculptures by Auguste Rodin, including *The Thinker*. This is the largest collection of his works outside France.

❶ ★ The Barnes Foundation
The gallery is famed for Impressionist and Modernist works such as Roger de La Fresnaye's *Married Life* (1913). The collection is revered for its depth and quality.

❸ Logan Square
Originally called Northwest Square, Logan Square is now centered by the Swann Memorial Fountain and flanked by the Free Library of Philadelphia.

❹ Cathedral of Saints Peter and Paul

| 0 meters | 200 |
| 0 yards | 200 |

❶ The Barnes Foundation

See pp88–9.

The Beaux-Arts façade of the Free Library of Philadelphia

❷ Free Library of Philadelphia

1901 Vine St Parkway (Central Branch). **Map** 2 E2. **Tel** (215) 686-5322. Suburban Station. Race-Vine. 38, Philly Phlash. **Open** 9am–9pm Mon–Thu, 9am–6pm Fri, 9am–5pm Sat, 1–5pm Sun. **Closed** Sun in summer, public hols. 2pm Mon, Wed, Fri; 10am Tue, Thu; 10am & 2pm Sat. Rare Book Dept: 11am Mon–Sat. freelibrary.org

Opened in 1894, this library first occupied rooms in City Hall. It relocated a few times before moving into its current Beaux-Arts building in 1927.

Today, the library has up to 1.75 million volumes, and its key collections include maps, children's books, social sciences and history books, and the largest public library chamber music collection in the eastern US. The Rare Book Department is also one of the nation's largest, with holdings that span 4,000 years and include Sumerian cuneiform tablets, medieval manuscripts, incunabula, early American children's books, and letters and manuscripts from authors such as Charles Dickens and Edgar Allan Poe *(see p98)*.

❸ Logan Square

19th St at Benjamin Franklin Parkway. **Map** 2 D3. Suburban Station. Race-Vine. 38, Philly Phlash.

Part of William Penn's original grid plan, Logan Square (then known as Northwest Square) was initially used as a burial ground, then for pastureland, and later for public executions. It was renamed Logan Square in 1825 in honor of Penn's secretary James Logan. The square changed dramatically during the 1920s, when the construction of the Benjamin Franklin Parkway turned it into a traffic circle, which is why it is today also referred to as Logan Circle.

At its center is the Swann Memorial Fountain, designed by Alexander Stirling Calder in 1924. It features three statues, meant to represent the city's three main waterways – the Delaware and Schuylkill Rivers, and Wissahickon Creek. The Sister Cities Park is also located here. This public park has many activities for kids, such as the Children's Discovery Garden, inspired by Philadelphia's Wissahickon Valley.

❹ Cathedral Basilica of Saints Peter and Paul

18th St at Benjamin Franklin Parkway. **Map** 2 E3. **Tel** (215) 561 1313. Suburban Station. Race-Vine. 38, Philly Phlash. **Open** 7am–4:30pm Mon–Sat. daily.

This grand cathedral, with a copper dome more than 60 ft (18 m) high, is a prominent city landmark. Designed by architects John Notman and Napoleon LeBrun, the Victorian Italianate basilica with Renaissance features was modeled after the Lombard Church of St. Charles in Rome and completed in 1864. The sanctuary is shaped in the form of a cross with a white marble floor, a marble altar, and six marble columns rising more than 40 ft (12 m) along the curved walls of the apse. Stained-glass windows add beauty to the main altar area, side altars, and the eight side chapels. Of particular note is the organ, one of the largest in the city, with 75 pipes and four manuals. The cathedral is now the seat of Philadelphia's Roman Catholic Archdiocese and was visited by Pope Francis in 2015.

Window of the Cathedral of Saints Peter and Paul

Logan Square's Swann Memorial Fountain, named after the founder of the Philadelphia Fountain Society

Exhibit at Dinosaur Hall, Academy of Natural Sciences

❺ Academy of Natural Sciences

1900 Benjamin Franklin Parkway.
Map 2 D3. **Tel** (215) 299-1000.
🚇 Suburban Station. Ⓢ Race-Vine. 🚌 38, Philly Phlash.
Open 10am–4:30pm Mon–Fri, 10am–5pm Sat & Sun. **Closed** Jan 1, Thanksgiving, Dec 25. 📷 ♿ 🏛 🖥
🌐 ansp.org

A natural history museum and research library, the Academy of Natural Sciences was founded in 1812 by seven naturalists, who pooled their fossils and specimens to foster education and research about the earth's diverse species. Its collection has since swelled to 18 million specimens. Exhibits are housed on four levels, and include mounted animals, ranging from birds native to Pennsylvania to bison from North America and Cape buffalo from Africa. Dinosaur Hall is a favorite with children, while the live butterfly exhibit is a reproduction of a tropical rainforest. The animals in the Live Animal Center cannot survive in the wild and are thus used for teaching purposes.

❻ Moore College of Art & Design

20th St & Benjamin Franklin Parkway.
Map 2 D3. **Tel** (215) 965-4027.
🚇 Suburban Station. Ⓢ Race-Vine. 🚌 38, Philly Phlash. **Open** galleries: 11am–5pm Mon–Sat. **Closed** Mon, public hols. ♿ 🏛 🌐 moore.edu

This school is the first and only women's art and design college in the United States, and one of only two in the world. It was founded as the Philadelphia School of Design for Women

in 1848 by Sarah Worthington Peter (1800–77). Her aim was to educate women for careers that would lead to financial independence, and in accordance with that the original curriculum provided training in the new fields spawned by the Industrial Revolution, such as textile design. Today, the college offers nine undergraduate degree programs in fine arts and design.

The galleries at Moore are open to the public. Rotating exhibitions highlight the works of alumnae and women artists. The Paley Gallery exhibits national and international artists, while the Levy Gallery showcases local artists and provides a center for exploration and experimentation for emerging and established talent. Past shows have featured work by Mary Cassatt, Karen Kilimnik, and Jacqueline Matisse.

❼ The Franklin Institute

222 N 20th St at Benjamin Franklin Pkwy. **Map** 2 D3. **Tel** (215) 448-1200. 🚇 Suburban Station. Ⓢ Race-Vine. 🚌 38, Philly Phlash. **Open** museum: 9:30am–5pm daily; IMAX theater: 10am–6pm daily (to 9pm Fri & Sat). 📷 🏛 ♿ 🌐 fi.edu

The oldest science and technology institution in continuous use in North America, this museum was founded in 1824. Named after Benjamin Franklin (see p55), the institute's first location was in the building that now houses the Philadelphia History Museum at the Atwater Kent (see p52). The current building opened in the 1930s and contains a spacious rotunda with a 21-ft (6-m) tall marble statue of Franklin. Exhibits highlight Franklin's accomplishments in medicine, astronomy, meteorology, and optics. Among the museum's attractions are Electricity Hall, which showcases his discovery of electricity, the Giant Walk-Through Heart (see p28) and the Brain with interactive devices, and the Train Factory, which has an original Baldwin steam locomotive.

Franklin's statue in the museum atrium

The KidScience exhibit, for five to eight year-olds, is designed to teach basic principles of science. Children are taken on a fictional journey across The Island of the Elements where they learn about Light, Water, Earth, and Air.

Moore College of Art & Design, housed in a modern building

❶ The Barnes Foundation

Established in 1922 by pharmaceutical magnate Albert C. Barnes and originally located on his estate in the Philadelphia suburb of Merion, the Barnes Foundation has one of the world's best displays of Impressionist, French Modern, and Postimpressionist paintings. There are more than 800 works, including pieces by Renoir, Cézanne, and Matisse. It also has ancient Egyptian and Greek art, American furniture, and African sculpture. Now located on the Benjamin Franklin Parkway, the collection is grouped into 96 ensembles, displayed without labels and with little regard for chronology, so as to highlight artistic affinities between diverse works. The collection is in keeping with the foundation's aim of promoting "the advancement of education and the appreciation of the fine arts." The original Merion site is now home to the arboretum and archives.

★ The Postman
Painted by Vincent van Gogh in 1889 in Arles, France, this is a portrait of postman Joseph Roulin. The foundation is home to seven van Gogh paintings.

Group of Dancers
Over half of the Impressionist Edgar Degas's pieces depict dancers; this painting, completed c.1900, is just one of the many fine examples of his work on view at the Barnes Foundation.

Walter and Leonore Annenberg Court

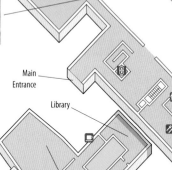

Main Entrance

Library

First Floor

Gardanne
Paul Cézanne, the renowned French artist, painted this scenic landscape of the town of Gardanne in the mid-1880s. It is located in Room 1. In total, 67 of Cezanne's works are at the Barnes, helping to make it one of the finest Impressionist collections in the world.

Auditorium

Lower Level

Gallery Guide
Artworks can be viewed on both the first and second floors. Galleries in the foundation display various paintings and sculptures that highlight different themes. An artist's oeuvre is not necessarily displayed together.

Dogone Couple
While many of his contemporaries viewed African art as "primitive" artifacts, Albert C. Barnes was an early and active collector of it. As a result, in addition to modern American and European art, the foundation holds a distinguished collection of African art.

VISITORS' CHECKLIST

Practical Information
2025 Benjamin Franklin Parkway.
Map 2 D2. **Tel** (215) 278-7000.
Open 10am–5pm Wed–Mon
(until 9pm, the first Fri of each
month). **Closed** Tue, public hols.
🖼 📷 🔊 📱 🖥
W barnesfoundation.org

Transport
🚉 Suburban Station. 🟩 Spring
Garden. 🚌 38, Philly Phlash.

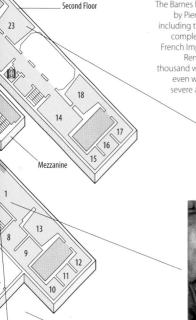

Second Floor

23

18

14

17

16

15

Mezzanine

1

13

8

9

12

11

10

Terrace

★ Leaving the Conservatory
The Barnes has over 180 works by Pierre-Auguste Renoir, including this one, which was completed by the famous French Impressionist in 1877. Renoir painted several thousand works over 60 years, even while suffering from severe arthritis toward the end of his life.

★ The Card Players
Often referred to as the father of modern art, Paul Cézanne completed this painting in 1892. Cézanne's compositions and use of color greatly influenced 20th-century art.

Models (1886-1888)
Georges Seurat was a pioneer of Pointilism, an Impressionist technique in which paintings are made from colored dots, as this piece shows.

Key
🟦 Joy of Life gallery
🟦 Permanent exhibition
🟦 Temporary exhibition
🟦 Non-exhibition space
🟦 Interior garden

Rodin's sculpture, *The Thinker*, outside the Rodin Museum

❽ Rodin Museum

2151 Benjamin Franklin Parkway.
Map 2 D2. **Tel** (215) 763-8100.
🚇 Suburban Station. Ⓢ Spring Garden. 🚌 38, Philly Phlash.
Open 10am–5pm Wed–Mon.
Closed Tue, public hols. 🎫 ♿ 📷
🌐 rodinmuseum.org

A cast of French sculptor Auguste Rodin's (1840–1917) most famous artwork, *The Thinker*, sits outside the columned façade that leads into the courtyard of this small, temple-like museum. With nearly 140 sculptures, it contains the largest collection of Rodin's work outside of Paris.

Opened in 1929, the Rodin Museum's garden showcases the impressive, 20-ft (6-m) high *The Gates of Hell*, which Rodin worked on for 37 years until his death. Also in the garden to the east of the building, is the life-sized sculpture of six heroes of the Middle Ages, known as *The Burghers of Calais*. Other notable works include *Apotheosis of Victor Hugo* and sculptures of kissing lovers, known as *Eternal Springtime*.

❾ The Oval

Benjamin Franklin Parkway.
Map 1 C1. 🚇 30th St Station. Ⓢ Spring Garden. 🚌 38, Philly Phlash. 🌐 theovalphl.org

Formerly named for prominent Philadelphia artist Thomas Eakins, this oval was part of the Benjamin Franklin Parkway project in the 1920s. Located opposite the entrance to the Philadelphia Museum of Art, The Oval has a prominent equestrian statue of President George Washington at its center. The center also features a fountain, which has figurines of wild animals surrounding four statues that symbolize four of the country's major rivers – the Delaware, Mississippi, Hudson, and Potomac. Two smaller fountains flank the large central one – the Ericsson fountain, named for the engineer who designed the USS *Monitor*, a Union naval vessel of the Civil War, and another named after Fairmount Park Commission chairman Eli Kirk Price (1797–1884), who led efforts to build the parkway. Today, the oval is at the center of a traffic circle and includes a shaded green area with park benches and a parking lot.

Washington's statue at The Oval

❿ Philadelphia Museum of Art

See pp92–5.

⓫ Fairmount Water Works Interpretive Center

640 Waterworks Dr. **Map** 1 B1.
Tel (215) 685-0723. 🚇 30th St Station. Ⓢ Spring Garden. 🚌 38, Philly Phlash. **Open** 10am–5pm Tue–Sat, 1–5pm Sun.
Closed Mon, public hols. ♿
🌐 fairmountwaterworks.org

Situated on the elevated banks of the Schuylkill River, these impressive Greek Revival buildings were constructed between 1812 and 1871 to supply drinking water to Philadelphia – the first American city to take on providing water as a municipal responsibility. When it opened in 1822, its huge water wheels, turbines, and pumps and the beauty of the site made it a destination for engineers and visitors from the US and Europe.

Water pumping ended in 1909, and today the restored buildings house old pumping apparatuses and an interpretive center with a number of fascinating interactive exhibits. All the exhibits here are based on the theme "Water Is Our World" and challenge children and adults alike to learn about water resources. Other exhibits include a real-time fish migration up the river, a virtual helicopter tour of the watershed, and a computer simulation of historic technology. Check the website for river cruises that run April to September.

Fairmount Water Works Interpretive Center, now a National Historic Landmark

Reconstruction of Al Capone's cell at the Eastern State Penitentiary

⓬ Eastern State Penitentiary

22nd St at Fairmount Ave. **Map** 2 D1.
Tel (215) 236-3000. 🚇 Spring
Garden. 🚌 38, Philly Phlash.
Open 10am–5pm daily. 🚸 children
under 7 not allowed. 🎫 ♿
🌐 **easternstate.org**

Named the "House" by inmates
and guards, the Eastern State
Penitentiary was a revolutionary
concept in criminal justice. Prior
to its opening, convicts lived
in despicable conditions and
suffered brutal physical
punishments. The Philadelphia
Quakers proposed an alternative
in the form of a facility where a
lawbreaker could be alone to
ponder and seek penitence for
his misdeeds. This led to the
opening of the penitentiary in
1829. During incarceration, with
sentences seldom less than five
years, prisoners were hooded
when outside their cells to
prevent interaction with others.

The prison, with its fortress-
like Gothic Revival façade, had
a single entrance and 30-ft
(9-m) high boundary walls.
Inside, seven cellblocks extended from a central rotunda, and
each solitary cell had a skylight
and private outdoor exercise
yard. In the early 20th
century, the isolation form of
imprisonment was abandoned,
and more cellblocks were
added. Over the years, the
prison has housed several
infamous personalities, including
the gangster Al Capone.

Officially closed in 1971, it
is now a National Historic
Landmark and museum. Today,

the structure's chipped walls
and aging cellblocks host
changing exhibitions from its
collections of old artifacts and
photographs. The prison also
conducts tours, with audio
excerpts from former guards
and inmates, and each
Halloween it hosts *Terror Behind
the Walls*, a "haunted" house
experience *(see p36)*.

⓭ Thomas Eakins House

1729 Mt Vernon St. **Map** 2 E1. **Tel** (215)
685-0750. 🚇 Spring Garden. 🚌 38,
Philly Phlash. **Open** hours vary.
🌐 **muralarts.org**

This brick row house was home
to the artist Thomas Eakins
for most of his life, with the
exception of the time he spent
abroad: first in Paris studying art

at the École des Beaux-Arts
from 1866 to 1868, and then
traveling to Spain in 1869 before
returning home in 1870. One of
the country's most renowned
Realist painters of the late 19th
and early 20th centuries, Eakins'
works often reflected life in
Philadelphia through portraits
and family paintings, as well
as through his popular city
and nature paintings, which
included sculling and sailing
scenes on the Schuylkill and
Delaware Rivers.

Today, the Thomas Eakins
House is home to the Lincoln
Financial Mural Arts Center.
Changing exhibitions in the
galleries highlight artwork
created by Philadelphia's youth
participating in the Mural Arts
and other outreach programs.

Façade of Thomas Eakins House, home to
the Lincoln Financial Mural Arts Center

Mural Arts Program

Philadelphia has America's largest collection of colorful, outdoor
and indoor murals, which are emblazoned on walls all across the
city. Through artists' visions and the sheer manpower of inspired
local youth, more than 3,600 variegated and vibrant murals have
been painted since the Mural Art Program's inception in 1984 as an

anti-graffiti initiative. With
extensive preparation,
including scaffolding and
undercoating, a typical
mural is completed within
two months and can cost as
much as $20,000. The murals
often highlight famous
community leaders, role
models, artistic cityscapes,
and themes of culture,
history, diversity, and anti-
drug messages.

Murals on city walls, a tradition in the city
of Philadelphia

❿ Philadelphia Museum of Art

Founded in the country's centennial year of 1876, Philadelphia's most prominent museum attracts major exhibitions to supplement its superlative permanent collections. More than 200 galleries showcase works of art spanning more than 2,000 years, with some Asian exhibits dating from the third millennium BC. The medieval cloister courtyard and fountain on the second floor is very popular, as are the French Gothic chapel and the pillared temple from Madurai, India. In addition to outstanding collections of Old Master, Impressionist, and Postimpressionist paintings, Pennsylvania Dutch and American decorative arts are also featured with American art. Scattered throughout the museum are computerized stations with information on the exhibits.

Mask of Shiva
A 9th-century copper alloy artifact from India.

★ Sunflowers
Impressionist painter Vincent van Gogh (1853–90) is perhaps best known for his series of sunflower paintings. This version was painted just 18 months before his death.

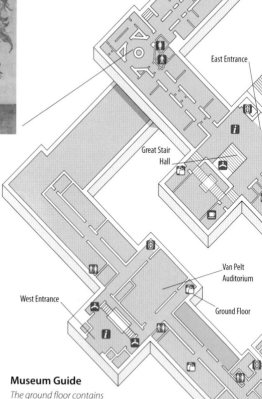

East Entrance

Great Stair Hall

Van Pelt Auditorium

West Entrance

Ground Floor

Key

Modern and Contemporary Art
Galleries 48–50, 166–188

European Art 1100–1500
Galleries 200–219

European Art 1500–1850
Galleries 250–299

European Art 1850–1900
Galleries 150–164

Special Exhibition Galleries

American Art
Galleries 110–119, 285–287, 289

Arms and Armor
Galleries 245–249

Asian Art
Galleries 220–244

Prints, Photographs, Drawings

Non-exhibition space

Museum Guide

The ground floor contains prints, drawings, photographs, and ceramics, while the first floor displays Impressionist, Postimpressionist, American, and contemporary art. The second floor has collections of European and Asian art. "First floor" refers to the floor above ground level.

The West Entrance of the Philadelphia Museum of Art

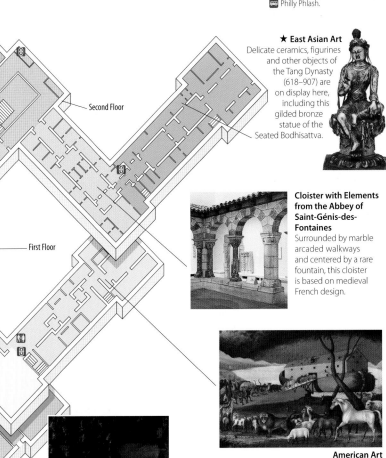

Second Floor

First Floor

★ East Asian Art
Delicate ceramics, figurines
and other objects of
the Tang Dynasty
(618–907) are
on display here,
including this
gilded bronze
statue of the
Seated Bodhisattva.

**Cloister with Elements
from the Abbey of
Saint-Génis-des-
Fontaines**
Surrounded by marble
arcaded walkways
and centered by a rare
fountain, this cloister
is based on medieval
French design.

American Art
The museum has an impressive
collection of American art that
includes *Noah's Ark*, painted in 1846
by Edward Hicks (1780–1849).

★ Thomas Eakins Collection
Several pieces from acclaimed Philadelphia artist Thomas
Eakins, such as *Portrait of Dr. Samuel D. Gross (The Gross
Clinic)* (1875) are on display in the American Art gallery.

Exploring the Philadelphia Museum of Art

The Museum of Art is home to over 240,000 objects from Europe, Asia, and the Americas, spanning more than 4,000 years. Its key exhibits include European paintings, from medieval and Renaissance to Impressionist and Postimpressionist pieces. Modern art collections feature works by Pablo Picasso and Henri Matisse, while Asian art includes furniture and ceramics. American art sections contain extensive works by Philadelphia artists Thomas Eakins and Charles Willson Peale, and the museum's collections of prints, drawings, and photographs feature works by 19th- and 20th-century US and European artists. It also has one of the oldest and largest collections of costumes and textiles in America.

Fra Angelico's *Dormition of the Virgin* (c.1427)

European Paintings, Sculpture, Decorative Arts, and Architecture

Most of the museum's second floor is devoted to European art from 1500 to 1850. In addition, it has rooms with sculpture, furniture, descriptive interiors, and original façades that highlight periods of European history from 1100 to 1800. The Portal from the Abbey Church of Saint-Laurent dates to 1125. Its imposing stone arched walls were once the main entrance to the Augustinian abbey church of Saint-Laurent in France.

The Cloister with Elements from the Abbey of Saint-Génis-des-Fontaines is based on one in a late 13th-century abbey in Roussillon in southwestern France. Other decorative arts include ceramic vases,

Jester Vase (1894) by Marc-Louis-Emmanuel Solon

stained and painted glass, stone sculptures, and metal and wooden objects ranging from candelabra to mahogany furniture and glass goblets. Key European paintings include masterpieces by Fra Angelico, Sandro Botticelli, Rogier van der Weyden, Peter Paul Rubens, and Nicolas Poussin, as well as classic European views and land- and cityscapes from 18th-century vedute artists Canaletto, his nephew and pupil Bernardo Bellotto, and Francesco Guardi. Renaissance portraits and religious paintings include Jan van Eyck's *Saint Francis of Assisi Receiving the Stigmata* (1428–30), Botticelli's *Saint Mary Magdalene Listening to Christ Preach* (c.1484–91) and Edouard Manet's *Basket of Fruit* (c.1864). Rubens' *Prometheus Bound* (1618) is a

centerpiece painting combining historical and mythological subjects.

The first floor has some excellent Impressionist and Postimpressionist paintings by artists such as Renoir, Monet, Cézanne, Pissarro, and van Gogh. Works include Renoir's *The Large Bathers* (1884–87), van Gogh's *Portrait of Camille Roulin* (1888), Cézanne's *Group of Bathers* (1895), and Monet's *Poplars* (1891), to name just a few.

American Art

One of the finest public holdings of American art, this collection is sourced from the Philadelphia area. Decorative arts, paintings, and sculptures include 18th- and 19th-century silver, ceramics, and porcelain, as well as Pennsylvania German items including toys, textiles, furniture, and illuminated folk art called Fraktur. Bookcases, desks, chairs, and chests made in colonial Philadelphia, along with other decorative arts, demonstrate the cultural links between European and early American

The Staircase Group (1795) by Charles Willson Peale

Japanese ceremonial teahouse, surrounded by a bamboo garden

Modern and Contemporary Art

The museum's modern art collection began with acquisitions of works by Pablo Picasso and Constantin Brancusi in the 1930s.

Today key holdings include Picasso's *Self-Portrait with Palette* (1906) and *Three Musicians* (1921), encompassing his decade-long study of Synthetic Cubism. Works by Marcel Duchamp include the *The Large Glass* (1915–23), applied on two planes of glass with lead foil, fuse wire and dust, and the 1912 *Nude Descending a Staircase (No. 2)*, a mechanical portrayal of a subject with Cubist qualities.

The museum's growing contemporary collection includes works by artists such as Cy Twombly, Jasper Johns, and Sol LeWitt.

Costumes and Textiles

Acquisitions from the 1876 Centennial Exposition initiated the museum's costume and textile collections. The first textiles showcased designs and techniques used in India, Europe, and the Middle East. The collections grew in the early 20th century with the addition of 18th- and 19th-century French textiles, and today number over 20,000 objects, including fashionable Philadelphia apparel, Pennsylvania Dutch quilts, weaving pattern books, and colonial-era clothing. One of the most famous costumes is the wedding dress worn by Princess Grace of Monaco, a Philadelphian. Other items include African-American quilts, 20th-century hats, 19th-century needlework, church embroideries and vestments, and three-century-old Japanese Noh robes, dating from between 1615 and 1867.

Gala Ensemble, Italy (late 19th to early 20th century)

lifestyles and designs. Key paintings include Charles Willson Peale's *Rachel Weeping* (1772) and *The Staircase Group* (1795), in which he painted his sons ascending a staircase. Thomas Eakins' works, including *The Gross Clinic* (1875), are the most significant part of the museum's collection of 19th-century paintings. However, *The Gross Clinic* rotates ownership with the Pennsylvania Academy of Fine Arts. Sculptures by the renowned artist are also housed here. Other paintings include Sanford Gifford's *A Coming Storm* (1863) and Edward Hicks' *Noah's Ark* (1846).

Bird Tree, Pennsylvania (1800–1830)

Middle East and Asian Art

Within the second-floor galleries of Asian Art are exquisite carpets, delicate jade carvings, porcelains, ink paintings, and sculptures forming part of the museum's collections of Southeast Asian, Korean, Chinese, Japanese, Persian, and Turkish art.

The Chinese Ming Dynasty (1368–1644) is represented by a room brought from China, the imposing Reception Hall from a Nobleman's Palace, and paintings and hardwood furniture. Works by Japanese artists from the 12th to 20th centuries include exquisitely painted scrolls and screens, decorative arts, and fine modern designs. A centerpiece exhibit is *Evanescent Joys*, a ceremonial teahouse acquired from Japan in 1928. Korean art includes ceramics, lacquer, and sculpture, of which an example is a rare 15th-century cast-iron tiger. Also on display are outstanding Persian and Turkish carpets, including the showpiece 16th- to 17th-century *Tree Carpet*. The carpets were gifted by collectors Joseph L. Williams and John D. McIlhenny in the 1940s and 50s. The museum's Indian art collection includes *Nandi, the Sacred Bull of Shiva*, a 13th-century schist carving from Mysore, and the impressive Pillared Hall from Madurai. Reconstructed from the ruins of three temples, its granite pillars are the only examples of stone architecture from India in an American museum.

FARTHER AFIELD

The growth of neighborhoods away from the historic center of Philadelphia only began in the 19th century, with the exception of areas such as Germantown and Fairmount Park, which were distinct areas even as far back as colonial times. These are home to some of the city's most renowned sights, including the University of Pennsylvania just beyond the Schuylkill River. Fairmount Park runs along the river, leading to the chic neighborhoods of Manayunk and Chestnut Hill. Sights to the south include the Italian Market and the Mummers Museum, while to the east, just across the Delaware River in the bordering state of New Jersey, are the varied attractions of the Camden Waterfront.

Sights at a Glance

Historical Buildings and Districts

① Edgar Allan Poe National Historic Site
② Germantown
③ Chestnut Hill
④ Main Street Manayunk
⑥ Boathouse Row and Kelly Drive
⑧ University of Pennsylvania and University City
⑩ Italian Market
⑬ Fort Mifflin
⑭ Camden Waterfront
⑮ Walt Whitman House

Parks, Gardens, and Zoos

⑤ Fairmount Park
⑦ Philadelphia Zoo

Museums and Galleries

⑨ University of Pennsylvania Museum of Archaeology and Anthropology
⑪ Mario Lanza Institute and Museum
⑫ Mummers Museum

Key

▓ Main sightseeing area
═ Highway
▬ Major road
═ Minor road
— Railroad
▬·▬ State border

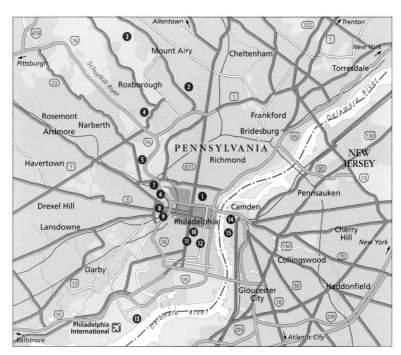

◀ House surrounded by autumnal trees in Fairmount Park, Philadelphia

For keys to symbols *see back flap*

Three-story brick house rented by Edgar Allan Poe in the mid-1840s

❶ Edgar Allan Poe National Historic Site

532 N 7th St. **Tel** (215) 597-8780.
🚇 Spring Garden. 🚌 47. **Open** 9am–noon & 1–5pm Fri–Sun. **Closed** Jan 1, Veterans Day, Thanksgiving, Dec 25.
🚻 limited. 🌐 nps.gov/edal

The great American writer Edgar Allan Poe (1809–49) lived in Philadelphia for six years from 1838 to 1844 in several residences. This three-story brick house was his rented residence for about a year between 1843 and 1844, and his only home that remains today in the city.

The inside, with original walls and creaking wooden floors, is empty, as there are no accurate descriptions of what the house looked like during Poe's time, and none of his personal belongings have survived. The visitor area, though, has exhibits and a video highlighting his life and a room decorated as depicted in his essay "The Philosophy of Furniture."

In fact, Poe's years in the city were some of his most productive, with the publishing of "The Murders in the Rue Morgue," "The Gold Bug," and "The Tell-Tale Heart." Poe's fans seem to think that the house's basement may have inspired him to write "The Black Cat." One wall has brick columns similar to where, in the story, the murderer had entombed his victim. The raven statue outside is a tribute to one of his poems, "The Raven."

❷ Germantown

Centered by Germantown Ave at Chelten Ave.
🚉 Chestnut Hill West SEPTA regional rail to Chelten Ave station. 🚌 23.

A few miles northwest of Philadelphia, this neighborhood was first inhabited in 1683 by German settlers wooed by Penn's promise of religious freedom. Its most prominent historical period was during and after the American Revolutionary War. It was the site of the Battle of Germantown in 1777, when British troops withstood an attack by the Continental Army, forcing the Americans to retreat to Valley Forge for the winter (see pp22–3). In 1793, President Washington and his family moved here to escape the yellow fever epidemic in the city. Several historic homes in this now urban neighborhood have been preserved and are open to visitors (see pp108–9).

At its center is Market Square, a busy marketplace in colonial times and now a small park dominated by a Civil War memorial. Flanking the square are the Germantown White House (where Washington stayed), and the **Germantown Historical**

Society Museum and Library. The center's museum features rotating exhibitions chosen from among its 50,000 historical artifacts and documents, some of which date back to the 1600s. About 1.5 miles (2.4 km) north is the **Awbury Arboretum**, a landscaped area with gardens, ponds, and a Victorian estate originally owned by a Quaker family, the Francis Cope House. This neighborhood is safest during the day.

🏛 **Germantown Historical Society Museum and Library**
5501 Germantown Ave. **Tel** (215) 844–1683. **Open** 9am–1pm Tue, 1–5pm Thu; call for Sun hours. 🚻 ♿

🌳 **Awbury Arboretum**
1, Awbury Rd. **Tel** (215) 849-2855.
Open dawn–dusk. ♿ limited access.

❸ Chestnut Hill

Centered by Germantown Ave at Chestnut Hill Ave. 🚉 Chestnut Hill East or Chestnut Hill West SEPTA regional rail to Chestnut Hill stations.

What began as a settlement of farmhouses and taverns in the mid-1700s is now one of Philadelphia's most upscale neighborhoods. Located on the city's northern border, Chestnut Hill is an urban village bisected by Germantown Avenue. Its shaded, cobblestoned streets

Boutiques and cafés line the sidewalks of Chestnut Hill

are lined with boutiques, fine-food restaurants, cafés, and galleries. Within its hilly terrain are the Wissahickon Gorge greenbelt and the **Morris Arboretum of the University of Pennsylvania**, an immense area that includes thousands of rare plants and "trees-of-record," greenhouses, ponds, and meadows. Some of the other attractions in this area include the **Woodmere Art Museum**, which is housed in a Victorian mansion and features a collection of more than 300 paintings and sculptures. The **Chestnut Hill Historical Society** has an archive of more than 20,000 items that date from the 1680s to the present, including artifacts, documents, and photographs.

Outdoor seating at a café along Manayunk's Main Street

drink." With the completion of the Manayunk Canal, the early 19th-century town grew into a thriving mill and industrial town. Today, the old mills are home to upscale apartments and an eclectic mix of storefronted shops. Main Street comes to life especially on weekends when sidewalk café tables fill up. The pedestrianized towpath along the canal is also popular with walkers.

❺ Fairmount Park

On both sides of the Schuylkill River & along Wissahickon Creek. **Tel** (215) 683-0200. 🚇 30th St Station. Ⓢ Spring Garden. Ⓦ myphillypark.org

Stretching along the shores of the Schuylkill River and Wissahickon Creek, Fairmount Park forms part of an extensive greenbelt. Its grassy fields and dense wooded areas are dotted with statues and crisscrossed by miles of hiking paths. The most popular path runs parallel to Kelly and Martin Luther King Jr. drives and stretches 8 miles (13 km) along both sides of the river.

West of the Schuylkill River is The Mann Center, an outdoor amphitheater and summer home of the Philadelphia Orchestra (see p164). The nearby **Horticulture Center** has elongated ponds with fountains, as well as the **Shofuso Japanese House and Garden**, a 17th-century-style Shoin mansion that has a koi pond.

The park's grand Memorial Hall, a centerpiece during the country's centennial celebration in 1876, was formerly the city's art museum. It was dedicated by President Ulysses S. Grant, but is now home to the **Please Touch Museum** for children (see p170).

Other park attractions include 18th- and early 19th-century mansions that were once the rural homes of prominent colonial families (see pp110–11).

🔼 **Morris Arboretum of the University of Pennsylvania**
100 E Northwestern Ave. **Tel** (215) 247-5777. **Open** 10am–4pm daily (Apr–Oct: to 5pm Sat & Sun). 🅿️ ♿ 📷 🖥️ Ⓦ morrisarboretum.org

🏛️ **Woodmere Art Museum**
9201 Germantown Ave. **Tel** (215) 247-0476. **Open** 10am–5pm Tue–Thu & Sun, 10am–8:45pm Fri, 10am–6pm Sat. 🅿️ 📷 📷 ♿ Ⓦ woodmereartmuseum.org

🏘️ **Chestnut Hill Historical Society**
8708 Germantown Ave. **Tel** (215) 247-9329. Archive **Open** 9:30am–1:30pm Tue & Fri, 1–3pm 1st Sat of month; appointments preferred. 🅿️ Ⓦ chhist.org

Rose at Morris Arboretum

❹ Main Street Manayunk

Main St, Manayunk. **Tel** (215) 482-9565. 🚇 Manayunk/Norristown SEPTA regional rail Manayunk Station. 🚌 61. Ⓦ manayunk.com

Once an industrial urban village known as Flat Rock, this neighborhood now has trendy stores, galleries, restaurants, and cafés lining the fashionable Main Street. In 1824, it changed its name to Manayunk, from the Lenape word manaiung, which means "Where we go to

🔼 **Horticulture Center**
100 N Horticultural Dr. **Tel** (215) 685-0096. **Open** 8am–6pm (Nov–Mar: to 5pm). 🅿️ ♿

🔼 **Shofuso Japanese House and Garden**
Tel (215) 878-5097. **Open** Apr–Oct: 10am–4pm Wed–Fri, 11am–5pm Sat & Sun. 🅿️ Ⓦ japanesehouse.org

🏛️ **Please Touch Museum**
Tel (215) 581-3181. **Open** 9am–5pm daily (from 11am Sun). 🅿️ 📷 🖥️ Ⓦ pleasetouchmuseum.org

Geese at Fairmount Park, part of Philadelphia's greenbelt

❻ Boathouse Row and Kelly Drive

West of Philadelphia Museum of Art along Kelly Drive. 🚇 30th St Station. 🚌 38, Philly Phlash.

This row of quaint stone and brick boathouses is home to what's affectionately known as the "Schuylkill Navy," namely rowing and sculling clubs patronized by area universities and high schools. Situated on the river's eastern shore, some feature Victorian Gothic architecture and date back to the 19th century. These boathouses, and others farther upstream, host the country's largest intercollegiate sculling contest in May, the annual Dad Vail Regatta (see p35).

At the south-eastern end of Boathouse Row is the Azalea Garden, where people picnic under the magnolias and large oaks. At the other end is the small 1887 Lighthouse on Turtle Rock, which once flashed beacons to warn barges and steamboats of the nearby Fairmount dam. Next to the lighthouse is Icelandic sculptor Einar Jonsson's 1918 statue of Thorfinn Karlsefni, the Viking explorer who is said to have landed in America a millennium ago. At night, strings of lights illuminating the boathouses reflect off the river, creating an idyllic scene often highlighted on calendars and postcards. A popular path along Kelly Drive offers miles of walking and biking on both sides of the Schuylkill River.

Hummingbird at Philadelphia Zoo

❼ Philadelphia Zoo

3400 Girard Ave. **Tel** (215) 243-1100. 🚇 30th St Station. 🚊 34th St. 🚌 38. **Open** Nov–Feb: 9:30am–4pm ; Mar–Oct: 9:30am–5pm. **Closed** Jan 1, Thanksgiving, Dec 24, 25, & 31. 🅿 📷 🔌 ♿ 🆆 philadelphiazoo.org

Boasting Victorian gardens and historic architecture, including the country home of William Penn's grandson John, the Philadelphia Zoo was opened in 1874. The zoo is the country's oldest and is home to almost 1,300 exotic animals from around the world. The zoo houses several rare species such as naked mole rats and blue-eyed lemurs. A walk-through giant otter habitat shows these animals at their playful best. The magnificent big cats – clouded leopards, lions, tigers (including rare Amur tigers), and jaguars – are kept in near-natural habitats or inside the Keybank Big Cat Falls exhibit, in weather-protected cages that provide a close-up view. Other features are an open birdhouse with uncaged finches and hummingbirds; the Reptile and Amphibian House with venomous king cobras, giant tortoises, and alligators basking in a tropical paradise; and a large reserve area for 10 primate species. The Zooballoon takes passengers aloft for panoramic views of the city (Apr–Oct only).

❽ University of Pennsylvania and University City

Main Campus between Chestnut St & University Ave and between 32nd & 40th Sts. **Tel** (215) 898-5000. 🚇 SEPTA Airport, Warminster, or Media/Elwyn line regional rail to University City Station. 🚊 34th St. 🚌 42. 📷 🆆 upenn.edu

This highly regarded Ivy League school has the honor of being America's first university. Founded by Benjamin Franklin in 1749, the University of Pennsylvania started classes two years later, beginning what would become the nation's first liberal arts curriculum. The university is also home to the country's first medical school, student union, and the oldest collegiate football field still in use.

Today, with more than 20,000 students enrolled in undergraduate, graduate, and professional school programs, it is often listed among America's top 10 universities. Its vast urban campus features 19th-century buildings along grassy areas and

Scenic Boathouse Row along Schuylkill River, to the west of the city

Shaded walkway at the University of Pennsylvania campus

stringed musical instruments, and an Alaskan umiak, a whaling boat with a skin hull.

⑩ Italian Market

Along 9th St between Christian & Wharton Sts. Ⓢ Ellsworth-Federal.
🚌 47. **Open** 8am–4pm Tue–Sat, 8am–1pm Sun. **Closed** Mon.
🅦 italianmarketphilly.org

Under numerous awnings and corrugated tin roofs, this open-air market is the largest and oldest of its kind in the country. The market dates to the late 1800s, when Italian immigrants sold meats and produce, and Jewish merchants sold clothing. Although still predominantly Italian, today it comprises a mix of nationalities. The sights and sounds of the market, however, have not changed much from a century ago. Several stalls offer fresh fruit and vegetables, butcher shops sell prime cuts, poultry and game meats, while seafood vendors stack fish and shellfish on ice. Other specialties include pastas, cheeses from all over the world, spices, coffees, and teas. Bakeries have pastries ranging from ricotta-filled Italian cannolies to Amish baked goods. Food stands and cafés dish up Philly cheesesteaks, pizzas, and traditional Italian dishes.

shaded walkways, including Locust Walk, its main pedestrian street. Among the notable sculptures on the campus are two of Franklin along Locust Walk, one with the statesman and inventor seated on a bench.

The Penn campus is located within University City, a revitalized neighborhood with one of the Philadelphia area's most ethnically diverse and educated populations. It has Victorian-era homes, as well as its own brand of galleries, cafés, and restaurants. Within University City are also several medical centers and other institutions of higher learning, including Drexel University.

⑨ University of Pennsylvania Museum of Archaeology and Anthropology

3260 South St. **Tel** (215) 898-4000.
🚇 Airport, Warminster, or Media/ Elwyn lines to University City Station.
Ⓢ 34th St. 🚌 42. **Open** 10am–5pm Tue–Sun (to 8pm, first Wed of each month). **Closed** Mon, public hols. 🅦 penn.museum

A world-class museum with nearly one million artifacts, this institute is one of Philadelphia's best. The museum's expansive 90-ft (27-m) rotunda is the largest unsupported masonry dome in the country, and

features Chinese art and early Buddhist sculpture. The museum's collections have been gathered since its founding in 1887 through more than 400 archaeological digs and research expeditions around the world. More than 30 galleries spread over three floors house impressive remnants of civilizations past and present spanning the earth, including a 13-ton (28,650-lb) granite Sphinx of Rameses II from 1200 BC, well-preserved mummies, an Etruscan warrior helmet from the 7th century BC, Zapotec figures from Mexico, African

A flower stall at the Italian Market

Mural depicting the Italian Market and Frank Rizzo, 1970s city mayor

Art Deco façade of the three-story Mummers Museum

⓫ Mario Lanza Institute and Museum

Columbus House, 712 Montrose St.
Tel (215) 238-9691. Ⓢ Ellsworth-Federal. 🚌 47. **Open** by appt only (see website for available dates). **Closed** Sun, public hols. 🅿️ 🏛️
W **mariolanzainstitute.org**

Housed in a former church rectory, the museum honors the world-famous Philadelphia tenor and movie star, Mario Lanza (1921–59). Lanza developed an interest in opera as he grew up, and his talents were soon recognized. His career flourished with best-selling recordings and starring roles in several major films of the 1940s and 50s, such as *The Great Caruso* and *For the First Time*.

Mario Lanza bust

Through posters, newspaper clippings, photographs, and other memorabilia, the museum charts his life from his childhood to his death in Rome from a heart attack. The museum shop sells many of the 460 songs Lanza recorded during his career.

⓬ Mummers Museum

1100 S 2nd St. **Tel** (215) 336-3050. 🚌 57. **Open** 9:30am–4pm Wed–Sat. **Closed** Sun–Tue & public hols. 🅿️ 🏛️ 🅰️ W **mummersmuseum.com**

Opened during the nation's bicentennial year in 1976, this museum celebrates the city's Mummers tradition and annual New Year's Day Mummers Parade where thousands of people strut to the rhythm of marching string bands (see

p37). Permanent and rotating exhibits showcase the museum's extensive collections. Artifacts from past parades are displayed to re-create the excitement of the event. They include floats, musical instruments used in the parades, and plumed and sequined costumes. The museum's library has newspaper clippings dating back to the late 19th century, and more than 6,000 manuscripts, photographs, works of art, and films that highlight the parade's history and tradition. Every Thursday, May through September, string bands perform a free concert at 8pm so that visitors can sample the sounds of the Mummers celebrations.

⓭ Fort Mifflin

Fort Mifflin Rd near Island Ave.
Tel (215) 685-4168. **Open** Mar–mid-Dec: 10am–4pm Wed–Sun; mid-Dec–Mar 1 (by appt). **Closed** public hols 🅿️ 🅰️ 🏛️ W **fortmifflin.us**

Historic Fort Mifflin, with its well-preserved ramparts and soldiers' barracks, is the only fort in Philadelphia. Surrounded by a moat, it overlooks the Delaware River and offers views of the city skyline, and the nearby and often noisy Philadelphia airport.

Construction of the fort began with the installation of sturdy granite walls in 1771 – the only remnants of the original fortification that remain today – and the fort stayed in continuous use through the Korean War in the 1950s.

Its most prominent moment, however, was during the Revolutionary War, when the Continental troops in the fort managed to keep the British at bay for seven weeks. This allowed Washington to retreat to Valley Forge and thwarted British efforts to open a supply route along the Delaware River for their troops who had occupied Philadelphia.

Today, Fort Mifflin is a popular tourist attraction. The former soldiers' barracks now house a

Mummers Tradition and Parade

The Mummers tradition in Philadelphia dates back to the 18th century, when European settlers ushered in the new year with parades and masquerades. The elaborate costumes were inspired by Greek celebrations of King Momus, the Italian feast of Saturnalia, and the British tradition of mummery plays. Today, the parade features the Comics, who dress as hobos and clowns and poke fun at the crowds; the Fancies, who dazzle in sequined outfits; the Fancy Brigades, who perform themed shows; and the String Bands, where marchers play banjos, drums, and glockenspiels. The parade is followed by the Fancy Brigade Finale, held at the Pennsylvania Convention Center.

Costumed revelers at a Mummers Day parade

Moat around 18th-century Fort Mifflin, Philadelphia's lone fort

small museum and a diorama depicting the siege of 1777. On display are tools, cannonballs, and grapeshot from the Revolutionary War, as well as items from the American Civil War, when Confederate soldiers, Union deserters, and civilian lawbreakers were imprisoned at the fort.

⓮ Camden Waterfront

Delaware River, NJ. **Tel** (856) 757-9154. 🚇 PATCO Speedline from Center City, New Jersey Transit. 🚌 New Jersey Transit. ⛴ RiverLink Ferry.
🌐 **camdenwaterfront.com**

This spacious riverfront area in New Jersey, opposite Penn's Landing, has gardens, a music venue, a minor league baseball stadium, art galleries, a theater, and other attractions.

One of the biggest draws is the **Adventure Aquarium**. It boasts one of the largest tanks in North America and contains over 8,500 aquatic creatures, such as sharks, seals, and stingrays. Nearby is the floating museum, the **Battleship New Jersey**, with nine 16-inch (40-cm) guns in three triple turrets. One of the nation's most decorated battleships, she served in World War II and the Vietnam War. The waterfront is also home to the 6,500-seat Campbell's Field, which hosts the Rutgers–Camden Scarlet Raptors baseball team. For concerts, head to the 7,000-seat BB&T Pavilion, an indoor and outdoor amphitheater. The **RiverLink Ferry** (*see p187*) offers a scenic ride across the Delaware River to and from Penn's Landing.

Adventure Aquarium, exterior detail

🐠 **Adventure Aquarium**
1 Riverside Dr. **Tel** (856) 365-3300. **Open** 10am–5pm daily. 🛢 📷 📱 🌐 **adventureaquarium.com**.

🚢 **Battleship New Jersey**
42 Battleship Pl, Clinton St at the waterfront. **Tel** (856) 966-1652. **Open** Feb 7–Mar 31, Nov–Dec 24: 9:30am–3pm Sat & Sun; Apr, Sep 8–Oct 31 & Dec 26–Dec 31: 9:30am–3pm daily; May 1–Sep 7: 9:30am–5pm daily. **Closed** Thanksgiving, Dec 25 & Jan 1–Feb 6 for Walk-up tours. 🛢 📷 📱 🌐 **battleshipnewjersey.org**

⛴ **RiverLink Ferry**
Tel (215) 925-5465. **Open** Memorial Day–Labor Day: 9:30am–4pm daily (to 7pm Fri–Sun). 🛢 📷 📱 ♿
🌐 **delawareriverwaterfront.com**

⓯ Walt Whitman House

330 Mickle Blvd (aka Martin Luther King Jr. Blvd), NJ. **Tel** (856) 964-5383. 🚇 PATCO Speedline, New Jersey Transit. 🚌 New Jersey Transit. ⛴ RiverLink Ferry. **Open** by appt only: 10am–noon, 1–4pm Wed–Sat; 1–4pm Sun. 📷 compulsory.

This modest, two-story house two blocks east of the Camden Waterfront is the only home that renowned American poet Walt Whitman (1819–92) ever owned. He lived here from 1884 until his death in 1892. Whitman left Washington, D.C. after suffering a stroke in 1873, coming to live with his brother George in Camden. When his brother decided to move to a nearby rural area, Whitman opted to stay on here. With the surprising success of the 1882 edition of his most famous volume of poetry, *Leaves of Grass*, he was able to purchase this home. Already a prominent poet, Whitman was visited in Camden by famous writers, such as Charles Dickens and Oscar Wilde, and Philadelphia artist and friend Thomas Eakins (*see p91*), who photographed and painted the aging poet.

Today, the house, a National Historic Landmark, contains some of Whitman's personal belongings, letters, and old photographs, including the earliest known image of the poet from 1848.

USS New Jersey, berthed at the dock adjacent to the BB&T Pavilion at Camden Waterfront

TWO GUIDED WALKS AND A DRIVE

Philadelphia's colonial history around Society Hill and Independence National Historical Park, also called "America's most historic square mile," is best explored on foot. However, for those who wish to explore other historical areas, this section introduces some neighborhoods that can be explored through a guided walk or drives.

The first is a walking tour around the Penn's Landing area along the scenic Delaware River. This tour includes stops at Gloria Dei (Old Swedes') Church, the oldest church in Pennsylvania, and the Irish, Korean, and Vietnam memorials.

The second walk explores colonial-era homes along Germantown, which was settled in 1683. This 90-minute walk includes the "White House," where the first president of the US, George Washington, and his family stayed to escape the city's 1793 yellow fever epidemic. The third is a drive through Fairmount Park, close to the Philadelphia Museum of Art on the banks of the Schyulkill River. This tour also highlights historic homes, many of which were once the summer retreats of the colonial elite. This drive includes splendid panoramic views of the city skyline at Belmont Plateau.

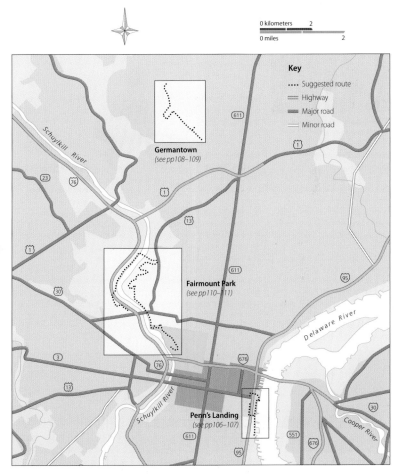

◀ Philadelphia's famed Boathouse Row along the Schyulkill River

A Two-Hour Walk Along Penn's Landing

Penn's Landing's plaza, piers, walkways, marina, and Spruce Street Harbor Park provide the setting for a scenic walk along the Delaware River, the natural boundary between the states of Pennsylvania and New Jersey. Docked along the riverside are some of Philadelphia's historic ships and popular dinner cruise boats, as this area is now a commercial and entertainment zone. The walk, which starts in the neighborhood of Old City and includes historic sights, stretches south along the river to the Gloria Dei Church and then doubles back to include the city's monuments to the Vietnam War and Korean War.

⑥ Independence Seaport Museum, showcasing US maritime heritage

② Corn Exchange National Bank, with a unique domed clock tower

Welcome Park to Irish Memorial

The walk begins in Welcome Park ① (see p57) at 2nd Street and the Sansom Street alley. Dedicated to William Penn, the park is located where his home, the Slate Roof House, once stood. Pass by the historic Thomas Bond House Bed and Breakfast (see p136) along 2nd Street to Chestnut Street, where the Corn Exchange National Bank building ② sits across the street. Designed in Georgian Revival style, the structure dates back to 1903

and now contains a branch of Citizens Bank, restaurants, and a pub.

Turn right onto Chestnut Street and stop in front of 126 Chestnut ③. A time capsule is buried at the site and a plaque on the sidewalk reads: "From the people of the Bicentennial to the Tricentennial – our mementos to be opened by the Mayor of Philadelphia on July 4, 2076."

Cross Front Street to the Irish Memorial ④, honoring those who suffered during the Irish Potato Famine (1845–50).

Irish Memorial to Spruce Street Harbor Park

Pass over I-95 and enter Penn's Landing ⑤ (see p68). Head down the curving walkway toward the river for great views of the Benjamin Franklin Bridge and the Camden Waterfront (see p103), home to the Adventure Aquarium and the Battleship New Jersey.

Walk past the RiverLink Ferry port and the Independence Seaport Museum ⑥ (see pp66–7), where the museum's cruiser

④ Detail of Irish Memorial Sculpture

Olympia and submarine *Becuna* are berthed. A dead-end walkway stretches out into the Delaware River offering splendid views of the river and the Benjamin Franklin Bridge. Continue around the marina to Spruce Street Harbor Park ⑦, which has as its centerpiece a tribute dedicated in 1992 to the 500th anniversary of Christopher Columbus's voyage to America. Across from the *Olympia* and *Becuna* is the Philadelphia Ship Preservation Guild.

Spruce Street Harbor Park to Korean War Memorial

Continue south along the waterfront to the *Moshulu* ⑧, a 1904 four-masted sailing ship that is now a floating restaurant (see p146). The *Spirit of Philadelphia*, a dinner cruise ship, is also berthed here. Then walk along Columbus Boulevard past the old Municipal Piers 38 and 40. Cross the boulevard at Christian Street to reach the Gloria Dei (Old Swedes') Church

⑤ Camden Waterfront, across Penn's Landing and along the scenic Delaware River

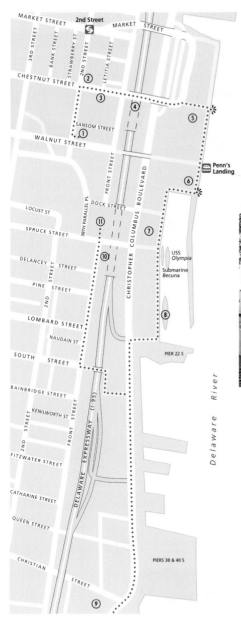

Starting point: Welcome Park on 2nd St between Chestnut and Walnut Sts.
Length: 2 miles (3 km).
Getting there: Philly Phlash.
Stopping points: Stop at the Irish Memorial, take in the views along the river at Penn's Landing, and relax under the trees at Spruce Street Harbor Park. Take time to explore the Gloria Dei Church and a few moments to reflect at the Vietnam War and Korean War memorials.

⑨ Exterior of the restored Gloria Dei (Old Swedes') church, founded in 1677

baptismal font and carved wooden cherubim holding a Bible, which were brought to the New World by the Swedish colonists. Among those buried in the church cemetery are soldiers of the Revolutionary War.

Head back up Columbus Boulevard and cross back over I-95 using the South Street overpass. Turn right on Front Street and continue to the Vietnam War Memorial ⑩. It pays tribute to the city's 80,000 veterans who served in the Vietnam War (1960–75), and has the names of more than 600 of those killed etched in stone. Cross Spruce Street and enter Foglietta Plaza, whose centerpiece is the Korean War Memorial ⑪ with the names of 610 local veterans killed or declared missing in action during the Korean War (1950–53).

⑨, the oldest in the state. Swedish Lutherans, who settled here in 1643, founded the church in 1677, before the arrival of William Penn. The brick building standing today was completed in 1700, with the steeple added in 1703. Now an Episcopal parish, the church still contains the original marble

Key

••• Suggested route

0 meters 200
0 yards 200

A 90-Minute Walk of Historic Homes in Germantown

Once a small country town a few miles northwest of Old City, Germantown (see p98) is now one of Philadelphia's oldest neighborhoods. It was settled in 1683 by immigrants from the Rhine Valley in Germany, who were attracted by Penn's promise of religious freedom. Within a century it evolved into a retreat for wealthy Philadelphia families. The homes on this walk, along cobblestoned Germantown Avenue, have been well preserved by the active Germantown Historical Society and are National Historic Landmarks. The stopping-points should be made during the day, as the area is best avoided at night. The route can be easily driven through, and tourism markers make the homes easy to find.

③ The Germantown White House, now a National Park Service property

① Germantown Historical Society and Visitor Center

Germantown Historical Society Museum and Library to Germantown White House

The walk starts at the Germantown Historical Society Museum and Library ①. This museum traces Germantown's history, in addition to selling maps of the region. The museum's rotating exhibits are culled from the society's 50,000-artifact collection of paintings, kitchenware, toys, and period clothing. Exit the center, turn left on Germantown Avenue, and walk a few blocks to Grumblethorpe ②, built in 1744 and home of wine merchant John Wister. Sally, his daughter, lived here during the American Revolution and kept a diary recording her impressions of the turbulent times. British General James Agnew died here after being mortally wounded in the fierce Battle of Germantown in 1777 (see p23) and a bloodstain remains on the first floor. The Georgian Grumblethorpe displays items that belonged to the family, and the gardens outside still retain their 19th-century appearance.

Head back up Germantown Avenue to one of the community's most famous homes, the Germantown White House ③. The house is situated opposite the Visitor Center and Market Square, which has a Civil War monument as its centerpiece. Built in 1752 by Quaker David Deshler, the home served as the headquarters of British General William Howe during the Battle of Germantown. After the

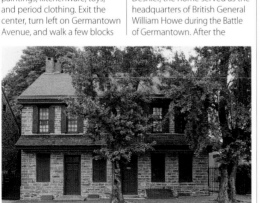

② Grumblethorpe, home to one family for 160 years

Revolutionary War, the building became known as the Germantown "White House" when President Washington and his family lived here to escape the 1793 yellow fever epidemic. Today, the house exhibits period furnishings and original paintings by colonial artists Gilbert Stuart and Charles W. Peale.

Chelten Avenue
250m

④ Back parlor of the Wyck House and Garden

Tips for Walkers

Starting point: Germantown Historical Society Museum and Library. **Tel** (215) 844-1683.
Length: 1.5 miles (2.5 km).
Getting there: Take the Chestnut Hill West SEPTA regional rail line to Chelten Avenue station.
Stopping points: Visits to all homes are recommended, though these would be dependent on opening hours.

Germantown White House to Ebenezer Maxwell Mansion

Continue up Germantown Avenue several blocks to the Wyck House and Garden ④, owned for three centuries by nine generations of the same Quaker family. It contains the family's belongings, collected from 1689 until 1973, including antiques, books, and manuscripts that highlight the family's history and its devotion to the Quaker faith.

Turning left on Walnut Lane, walk two blocks to turn right on Greene Street to the Ebenezer Maxwell Mansion ⑤. Built in 1859, it is the city's only authentically restored Victorian residence. It features original 19th-century

stenciled designs in the upstairs rooms, Rococo furniture in the dining room and parlor, and various other period items that reflect life in the 1860s.

Ebenezer Maxwell Mansion to Cliveden

Turn right on Tulpehocken Street back to Germantown Avenue and turn left for the Johnson House ⑥, built in 1768. This stone house was owned by three generations of an

⑤ Ebenezer Maxwell Mansion, a 19th-century Victorian house

abolitionist Quaker family, who made it into the city's only stop on the Underground Railroad that led slaves to freedom in Canada and the northern states *(see p62)*.

Continuing up Germantown Avenue, the next home on the walk is Upsala ⑦. Dating from around 1740 and expanded in the 1790s, the home is an outstanding example of Federal architecture, with wooden and marble mantels inside *(see p30)*. This house is where the Continental Army made its stand during the Battle of Germantown on October 4, 1777. Across the street is Cliveden ⑧. Built in 1767, it is one of the finest surviving colonial homes in the city. During the Battle of Germantown, British troops occupied the Georgian-style Cliveden and repulsed the colonial army. Chipped bricks from rifle shots are still evident on the home's façade, and one room has an original musket-ball hole from the battle that raged in the street outside. Reenactments of the battle are held on the grounds on the first Saturday of every October.

Germantown

① ③ ②

Key

• • • Suggested route

0 meters 400
0 yards 400

⑧ The study at Cliveden, an example of a colonial-era house

For keys to symbols *see back flap*

A Three-Hour Drive Around Fairmount Park Historic Mansions

Prominent colonial Philadelphia families took note of the trees and rolling hills in the landscape just west of the city along the Schuylkill River, and built mansions in what is today Fairmount Park *(see p99)*. Some of the homes had working farms with grazing lands and orchards, while others were upscale summer retreats. The park was established when the city began purchasing these properties in the mid-19th century, thus preserving scenic land and the homes in their architectural splendor. They are open for tours and are best seen as part of a driving tour. During the Christmas holiday season, those without vehicles can take a trolley tour.

Boathouse Row along Kelly Drive

Lemon Hill to Laurel Hill

Begin the drive from the parking lot at the Philadelphia Museum of Art's West Entrance ①. Turn left at the traffic light onto Kelly Drive, then drive straight on. At the seated statue of President Lincoln ②, take the fork to the right, and then make a sharp left to reach Lemon Hill ③. The house was named after the lemon trees that once grew here when Revolutionary War financier and signer of the Declaration of Independence Robert Morris owned the land. A later owner, Henry Pratt, built the mansion in 1800. The oval rooms, with curved doors, fanlights, and fireplaces on all three levels, are Federal elements, while the Palladian windows are Georgian remnants. Return to the

Lincoln statue, and turning right, continue up Kelly Drive past Boathouse Row. At the statue of Ulysses S. Grant, turn right onto Fountain Green Drive and then left for Mount Pleasant ④. Once described by President John Adams as "the most elegant seat in Pennsylvania," this Georgian house has ornate woodwork and classical motifs in the entrance hall and stairway. Returning to Fountain Green Drive, which merges with Reservoir Drive, continue to Ormiston ⑤. Built in the

1790s in Georgian style, the house has an original Scottish oven and an open fireplace. Events and rotating exhibits at Ormiston highlight the area's British heritage.

Drive down Reservoir Drive and turn left onto Randolph Drive. Continue to Edgeley Drive for Laurel Hill ⑥, a 1767 Georgian-style country house with a two-story octagonal wing, perched on a prominent bluff overlooking the river.

④ Mount Pleasant, built between 1762 and 1765

(7) Woodford, a National Historic Landmark

Laurel Hill to Memorial Hall

Continue through an intersection that has an equestrian statue of a Native American, and onto Dauphin Drive. Turn left before 33rd Street onto Greenland Drive to reach Woodford (7), built in 1758 by William Coleman, a merchant and friend of Benjamin Franklin. The Georgian house has an array of exquisite colonial decorative arts and furniture, donated by Naomi Wood, a Philadelphian collector. Continue up Greenland Drive a short distance to Strawberry Mansion (8), with its Federal-style center wing built by Judge William Lewis in 1789. Two large wings, in Greek Revival style, were added later. The house displays Empire and Federal period furnishings. Key exhibits include a doll collection and a well-preserved Victorian dollhouse. Drive down Strawberry Mansion Drive, turn right at Woodford Drive, and cross the Strawberry Mansion Bridge. Make a quick left onto Martin Luther King, Jr. Drive, continue for about a mile (1.6 km) and turn right onto Black Road toward the Smith Civil War Memorial (9). Turn right at the Memorial onto North Concourse Drive to reach Memorial Hall (10). Built in Beaux-Arts style, it was the city's first art museum and now houses the Please Touch Museum for children *(see p172)*. Guided tours of Memorial Hall allow visitors to view the building behind the scenes.

Memorial Hall to Sweetbriar

Returning to the Smith Civil War Memorial, turn left, and then make a quick right onto Cedar Grove Drive and head to Cedar Grove (11), a house that was built elsewhere and reassembled in Fairmount Park in the 1920s. This Georgian house has an unusual two-sided wall of closets on the second floor, and much of its original, early Pennsylvania furniture. It is now maintained by the Philadelphia Museum of Art. For the last stop, turn right after Cedar Grove towards the Federal-style Sweetbriar (12), the home of merchant Samuel Breck, built in 1797. The Etruscan Room is decorated in keeping with Breck's interest in classical forms and ancient Etruscan wall painting.

Tips for Drivers

Starting point: Philadelphia Museum of Art, West Entrance parking lot.
Length: 5 miles (8 km) to visit homes, then another 2 miles (3 km) back to the museum.
Stopping points: Homes open to the public can be visited, depending on opening hours and time.
Trolley tour: Tours during the Christmas holiday season leave from the Philadelphia Museum of Art and the Independence Visitor Center (6th & Market Sts).
Tel (215) 925-8687. ♿ 🅿
May–Dec 15: 10:30am & 1:45pm Wed–Sun.

(12) Sweetbriar, a three-story house built in Federal style

Key

••• Suggested route

0 meters 500
0 yards 500

(11) Cedar Grove, built as a summer home in the 1740s

BEYOND PHILADELPHIA

Exploring Beyond Philadelphia

To the west of Philadelphia, the area encompassing Lancaster County is known as the Pennsylvania Dutch Country, and is made up of bucolic hills and farmland as far as the eye can see. The region is home to the Amish *(see p117)* who wear traditional clothing and are often seen riding in horse-drawn buggies. Farther west is the town of Hershey, home of the chocolates, and Gettysburg, site of the American Civil War's bloodiest battle. To the east, the glitzy casinos of Atlantic City are just over an hour's drive away, and a little farther is the idyllic beach resort of Cape May.

Fountains at Longwood Gardens

Sights at a Glance

Boy outside a candy and ice cream store in Strasburg

◀ Farmhouse, barn and outlying buildings amid the rolling hills of southern York County, Pennsylvania

Key

▬▬ Highway
▬▬ Major road
— Other roads
— Major rail
— Minor rail
▬▬ State boundary

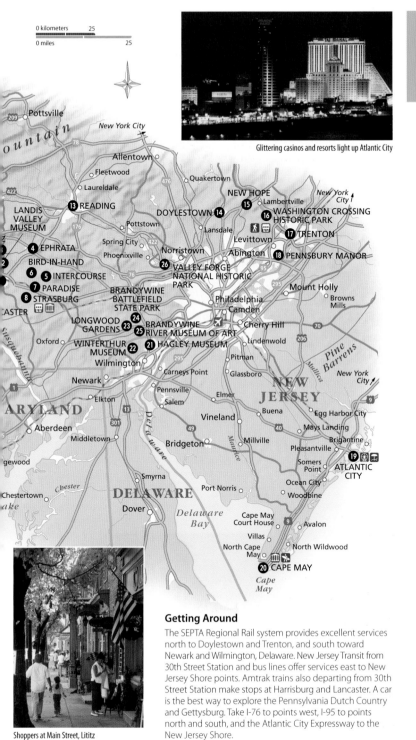

0 kilometers 25
0 miles 25

Glittering casinos and resorts light up Atlantic City

Shoppers at Main Street, Lititz

Getting Around

The SEPTA Regional Rail system provides excellent services north to Doylestown and Trenton, and south toward Newark and Wilmington, Delaware. New Jersey Transit from 30th Street Station and bus lines offer services east to New Jersey Shore points. Amtrak trains also departing from 30th Street Station make stops at Harrisburg and Lancaster. A car is the best way to explore the Pennsylvania Dutch Country and Gettysburg. Take I-76 to points west, I-95 to points north and south, and the Atlantic City Expressway to the New Jersey Shore.

For keys to symbols *see back flap*

Soldiers and Sailors Monument in Penn Square, Lancaster

❶ Lancaster

Lancaster County, PA. 🗺 55,000.
🚆 🚌 ℹ️ Discover Lancaster
Visitors Center: Route 30 at Greenfield Exit, 501 Greenfield Rd, (717) 299-8901. 🌐 **discoverlancaster.com**

Founded by John Wright in 1730 and named after his birthplace in England, today Lancaster is the county seat. Its tree-shaded streets are still lined with 18th- and 19th-century buildings. In the heart of downtown is Penn Square with its centerpiece Soldiers and Sailors Monument, dedicated in 1874 to local men who fought in the American Civil War between 1861 and 1865. Just a few minutes' walk from the square, the **Rock Ford Plantation** is located in the Lancaster County Central Park. This estate is the 18th-century home of General Edward Hand, adjutant general to George Washington during the Revolutionary War, and the estate remains an authentic example of refined country living.

At the **Lancaster Central Market**, vendors and Amish farmers sell cheeses, meats, flowers, fresh produce, and treats such as homemade cider. Nearby is the **Fulton Theatre,** Lancaster County's professional regional theater and a National Historic Landmark. For over 150 years, audiences from central Pennsylvania have been entertained at America's oldest continuously operating theater.

Located west of downtown is **Wheatland**, the estate of the

15th president of the US, James Buchanan, who served during the tumultuous years leading up to the Civil War. The house, named for the wheat fields it once overlooked, features most of Buchanan's original belongings, and has a beautiful 19th-century garden.

An old-fashioned pretzel

🏛 Rock Ford Plantation
881 Rockford Rd. **Tel** (717) 392-7223.
Open Apr–Oct: 10am–3pm Tue–Sun (last tour begins at 3pm). 🗿

🏛 Fulton Theatre
12 North Prince St. **Tel** (717) 397-7425.
Open 10am–5pm Mon–Fri (box office). 🗿

🎭 Wheatland
1120 Marietta Ave. **Tel** (717) 392-4633. **Open** Apr–Oct: 10am–4:30pm Mon–Sat, noon–4pm Sun; Nov & Dec: 10am–4:30pm Fri & Sat. **Closed** Jan–Mar, Thanksgiving, Dec 25. 🗿

❷ Landis Valley Museum

See pp118–19.

❸ Lititz

Lancaster County, PA. 🗺 9,000. 🚌
ℹ️ Lititz Welcome Center: 18 N Broad St, (717) 626-7960. 🌐 **lititzpa.com**

Named after a castle in Bohemia (now Litice in the Czech Republic), Lititz was founded by Moravians in 1756 and remained a closed settlement for nearly a century. The town boasts 18th-century

buildings, a quaint Main Street, and the Lititz Springs Park, which has a natural spring-fed creek. Today, Moravian Church Square includes the centerpiece church. Nearby is the **Lititz Museum** with its star exhibit, the Johannes Mueller House, a restored 1792 Moravian stone house named for a local tanner and dyer. A room in the museum is dedicated to General John Sutter, founder of Sacramento and a Lititz resident. It was the discovery of gold on his land that led to the 1849 California Gold Rush.

The **Julius Sturgis Pretzel Bakery**, in a house dating from 1784, offers pretzel tours. The **Wilbur Chocolate Candy Store and Museum** displays 19th-century chocolate molds that highlight the company's history since 1884, though the chocolate factory closed in 2015.

🏛 Lititz Museum
137–145 East Main St. **Tel** (717) 627-4636. **Open** Memorial Day–Oct: 10am–4pm Mon–Sat; special weekends in May, Nov, & Dec. 🗿 🏛

🎭 Julius Sturgis Pretzel Bakery
219 East Main St. **Tel** (717) 626-4354.
Open Martin Luther King Day–Mar 15: 10:30am–3:30pm (tours), 10am–4pm (store); Mar 16–Dec 31: 9:30am–4:30pm (tours), 9am–5pm (store). 🗿 ⬛ 🏛

🏛 Wilbur Chocolate Candy Store and Museum
45 N Broad St. **Tel** (717) 626-3249.
Open 10am–5pm Mon–Sat.
🌐 **wilburbuds.com**

Lititz's historic Main Street shopping district

The Amish, Mennonites, and Brethren

The Mennonites and the Amish trace their roots to the Swiss Anabaptist ("New Birth") movement of 1525, an offshoot of the Protestant Reformation, whose creed rejected the formality of the established churches. Lured by the promise of religious freedom held out to them by William Penn, the Mennonites were the first to arrive in Germantown in the late 17th century. They were soon followed by the Amish, who settled in what is now Lancaster County in the early 18th century. However, not all Pennsylvania Dutch are Amish or Mennonites; German Baptist Brethren and other subgroups are also part of the community. The mostly German heritage of these groups has given rise to a popular myth about the name "Pennsylvania Dutch" – it is thought that it came from other early colonists mispronouncing "Pennsylvania Deutsch."

Amish

The Amish sect began in the 1690s when Jacob Amman, a Swiss bishop, split from the Mennonites. The conservative Old Order Amish disdain any device that would connect them to the larger world, including electricity, cars, modern farm tools, and telephones.

Amish farms have changed little since the 17th century. Farming is usually done with horse-drawn equipment with bare metal wheels.

Amish families dress in plain, dark attire, with women in white caps and men in straw hats.

Buggies are used even today

Mennonites in traditional dress

Mennonites

Taking their name from Menno Simons, a young Dutch priest who advocated adult baptism by faith in the 1530s, Mennonites are pacifists and believe in simple living. However, they do not segregate themselves from society, and in recent years urbanization has lured many to the cities.

German Baptist Brethren

Alexander Mack founded this movement in 1708, breaking away from the established and reformed faiths of the time and following the German Pietists in espousing worship on a more personal level. The pacifist Brethren migrated to America in the late 1720s. They believe in adult baptism and adhere only to the teachings of the New Testament.

Old Order Brethren at a Pennsylvania Dutch Country covered bridge

The Brethren church is where the community worships and baptizes adults by "dunking" them thrice in the name of the Holy Trinity.

❷ Landis Valley Museum

The descendants of German settlers, brothers George and Henry Landis, started the Landis Valley Museum in the 1920s. At that time, it included more than 75,000 objects from the 18th and 19th centuries, featuring the traditions and farming culture of the Pennsylvania German community. Now supported and run by the state Historical and Museum Commission, Landis Valley is a living history village of Pennsylvania German life and home to nearly 100,000 artifacts such as quilts, rugs, leather goods, carriages, kitchen utensils, baskets, and lace. More than 30 homes, barns, sheds, shops, and other structures highlight the trades and crafts of earlier generations, complemented by regular demonstrations by craftspeople.

Maple Grove Schoolhouse
This 1890 Amish school features authentic wooden desks.

★ **Landis Collections Gallery**
Items like this silver lamp are displayed in the museum's historic collection, which dates from 1740 to 1940.

Country Store
A wide range of items, including farm tools, saddles, phonograph records, and glass-jarred licorice, stock the shelves of this reconstructed store.

Firehouse and Surveyor Shop
The larger firehouse, which has original pumpers inside, resembles a late 19th-century fire company.

★ Farm Machinery and Tool Barn

This building houses a major exhibit of Pennsylvania German farm machinery and tools dating back to the Colonial era and into the 20th century.

VISITORS' CHECKLIST

Practical Information
Route 272, 2451 Kissel Hill Rd, Lancaster, PA. **Tel** (717) 569-0401; Museum Store (717) 569-9312.
Open Jan 1–Mar 8: 9am–5pm Wed–Sat, noon–5pm Sun; Mar 9–Dec 31: 9am–5pm Mon–Sat, noon–5pm Sun.
Closed Jan 1, Thanksgiving, Dec 25. 🅿 🚻 & call to arrange. 📷
🆆 landisvalleymuseum.org

Transport
🚆 Amtrak from 30th St Station to Lancaster.

★ Landis House and Stable

This 1870s Victorian house is the original homestead of the museum's founders, brothers George and Henry Landis. Decorated with late 1800s and early 1900s furnishings, it exemplifies the Pennsylvania farmhouse of this period.

Tavern

The spacious brick-paved kitchen of the inn, with its enormous walk-in fireplace and displays of baskets, utensils, and stoneware jugs, reflects 18th-century cooking methods.

★ Gun Shop

An elaborate exhibit of Pennsylvania long rifles, powder horns, and gunsmithing tools sits within this stone structure. Early settlers used such shops to perfect the accuracy of their weapons.

Austere interior of the Saal, the meetinghouse in Ephrata Cloister

❹ Ephrata

Lancaster County, PA. 🚗 13,000. 🚌
ℹ️ 16 E Main St; (717) 738-9010.
🌐 ephrataareachamber.org

This northern Lancaster County community was settled in 1732 by a German religious order led by Conrad Beissel, who founded one of America's earliest communal societies. The order built the medieval-style buildings that make up the **Ephrata Cloister**. Today, nine structures from the mid-1700s remain. The Sisters' House, next to the meetinghouse, has rows of windows for each small chamber where members slept on narrow benches. Other buildings include a schoolhouse, bakery, woodshop, and print shop. The cloister visitor center displays artifacts, such as the Mennonites' 1,500-page *Martyrs' Mirror*. Just north of town, on State Street, vendors at the Green Dragon Farmers' Market sell antiques, Pennsylvania Dutch treats, and crafts every Friday (9am–9pm).

🎫 **Ephrata Cloister**
632 W Main St. **Tel** (717) 733-6600. **Open** Jan–Feb: 9am–5pm Wed–Sat, noon–5pm Sun; Mar–Dec: 9am–5pm Mon–Sat, noon–5pm Sun. 🈁

🕒 10am, noon, 2pm & 3:30pm Mon–Sat; 12:30pm, 1:30pm, 2:30pm & 3:30pm Sun. 📷 🈵 limited.
🌐 ephratacloister.org

❺ Intercourse

Lancaster County, PA. 🚗 900. 🚌
🌐 villageofintercourse.com

Theories abound on how the village acquired its interesting name, including it coming from the intersection of the two main roads, from an old racecourse, or even from Intercourse being a center for social interaction. Founded in 1754, the village is one of the main centers for Amish business. Key to its success are the extensive gift shops and stores that lure tourists by the busloads. For instance, Kitchen Kettle Village, a mini-shopping center, has over 30 restaurants and country shops selling everything from quilts and baskets to woodcraft. One store delights customers with homemade jellies and relishes bottled on the spot by Amish women. In the center of town, along Old Philadelphia Pike, is **The Old Country Store**. Opened in 1978, the store sells locally made Mennonite and Amish quilts, plus pottery, Amish dolls, and crafts.

West of the town center is the **Amish Experience at Plain &**

Exhibit detail at The Old Country Store

Fancy Farm, where visitors can tour a traditional Amish home and view the multimedia show, *Jacob's Choice*, which chronicles an Amish family's efforts to preserve its lifestyle.

🏬 **The Old Country Store**
3510 Old Philadelphia Pike. **Tel** (717) 768-7101. **Open** Jun–Oct: 9am–6:30pm Mon–Sat; Nov–May: 9am–5pm Mon–Sat. 🈁
🌐 theoldcountrystore.com

🏬 **Amish Experience at Plain & Fancy Farm**
3121 Old Philadelphia Pike, Route 340, Bird-In-Hand. **Tel** (717) 768-8400, ext 210. **Open** Times vary by tour type. Visit the website or call for details. 🈁
🈁 🌐 amishexperience.com

❻ Bird-in-Hand

Lancaster County, PA. 🚗 300. 🚌
🌐 bird-in-hand.com

This village is said to have received its unusual name from an historic 1734 inn that once dangled a tavern sign depicting a man with a perched bird in his hand. The village contains a cluster of restaurants, stores, hotels, and quaint farmhouses.

The **Farmers' Market** bustles with stalls packed with foods ranging from farm vegetables to fresh bacon and sausage. Across the street, the beautifully restored **Peddler's Cottage** features twelve rooms stocked full of antique furniture (including classic primitive and colonial styles), handicrafts, and a wide selection of specialty gifts. Set up in 1877, the Weavertown One-

Amish boys ride a buggy into the village of Intercourse

Room School showcases a typical schoolhouse, now reopened as a craft store.

🏠 Farmers' Market

2710 Old Philadelphia Pike. **Tel** (717) 393-9674. **Open** Apr–Jun & Nov: 8:30am–5:30pm Wed, Fri, & Sat; Jul–Oct: 8:30am–5:30pm Wed–Sat; Dec–Mar: 8:30am–5:30pm Fri & Sat.

W birdinhandfarmersmarket.com

🏛 Peddler's Cottage

2709 Old Philadelphia Pike.
Tel (717) 397-7787.
Open 9am–5pm Mon–Sat. 📷

❼ Paradise

Lancaster County, PA. 🚶 1,000. 🚌
W lancasterpa.com/paradise

The origins of this small village along Route 30 date from colonial times, when the road served as a link between Lancaster and Philadelphia. Paradise grew as the number of inns and taverns increased along Route 30. One of them, the Historic Revere Tavern, was built in 1740 and is still a working restaurant *(see p139)*. President James Buchanan purchased it in 1841 as a home for his brother, a reverend, whose wife was the sister of songsmith Stephen Foster, writer of such American favorites as "Oh! Susanna" and "My Old Kentucky Home."

A short drive east is the one-of-a-kind **National Christmas Center**, where the spirit of Yuletide is always in the air. Spread over 20,000 sq ft (1,860 sq m) are life-sized scenes depicting Christmas feasts and snowy villages, toy train and nativity displays, and several versions of St. Nicholas from around the globe.

Signage at the National Christmas Center

🏛 National Christmas Center

3427 Lincoln Hwy East.
Tel (717) 442-7950. **Open** May 1–Jan 1: 10am–6pm daily; Mar & Apr: 10am–6pm Sat & Sun. **Closed** Jan–Feb, Thanksgiving, Dec 25. 📷 📷
W nationalchristmascenter.com

An Amish house and buggy in Strasburg

❽ Strasburg

Lancaster County, PA. 🚶 2,800. ℹ
Chamber of Commerce, 132 W King St (10am–3pm Mon–Fri); (540) 465-3187. **W** strasburgpa.com

Initially settled by French Huguenots in the early 18th century, Strasburg is named after the cathedral city of Strasbourg in France. The first structures, built in 1733, are now part of the historical district along with numerous colonial stone and log homes. The town developed as an educational and cultural center as followers of different faiths chose to settle here. But, by the mid-19th century, it had become home to the railroads that are today its most popular attraction. Set up in 1832, the **Strasburg Railroad** offers 45-minute rides in refurbished railcars pulled by early 20th-century coal-fired, smoke-belching locomotives. Directly across the highway is the **Railroad Museum of Pennsylvania**, with spacious hangars housing one of the nation's largest collections of classic railroad cars, locomotives, and colorful cabooses. The **National Toy Train Museum** has exhibitions of collector-item locomotives and exquisite model train layouts, while the **Choo Choo Barn** has one of the most unique model railroads in the world, with 22 trains running through scenes of Lancaster County.

North of town is the **Amish Village** with an 1840s Amish house, smokehouse, blacksmith shop, and water wheel. The Millennium Theater nearby is home to inspirational, Biblical-themed stage productions.

🚂 Strasburg Railroad

301 Gap Rd, Ronks, Rte 741, E of Strasburg. **Tel** 1-866-725-9666.
Open Feb–Dec; check website or call for times. **Closed** Jan. 📷 📷 📷
W strasburgrailroad.com

🏛 Railroad Museum of Pennsylvania

300 Gap Rd. **Tel** (717) 687-8628.
Open Apr–Oct: 9am–5pm Mon–Sat, noon–5pm Sun; Nov–Mar: 9am–5pm Tue–Sat, noon–5pm Sun. **Closed** Jan 1, Thanksgiving, Dec 25. 📷 📷
W rrmuseumpa.org

🏛 National Toy Train Museum

300 Paradise Lane, off Rte 741, E of Strasburg. **Tel** (717) 687-8976. **Open** Apr–Dec: check website or call for times. 📷 📷 **W** nttmuseum.org

🏛 Choo Choo Barn

226 Gap Rd, Rte 471, E of Strasburg.
Tel (717) 687-7911. **Open** early Jan, early Mar–Dec: 10am–5pm daily.
Closed Jan 1, mid-Jan–early Mar, Easter, Thanksgiving, Dec 25. 📷 📷
W choochoobarn.com

🚂 Amish Village

199 Hartman Bridge Rd, Ronks, Rte 896, N of Strasburg. **Tel** (717) 687-8511. **Open** days and times vary.
Closed Jan 1, Thanksgiving, Dec 24 & 25. 📷 📷 **W** theamishvillage.net

Gettysburg

This south-central Pennsylvania town amidst gently sloping hills is home to the greatest military encounter ever fought in North America, the Battle of Gettysburg in 1863, during the Civil War (1861–65). Shaded streets are lined with well-preserved Civil War-era buildings, which served as makeshift hospitals during the conflict. Many of these have today been converted into museums, restaurants, and hotels. Shops sell Civil War souvenirs and artifacts, including authentic rifles and a seemingly unending supply of cannon balls and bullets unearthed from the battleground. Other attractions include museums with dioramas – some with waxwork figures – depicting events of the Gettysburg battle and the Civil War.

The *Gettysburg Cyclorama*, a 360-degree painting of Pickett's Charge

Gettysburg Museum and Visitor Center

1195 Baltimore Pike. **Tel** (717) 338-1243. **Open** Apr–Oct: 8am–6pm daily; Nov–Mar: 9am–5pm daily. **Closed** Jan 1, Thanksgiving, Dec 25. **W** gettysburgfoundation.org

The Gettysburg Museum and Visitor Center opened in 2008 at the Gettysburg National Military Park. The 139,000-sq ft (12,900-sq m), awe-inspiring facility houses a modern visitor center that serves to navigate visitors around the park. A 20-minute film, introducing the Battle of Gettysburg, is repeated here every 30 minutes throughout the day. The facility also houses the Museum of Civil War where wide-ranging military artifacts, including an impressive display of artillery shells and fuses, are on display. Also on view is the *Gettysburg Cyclorama*. First exhibited in Boston in 1883, this colossal panoramic painting depicts Pickett's Charge, the conflict's climactic moment *(see pp124–5)*.

Dobbin House Tavern

89 Steinwehr Ave. **Tel** (717) 334-2100. Restaurant **Open** 11:30am onward. usually 10am Fri–Sun (but check in advance). **W** dobbinhouse.com

Built in 1776, this stone house is Gettysburg's oldest standing structure. Tours include all the rooms and an account of what the Zeigler family experienced here during the Battle of Gettysburg. Now a restaurant, the building has original fireplaces, hand-carved woodwork, and a colonial wooden bar in the downstairs tavern *(see p152)*.

Eisenhower National Historic Site

250 Eisenhower Farm Drive. **Tel** (717) 338-9114. **Open** check website or call for times. **Closed** Jan 1, Thanksgiving, Dec 25. tickets available at Gettysburg Visitor Center. mandatory. **W** nps.gov/eise

Before being elected president in 1952, Dwight D. Eisenhower had served as Supreme Commander of the Allied Forces during World War II. While president, he and his wife Mamie owned this farm on the outskirts of Gettysburg and used it for weekend retreats. Inside are original furnishings and exhibits highlighting his career as president.

Farnsworth House Inn

401 Baltimore St. **Tel** (717) 334-8838. **Open** hours vary. **W** farnsworthhouseinn.com

Dating from 1810, this historic home sheltered Confederate sharpshooters, one of whom is thought to have shot Jennie Wade. Most impressive are the more than 100 bullet piercings still evident on the house's brick façade from Union soldiers returning fire. Now an inn *(see p139)*, the house offers ghost tours and a Mourning Theatre in the cellar with Civil War-related ghost tales told around a coffin by candlelight.

General Lee's Headquarters Museum

401 Buford Ave. **Tel** (717) 334-3141. **Open** mid-Feb–Nov: 9am–5pm, longer summer hours (call for details). **Closed** Dec–mid-Feb.

Confederate General Robert E. Lee spent the night of July 1, 1863, at this house so he could see the Union line with his fieldglasses. After a major renovation, the house reopened as a museum in 2016.

General Lee's Headquarters, today a museum

Entrance to the Pennsylvania Memorial in Gettysburg

VISITORS' CHECKLIST

Practical Information

Gettysburg Convention & Visitors Bureau: 35 Carlisle St, PA. **Tel** (717) 334-6274. **Open** 9am–5pm Mon–Fri. Apple Blossom Festival (May), Gettysburg Anniversary Civil War Battle Reenactments (Jul), Apple Harvest Festival (Oct), Remembrance Day (Nov).
w destinationgettysburg.com

Jennie Wade House

528 Baltimore St. **Tel** (717) 334-4100.
Open Mar–Nov: daily.
w jennie-wade-house.com

Twenty-year-old Jennie Wade was the only civilian killed during the Battle of Gettysburg. A sharpshooter's bullet pierced two doors and struck her while she baked bread for Union soldiers.
The home contains original furnishings, and a statue of her stands outside.

Lincoln Railroad Station

35 Carlisle St. **Tel** (717) 334 6274. **Open** Memorial Day–Labor Day: 10am–5pm daily; Mar–May & Sep–Oct: 10am–5pm Fri–Sun. **Closed** Jan 1, Thanksgiving, Dec 25.

This 1858 Italianate-styled railroad depot is where President Lincoln stepped off the train from Washington, a day before delivering the Gettysburg Address. Inside is an interpretive center, with exhibits about the train station and town history, and information on sights, attractions, and tours.

Soldiers' National Cemetery

Taneytown Rd, across Visitor Center.
This peaceful and shaded cemetery contains the graves of 6,000 US servicemen killed in various conflicts in America's history, from the Civil War to the Vietnam War. More than 3,500 are Union soldiers killed at the three-day Battle of Gettysburg. They are buried in a semicircle around the Soldiers' National Monument, which marks the spot where President Lincoln delivered his moving Gettysburg Address. The now-famous address is commemorated by the nearby Lincoln Speech Memorial, which contains an inscription of his speech and his bust.

Soldiers' National Monument

Shriver House Museum

309 Baltimore St. **Tel** (717) 337-2800.
Open Mar: 10am–5pm Sat, 10am–3pm Sun; Apr–Oct: 10am–5pm Sun–Thu, 10am–6pm Fri & Sat; Nov: noon–5pm Mon–Fri, 10am–5pm Sat, 10am–3pm Sun.

This 19th-century home portrays the life of a family under the three-day Confederate occupation. The third-story attic has original holes in the brick wall where rebel sharpshooters stood poised. A small museum displays artifacts of the time.

Wills House and Lincoln Room Museum

8 Lincoln Square. **Tel** (877) 874-2478.
Open May–Aug: 10am–5pm daily; Mar, Apr, Sep & Oct: 10am–4pm Wed–Mon; Nov & Dec: 10am–4pm Sat & Sun.
Closed Thanksgiving, Dec 25.

President Abraham Lincoln slept in this corner house on the town's center square the night before he delivered the Gettysburg Address. His bedroom is part of the Lincoln Room Museum. It has copies of the letter sent by attorney David Wills inviting Lincoln to visit the town.

Lincoln's Gettysburg Address

Four months after the battle, President Abraham Lincoln visited Gettysburg to dedicate a cemetery for Union soldiers. Although not the main speaker, and asked only to make "a few appropriate remarks," Lincoln's 272-words two-minute speech on November 19, 1863 not only gave new meaning to the war's losses, but was an inspiration to preserve a nation divided. His words conferred significance on the sacrifice of the thousands who died during the battle, urging for the "resolve that these dead shall not have died in vain."

Lincoln's bust at Soldiers' National Cemetery

A Tour of Gettysburg National Military Park

The Battle of Gettysburg was fought on the first three days of July 1863. Not only was it the turning point of the American Civil War between the North and South, it was also the war's largest battle, leaving more than 51,000 Union and Confederate soldiers killed, wounded, captured, or missing. Although the Union army won this critical battle, it took a further two years for them to decisively win the Civil War on April 26, 1865. This self-guided tour traces the course of the three-day battle.

② Eternal Light Peace Memorial
From Oak Hill, Confederates attacked Union forces on the first day. This memorial to "Peace Eternal in a Nation United" was built in 1938.

③ Oak Ridge
Union troops held this ridge but retreated to Cemetery Hill on July 1 as their defenses collapsed.

① McPherson's Ridge
This quiet farm with McPherson's barn is where the Battle of Gettysburg began early in the morning on July 1, 1863. Confederate infantry advanced eastward and engaged in heavy fire with Union Cavalry.

④ North Carolina Memorial
On the second day, the Confederates stood on Seminary Ridge. Union troops held Culp's and Cemetery Hills.

⑤ Virginia Memorial
This monument on Seminary Ridge overlooks the field where, on July 3, 12,000 Confederates launched their last major assault, known as "Pickett's Charge." In less than an hour, 10,000 of them were dead or wounded.

⑥ Pitzer Woods
Confederates occupied these woods on the second day. An observation tower offers grand views of the "Pickett's Charge" battlefield.

Eisenhower National Historic Site

0 meters 500
0 yards 500

Emmitsburg

Key

▬▬ Suggested route

── Other roads

⑦ Warfield Ridge
On the battle's second day, Confederates charged Union troops at Devil's Den and Little and Big Round Tops.

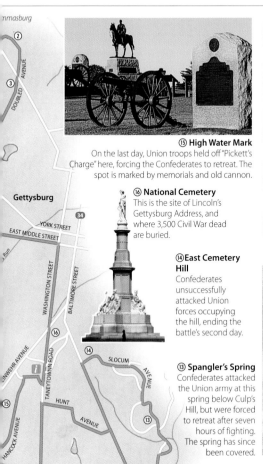

⑮ High Water Mark
On the last day, Union troops held off "Pickett's Charge" here, forcing the Confederates to retreat. The spot is marked by memorials and old cannon.

⑯ National Cemetery
This is the site of Lincoln's Gettysburg Address, and where 3,500 Civil War dead are buried.

⑭ East Cemetery Hill
Confederates unsuccessfully attacked Union forces occupying the hill, ending the battle's second day.

Gettysburg

⑬ Spangler's Spring
Confederates attacked the Union army at this spring below Culp's Hill, but were forced to retreat after seven hours of fighting. The spring has since been covered.

⑪ Plum Run
Union forces crossed this area as they retreated from Peach Orchard to Cemetery Ridge.

⑫ Pennsylvania Memorial
An ornate, stately memorial marks the Union position along Cemetery Ridge.

⑩ Peach Orchard
On the second day, Confederate soldiers overran this position despite heavy Union cannon fire.

⑨ The Wheatfield
Charges and countercharges here on the second day left over 4,000 men dead and wounded.

⑧ Little Round Top
At first undefended on the second day, this position was reinforced when an alert Union general called for help. Monuments, such as this one to the 155th Pennsylvania Volunteer Infantry, dot the hill.

Tips for Drivers
Tour length: 18 miles (29 km).
Duration of tour: About 3 hours.
Distance from Philadelphia: 118 miles (189 km). This is usually a 2-hour drive.
Starting point: Gettysburg National Military Park and Visitor Center.
Stopping points: The tour has 16 stops, all of which have plaques explaining historical significance. Some stops have a scattering of monuments.
When to go: Mar–Dec.
Tourist information: Destination Gettysburg, 571 W Middle St, PA.
Tel (717) 334-6274.
W destinationgettysburg.com

The Golden Plough Tavern, one of York's historic establishments

⑩ York

York County, PA. 🚹 40,500. 🚍 🚌 ℹ️
Downtown York Visitor Information
Center: Central Mkt, 34 W Philadelphia
St , (717) 852-9675, open 7:30am–2pm
Tue–Sun. 🆆 yorkpa.org

The first Pennsylvania town west
of the Susquehanna River, York
was laid out in 1741, the inhabitants mainly tavern-keepers
and craftspeople catering to
pioneers heading west. Since
then, manufacturing has been
the town's economic strength.

East of York is the **Harley-
Davidson Final Assembly Plant**,
noisy, colorful, and the size of
two football fields. Its giant
presses mold steel while
motorcycles fly overhead. A
small museum depicts Harley
Davidson's history from 1903
to the present.

🏛️ **Harley-Davidson Final
Assembly Plant**
1425 Eden Rd. **Tel** (717) 852-6590.
Open 9am–2pm Mon–Fri. 🔒
9am–2pm Mon–Fri; some Saturdays
in summer; no under-12s. 📷

⑪ Harrisburg

Dauphin County, PA. 🚹 47,000. 🚍
🚌 ℹ️ Hershey Harrisburg Regional
Visitors Bureau: 3211 N Front St, (877)
727-8573. 🆆 **visithershey
harrisburg.org**

First settled in the early 1700s
by Englishman John Harris,
Harrisburg is situated along the
Susquehanna River. The city was
not planned until the 1780s and
became Pennsylvania's capital
in 1812. Today, the state
government is the biggest
employer in the city, which has
the impressive **State Capitol** as
a focal point. The Renaissance-
style building was dedicated in
1906 by President Roosevelt.

The **National Civil War
Museum** tells the story
of the war through
permanent displays
of artifacts,
photographs,
manuscripts,
and
documents
from its 24,000-
item collection.
City Island, located in
the middle of the
Susquehanna, offers panoramic
views of the city. It includes
marinas, parks and nature areas,
riverboat rides and dinner cruises,
and a replica of John Harris's
18th-century trading post.

🏛️ **State Capitol**
3rd & State Sts. **Tel** (717) 787-6810.
Open 8:30am–4:30pm Mon–Fri. 🔒
8:30am–4pm Mon–Fri, 9am,

11am, 1pm, 3pm Sat–Sun & hols.
Closed Jan 1, Easter, Thanksgiving,
Dec 25. 🔒 📷 ♿ 🆆 **pacapitol.com**

🏛️ **National Civil War Museum**
One Lincoln Circle (Reservoir Pk). **Tel**
(717) 260-1861. **Open** 10am–5pm
Mon–Sat (8pm Wed), noon–5pm Sun
(Jun–Aug: 10am Sun). **Closed** Jan 1,
Easter, Thanksgiving, Dec 25. 📷 📷 📷
♿ 🆆 **nationalcivilwarmuseum.org**

⑫ Hershey

Dauphin County, PA. 🚹 12,800. 🚍
🚌 🆆 **hersheypa.com**

This factory town, now a tourist
destination, revolves around
chocolate – even its streetlights
are shaped like foil-wrapped
Hershey Kisses. The town's main
attraction is **Hershey
Park**, an amusement
park that has 80
rides on
offer, and a
fine, four-row
carousel. There
are also two resort
hotels in the park.
Nearby is Hershey's
Chocolate World,
featuring a 15-minute
ride through animated tableaux
that reveal Hershey's chocolate-
making process. A free sample
awaits at the end of the tour.

Hershey's Chocolate World
signage

🎡 **Hershey Park**
100 W Hersheypark Drive.
Tel (717) 534-3900. **Open** May 21–Sep
1: 10am–8pm daily (for other times
check website). 📷 📷 📷
🆆 **hersheypark.com**

State Capitol complex in Harrisburg, the seat of Pennsylvania's government

The towers and parapets of Mercer Castle, Doylestown

⑬ Reading

Berks County, PA. ⚠ 80,000. 🚉 🚌
ℹ Greater Reading Visitors Center,
GoggleWorks Center for the Arts, 201
Washington St, (610) 375-4085.
w gogreaterreading.com

Once a center of industry,
Reading reinvented itself as a
discount-store capital in the
1970s (see p157) and is now a
mountain-biking destination.
The pagoda, on the outskirts of
the town, is the main attraction
here. Built in 1908, it is modeled
in a traditional Japanese style.
  The **Mid-Atlantic Air
Museum**, at Reading Regional
Airport, has over 60 different
military and civilian aircraft.

🏛 **Mid-Atlantic Air Museum**
11 Museum Drive. **Tel** (610) 372-7333.
Open 9:30am–4pm. **Closed** major
holidays. 🅿 w maam.org

⑭ Doylestown

Bucks County, PA. ⚠ 9,200. 🚉 🚌
ℹ Bucks County Visitors Center: 3207
Street Road, Bensalem, (215) 639-0300.

Doylestown's origins date to
1745, when William Doyle built
a tavern here. The town later
developed as a cultural and
commercial center, and today it
is also the Bucks County seat.
  The biggest attractions in town
are the castle-like museums that
tower over shaded grassy areas
close to the town center. The
Mercer Museum, built by
archaeologist Henry Mercer in

1916, displays his collection of
folk art, woodwork, textiles, and
furnishings. Since 1976, Mercer's
44-room home, **Fonthill Castle**,
has been preserved as a museum.
  Named for a famous writer
from this area, the **James A.
Michener Art Museum**, in a 19th-
century county jail, has a superb
collection of Pennsylvania
Impressionist paintings. Michener
donated $1 million to the
museum upon its 1988 opening
and supported it for the rest of his
life. Highlights include Edward W.
Redfield's *The Trout Brook*, Charles
Rosen's *Opalescent Morning*, and
the 22-ft (6.7-m) mural by Daniel
Garber, *A Wooded Watershed*.

🏛 **Mercer Museum**
84 S Pine St. **Tel** (215) 345-0210. **Open**
10am–5pm daily (from noon Sun). 🅿
🎥 w mercermuseum.org

🏛 **Fonthill Museum**
525 E Court St and Rte 313. **Tel** (215)
348-9461. **Open** 10am–5pm daily
(from noon Sun). 🅿 🎥 mandatory;
reservations required. w mercer
museum.org

🏛 **James A. Michener Art Museum**
138 S Pine St. **Tel** (215) 340-9800.
Open 10am–4:30pm Tue–Fri (to 5pm
Sat), noon–5pm Sun. 🅿 🖥 🎥
w michenerartmuseum.org

⑮ New Hope

Bucks County, PA. ⚠ 2000. ℹ Visitor
Center: 1 W Mechanic St, at S Main St,
(215) 862-5030, open daily. w new
hopevisitorscenter.org

This delightful waterfront village
and shoppers' paradise teems
with upscale boutiques and
restaurants. Tracing its roots to
the early 18th century, it gained
its name when Benjamin Parry's
gristmill, which ground grain,
burned down in 1790. He rebuilt
it and named it "New Hope Mills."
  Today, that prosperity is
evident with more than 200 art
galleries, boutiques, and craft
and antiques shops. Train rides
aboard restored 1920 passenger
cars, horse-drawn carriages, and
mule-drawn barge trips down
the 19th-century Delaware Canal
add to the town's ambience.
  Parry, who also helped
finance the first bridge across
the Delaware, built a house in
1784 that was occupied by
successive generations of his
family until 1966. Today, the
Parry Mansion Museum is
decorated according to different
periods of its history.

🏛 **Parry Mansion Museum**
45 S Main St. **Tel** (215) 862-5652.
Open early May–late Nov: 1–5pm Sat
& Sun. 🎥 by appointment.

Storefronts line New Hope's old-world, picturesque streets

⑯ Washington Crossing Historic Park

1112 River Rd, PA. **Tel** (215) 493-4076. Visitor Center **Open** 10am–5pm daily. **Closed** public hols exc Jul 4, Memorial Day, Labor Day, Dec 25. 🚻 📷 10am–4pm daily (seasonally). ♿ 🌐 **washingtoncrossingpark.org**

This waterfront park, set up in 1917 to commemorate Washington's historic crossing of the Delaware River, is divided into two sections. The Village section includes the McConkey Ferry Inn, a local 18th-century tavern, the visitor center, and the riverbank from which Washington and his army departed in Durham boats. Nearby is a 19th-century boathouse that contains replicas of the boats; these vessels are now used for the annual Christmas Day reenactment of the crossing.

About 4 miles (6 km) upstream is the Thompson-Neely section, which includes historic buildings, a gristmill, Bowman's Hill Tower, and a cemetery along the peaceful Delaware Canal containing the graves of Revolutionary War soldiers.

On the New Jersey side of the river, Washington Crossing State Park marks the site where Washington landed. This forested area includes historic homes, a visitor center and museum, and miles of hiking, riding, and biking trails.

⑰ Trenton

Mercer County, NJ. 🚗 85,000. 🚆 🚌 🚏 Trenton Visitors Center, 102 Barrack St (open 11am–2:30pm Mon–Fri, 10am–4pm Sat & Sun), (609) 777-1770. 🌐 **destinationtrenton.com**

The capital of New Jersey, Trenton's origin dates to 1679, when Quaker Mahlon Stacy built a gristmill along the Delaware. In 1714, his son sold land to merchant William Trent who laid out a new city called "Trent's Town" in 1721. Today, the state is governed from the

Delaware River at Washington Crossing Historic Park

New Jersey State House, an elegant gold-domed building in the heart of the city, dating back to 1792. Tours include the senate and assembly chambers, the rotunda, and the governor's reception office. Nearby, the **New Jersey State Museum** chronicles the often turbulent history of the state, with 13,000 historic artifacts and 12,000 works of art, ranging from ceramics produced by Trenton potteries to flags carried into battle by New Jersey Civil War regiments. Further north, the **Trenton Battle Monument** pays tribute to the Battle of Trenton, in which General Washington and 2,400 men crossed the ice-clogged Delaware River on December 25, 1776, to defeat a British and Hessian force. The Old Barracks, dating to 1758, were occupied by Hessian soldiers during the encounter, and now house a museum.

🏛 **New Jersey State House**
125 W State St. **Tel** (609) 847-3150. 📷 hourly: 10am–3pm Mon–Fri, noon–3pm 1st and 3rd Sat. **Closed** state hols.

🏛 **New Jersey State Museum**
205 W State St. **Tel** (609) 292-6300. **Open** 9am–4:45pm Tue–Sun. **Closed** state hols. 🚻 ♿

Plaque marking the river crossing 🏛 **Old Barracks Museum**
101 Barrack St. **Tel** (609) 396-1776. **Open** 10am–5pm Mon–Sat. **Closed** Jan 1, Easter, Thanksgiving, Dec 24–25. 📷 🌐 **barracks.org**

⑱ Pennsbury Manor

400 Pennsbury Memorial Rd, Morrisville, PA. **Tel** (215) 946-0400. **Open** Jan 1–Feb 29: by appt only; Mar 1–Dec 31: 9am–5pm Tue–Sat, noon–5pm Sun. **Closed** Mon. 📷 🚻 🌐 **pennsburymanor.org**

An elegant brick Georgian house 26 miles (42 km) north of Philadelphia, this manor is a re-creation of William Penn's country home and estate from the 1680s. The plantation sits on the site chosen by Penn, and this manor was built in 1939 on original foundations, where some 17th-century bricks are the only remnants of Penn's initial home. Inside, a hall served as a waiting room between the family's quarters and governor's parlor, while the second floor had three bedrooms and a nursery.

The estate today includes farm animals similar to those owned by Penn. Other recreated structures include a blacksmith shop, brew house, smokehouse, and horse shelter. The visitor center offers activities for schools, a gallery, office space, an auditorium, and facilities for videoconferencing.

Gardens at Pennsbury Manor, Penn's country estate

Atlantic City's glamorous resorts by night – lighting up the Jersey coast

⑲ Atlantic City

Atlantic County, NJ. 40,000.
ℹ️ Boardwalk Information Center:
Boardwalk Hall, Mississippi Ave.
Tel 1-888-228-4748.
W atlanticcitynj.com

Called the "Queen of the Coast" by generations of beachgoers, Atlantic City has been a favored vacation spot since the mid-1800s. The first casino opened on the famous Boardwalk in 1978, and since then the town has become one of the most popular destinations on the eastern seaboard. All gambling – referred to as "gaming" – takes place in the large, ostentatious casino hotels that lie within a block of the beach and Boardwalk, which is lined with shops and amusement arcades.

Playing cards used in gaming

Seven casino resorts – with their towers shooting up along the Boardwalk – make up the dazzling city skyline. They include Caesars, Bally's, Harrah's, Golden Nugget, Resorts, and Tropicana, though the properties owned by developer-turned-president Donald Trump, such as the 51-story Trump Taj Mahal, have all closed. Among the flashier hotels are the Borgata Hotel Casino and Spa, a 2,000-room hotel, and its companion property, The Water Club. Visitors not enchanted by the casinos instead head for the lively local attractions.

Amusement parks jut out over the ocean on the Central Pier Arcade and Speedway, and the Steel Pier. Another attraction is the Absecon Lighthouse, the tallest lighthouse in New Jersey, which offers views of the city and waterfront. Atlantic City also hosts the annual Miss America Pageant, held here since 1928. Shopping is also a big draw, with the arrival of Tanger Outlets – The Walk – housing stores like Banana Republic and Coach. In the nearby Margate City, **Lucy the Elephant** stands tall in celebration of American marketing ingenuity. Built by a real-estate developer in 1881 to draw prospective buyers to his holdings, "Lucy" has served as a residence and a tavern over the years. Today, guided tours take visitors into the structure that has become instantly recognizable as part of the Jersey shoreline.

🔲 **Lucy the Elephant**
3200 Atlantic Ave, Margate. **Tel** (609) 823-6473. **Open** Jan–Mar: 11am–4pm Sat & Sun; Apr, Nov, Dec: 11am–4pm Wed–Fri, 10am–5pm Sat & Sun; May–mid-Jun, Sep, Oct: 11am–4pm Mon–Fri, 10am–5pm Sat & Sun; mid-Jun–Labor Day: 10am–8pm Mon–Sat, 10am–5pm Sun. 🈺 🈳
W lucytheelephant.org

⑳ Cape May

Cape May County, NJ. 4,000.
ℹ️ Cape May Welcome Center: 609 Lafayette St, (609) 884-5508.
W capemay.com

First explored by Cornelius Mey for the Dutch West India Company in 1621, Cape May is one of the oldest resorts on the Atlantic coast. Popular with Philadelphia socialites during the late 1800s, it has, since then, continued to enjoy a fine reputation among beach lovers. The building boom of the Victorian era characterizes Cape May today. **Historic Cold Spring Village** is a living history museum showcasing 25 restored buildings, with costumed actors portraying 19th-century lifestyles.

🏛️ **Historic Cold Spring Village**
720 US 9. **Tel** (609) 898-2300.
Open mid-Jun–Labor Day: 10am–4:30pm Tue–Sun; Labor Day–mid-Sep & Memorial Day–mid-Jun: weekends only. 🈺 🈳 🈳 🈳 🈳
W hcsv.org

Brightly painted façade of a house at Cape May, America's largest Victorian district

㉑ Hagley Museum

200 Hagley Creek Rd, Rte 141, Wilmington, DE. **Tel** (302) 658-2400. **Open** early Nov–mid-Mar: 10am–4pm daily; Mar 14–early Nov: 10am–5pm daily. **Closed** Thanksgiving, Dec 25. 📞 call or check website for times. 🏢 📷 ♿ 🅦 hagley.org

Not a museum in the conventional sense, this forested site along the rocky Brandywine River is where the DuPont Company was founded. In 1802, French immigrant Éleuthère Irénée du Pont built a factory to manufacture gunpowder and "black powder" used in explosives. The earliest buildings included the first du Pont family home, gardens, and company office. Through its 119-year-history, overseen by five generations of du Ponts, the mill expanded downriver, with water- wheels powering production facilities that sifted, mixed, and crushed raw materials into fine powder.

Today, only the façades of the original buildings remain. Some have working exhibitions, such as a rolling mill using safe charcoal. Staff members demonstrate the workings of a steam engine and the operations in a machine shop, but most impressive is the ignition of a powder sample. Some buildings house artifacts, original furniture, and rare du Pont cars, including a 1911 electric car and a 1928 Phaeton.

View of the Brandywine River at Hagley Museum

Interior of the conservatory at Longwood Gardens

㉒ Winterthur Museum

5105 Kennett Pike, Rte 52, Winterthur, DE. **Tel** (302) 888-4600. **Open** 10am–5pm Tue–Sun. **Closed** Mon (except hols), Thanksgiving, Dec 25. ♿ 📞 🏢 📷 🅦 winterthur.org

Once the home of Henry Francis du Pont, great-grandson of Éleuthère Irénée du Pont, this vast estate contains an extraordinary 175-room mansion. The original home, the core of the current mansion, dates to 1839. It was built by J.A. Bidermann and his wife, Evelina, Éleuthère du Pont's daughter. Henry Francis inherited the estate in 1926, expanding it during the two-decade-long conversion of his home into a museum. Today, it houses nearly 90,000 items from the 17th to the 19th centuries, including paintings, textiles, furniture, ceramics, and Chinese porcelain. The main dining room features original silver tankards crafted by Paul Revere, and works of art by Gilbert Stuart and Benjamin West. The parlor features a unique oval Montmorency staircase and is elegantly decorated with Chippendale furniture. The estate contains meadows, streams, and woods, including a tulip-poplar tree, which has been around since William Penn's days, and the fairy-filled Enchanted Woods.

㉓ Longwood Gardens

1001 Longwood Rd, Rte 1, Kennett Sq, PA. **Tel** (800) 737-5500, (610) 388–1000. **Open** Apr– Oct: 9am–6pm; Nov–Mar: 9am–5pm. **Closed** Mon (except hols), Jan 1, Thanksgiving, Dec 25. ♿ 📷 📞 🏢 ♿ 🅦 longwoodgardens.org

This well-manicured horticultural wonderland consists of colorful gardens, woodlands, lush meadows, greenhouses, and spectacular fountains amid idyllic bucolic scenery. Settler George Pierce acquired the land in 1700, and in 1798 his descendants established an arboretum that, by the mid-19th century was one of the nation's finest.

Industrialist Pierre S. du Pont bought it in 1906 and it is his design that remains today. It includes over 11,000 plant varieties in both indoor and outdoor displays, whimsical topiaries, and a children's garden. The massive main greenhouse and conservatory are engineering marvels that shelter an array of exotic plant life. But the most breathtaking sights are the fabulous fountains with choreographed eruptions highlighted at night by colored lights, which create dazzling displays that are often the backdrop of musical events.

② Brandywine Battlefield State Park

1491 Baltimore Pike, Rte 1, Chadds Ford, PA. **Tel** (610) 459-3342. **Open** 9am–5pm Tue–Sat, noon–5pm Sun. 🏛 📷 **W** brandywinebattlefield.org

The Battle of Brandywine, fought on these rolling hills on September 11, 1777, was the biggest engagement of the American Revolution. General Washington stationed his troops atop this high ground at Chadds Ford along the Brandywine River in an attempt to stop the advancing British. The Americans were outmaneuvered as the British crossed the Brandywine River at an unguarded ford to the north of Washington's troops, forcing them to retreat.

Today, the battlefield is a state park with a visitor center and two historic houses, both restored to the way they were in 1777. The Benjamin Ring House was owned by a Quaker farmer and served as Washington's headquarters on the eve of the battle. The French patriot and American Revolution hero, Marquis de La Fayette, stayed in the farmhouse of Quaker Gideon Gilpin. The visitor center includes a small museum.

Revolutionary War hero La Fayette's quarters at Brandywine Park

② Brandywine River Museum of Art

1 Hoffman's Mill Rd, Chadds Ford, PA. **Tel** (610) 388-2700. **Open** 9:30am–5pm. **Closed** Dec 25. 🗓 Apr–mid-Nov: timed tours of N.C. Wyeth House & Studio, and Kuerner Farm Wed–Sun. 🏛 🖼 📷 **W** brandywinemuseum.org

Located in a Civil War-era gristmill along Brandywine River, this museum is best known for housing artworks by three generations of the Wyeths – N.C., Andrew, and Jamie. Galleries showcase landscapes inspired by the Brandywine River Valley, and paintings and illustrations by the Wyeths and other artists.

N.C. Wyeth (1882–1945) was a famous illustrator of the early 20th century, completing more than 1,000 illustrations, including some for classics such as *Treasure Island* and *Robin Hood*. N.C.'s son Andrew is known for mastering drybrush watercolor and egg tempera mediums. His son Jamie painted portraits of figures such as President John F. Kennedy and artist Andy Warhol.

Tours are organized to the N.C. Wyeth House and Studio, and the Kuerner Farm, which inspired Andrew for over 70 years. A farmhouse and barn display his works related to the farm.

National Memorial Arch at Valley Forge

George Washington's restored headquarters at Valley Forge

② Valley Forge National Historic Park

1400 N Outer Line Dr, King of Prussia, PA. **Tel** (610) 783-1077. **Open** Visitor Center: 9am–5pm daily (mid-Jun–Aug: to 6pm daily). **Closed** Jan 1, Thanksgiving, Dec 25. ♿ 📷 **W** nps.gov/vafo

George Washington and his soldiers spent the harsh winter of 1777–78 at Valley Forge, retreating to these hills after losing to British forces at Brandywine and Germantown (see pp108–9). No battles were fought here, but nearly 2,000 soldiers died of typhus, typhoid, pneumonia, and dysentery. Today, reconstructed cabins, statues, and cannon are scattered through the park. Key sites are the National Memorial Arch, designed by Paul Cret, and built in 1917 in the memory of those who died in the winter of 1777–78, and stone farmhouses that once served as officers' quarters. The park has miles of fields and woods crisscrossed by hiking paths, and a visitor center with artifacts such as muskets and powder horns.

The Visitor Center is home to the park's museum collection and contains exhibits pertaining to the 1777–78 winter encampment and the Revolutionary War, as well as the cultural and natural history of Valley Forge.

TRAVELERS'
NEEDS

WHERE TO STAY

The Philadelphia area offers a wide selection of hotel rooms to suit every style and budget. More expensive hotels include high-rises with scenic Center City and riverfront views, boutique and upscale chain hotels, as well as smaller but luxurious bed-and-breakfasts (B&Bs).

The more budget-conscious traveler can find a range of comfortable chain hotels, inns, and B&Bs within the city and beyond, plus roadside motels and urban hostels. Hotel rates are typical for the US, though they tend to be higher in the more popular business districts and tourist areas.

Locations

The Center City district has the highest concentration of hotel rooms in the Philadelphia metropolitan area, with over 10,000 rooms available. Business travelers prefer to stay in these properties, which include upscale hotel chains, such as the Logan Hotel and the Ritz Carlton. In particular, hotels are clustered near Logan Square and on Market, Chestnut and Walnut Streets, with many in and around Rittenhouse Square, the Pennsylvania Convention Center, and along the Avenue of the Arts in the theater district.

A few hotels can be found in Old City and Society Hill, while some are located along the Delaware River. Quality hotels are also situated in University City, the northwestern suburbs near Germantown, satellite towns such as Valley Forge and King of Prussia, and at the Philadelphia Airport.

Facilities and Amenities

All hotels in Philadelphia have standard air conditioning, cable TV, and Wi-Fi. Upscale properties and some chain hotels also provide 24-hour business services, including computer and fax facilities.

Chain hotels, in particular, have fitness centers and some of the larger establishments have pools. At times, hotels also tie-up with nearby health clubs for the use of their facilities by hotel guests. Additional charges may apply for certain amenities, which may be costly. It is best to call and clarify when booking accommodation.

Reservations

Well-known chain hotels usually have toll-free reservation numbers. Visitors can also book hotel rooms online through their official websites. The quoted prices are often for double occupancy and do not include taxes or parking charges. Online hotel reservation service companies offer reduced rates for rooms, but often add hidden fees and taxes. A good resource is the official visitor and travel site of the **Greater Philadelphia Tourism and Marketing Corporation**, which displays all the available hotel packages, including tours, and other offers.

Hidden Costs

If traveling solo, always make sure that the quoted rate is for one person, as hotels normally quote room rates for double occupancy. Room taxes in Philadelphia amount to around 14 percent, while parking rates range anywhere from $10 to $30 per day. Rooms with views can also cost more.

Discounts

Discounts are often available when booking packages. Most chain-hotels offer discounted online booking on their websites. The "Visit Philly Overnight Hotel Package" promotion runs at different times during the year and offers free parking, gifts, and other discounts. It is available through the website of the Greater Philadelphia Tourism and Marketing Corporation.

Bed-and-Breakfasts

B&Bs in Philadelphia are mostly intimate, family-run enterprises in beautifully decorated 18th- or 19th- century houses. The prices vary depending on their offered location and range of services. B&Bs tend not to have restaurants, business facilities or fitness centers. Most B&Bs are located

View of the First Bank of the United States from a Ritz-Carlton Hotel room *(see p137)*

◀ The Wanamaker Organ at Macy's on Market Street

Entrance to the Warwick Rittenhouse Square *(see p137)*

in the University City area, Center City, Chestnut Hill, and near City Line Avenue. **A Bed and Breakfast Connection of Philadelphia** can be contacted for reservations.

The online booking service **Airbnb** offers apartments and rooms in homes at good rates.

Hostels

Younger travelers and students often stay in hostels, as they offer cheaper accommodation than hotels. Hostels in and around Philadelphia are equipped with all modern amenities, and offer dormitories, private rooms, as well as shared cooking and washing facilities. Some good hostels are: the **Apple Hostel**, situated near Liberty Bell and Independence Hall in Old City; and the **Hosteling International Chamounix Mansion**, a historic country house in Fairmont Park.

Traveling with Children

Philadelphia's historic attractions and science museums make the city an exciting place for children. Most city hotels warmly welcome children. The younger ones can usually stay for free in their parents' rooms, but it is best to check when making reservations. Family hotel packages are available through the **Greater Philadelphia Tourism and Marketing Corporation**. These may include accommodation, meals, tickets for historic tours and free parking.

Disabled Travelers

Most of the larger hotels accommodate wheelchairs, while smaller establishments, such as B&Bs, may not have full amenities for the disabled, as they may be housed in 18th- and 19th- century homes. For more information, contact the hotels or call the **Mayor's Commission on People with Disabilities**.

Recommended Hotels

The hotels on pages 136–9 of this guide are a selection of the best luxury, business, and budget hotels in in Philadelphia. The city's famous luxury establishments include high-end hotel chains known for the quality of their services and amenities. They also have excellent restaurants and spa facilities. For those on business visits, the city has several fine hotels that provide comfortable lodging and fully-equipped business centers. These hotels are located in the vicinity of all major convention centers and transport hubs. Vistors can also choose to stay at historically themed inns, which are quite large and have pleasant accommodations. The selection is not just confined to hotels and inns. There are also motels, B&Bs, and hostels which offer simple, but adequate rooms and are perfect for those on a tight budget. Within these six categories, the hotels are divided by areas, first those in the city and then beyond Philadelphia. Throughout the listings, certain establishments carry the DK Choice label. They have been highlighted for the exceptional experience they offer – be it through their superlative services, beautiful rooms, top-notch amenities, spectacular views, and great on-site restaurants, or a combination of these.

DIRECTORY

Online Booking Services

Hotels.com
W hotels.com

Hotel Packages and Promotions

Greater Philadelphia Tourism and Marketing Corporation
W visitphilly.com

Bed-and-Breakfast Booking

A Bed and Breakfast Connection of Philadelphia
Tel (800) 448-3619, (610) 687-3565. W bnbphiladelphia.com

Airbnb
W airbnb.com

Hostels

Apple Hostel
32 S Bank St. **Map** 4 E3. **Tel** (215) 922-0222. W applehostels.com

Hosteling International Chamounix Mansion
3250 Chamounix Dr, W Fairmount Park. **Tel** (800) 379-0017, (215) 878-3676. W philahostel.org

Disabled Travelers

Mayor's Commission on People with Disabilities
1401 JFK Blvd. **Map** 2 F4. **Tel** (215) 686-3480. W phila.gov/aco/index.html

Cosy setting of a room at the Inn at Westwynd Farm *(see p139)*

Where to Stay

Philadelphia
Old City

DK Choice

Apple Hostel $
Hostel Map 4 E3
32 S Bank St, 19106
Tel *(215) 922-0222*
W applehostels.com
Centrally located, this friendly
hostel has exclusive male and
female dorms, as well as mixed.
It has private rooms, too. Offers
free pub crawls, walking tours,
and high-speed Wi-Fi. No curfew.

**Franklin Hotel at
Independence Park** $$
Luxury Map 4 D3
401 Chestnut St, 19106
Tel *(215) 925-0000*
W marriott.com
The Franklin's elegant rooms
overlook the Independence Mall.
It also has a restaurant and spa.

**Holiday Inn Express
Philadelphia–Penns Landing** $$
Business Map 4 F2
100 N Columbus Blvd, 19106
Tel *(215) 627-7900*
W hiepennslanding.com
This riverfront inn has nice, well-
furnished rooms with beautiful
views and a business centre.
Close to many historic sights.

Penn's View Hotel $$
Inn Map 4 E3
14 N Front St, 19106
Tel *(215) 922-7600*
W pennsviewhotel.com
Opposite Penn's Landing, this
family-run European-style hotel
has stately, spacious rooms.
Offers great deals online.

The Thomas Bond House $$
B&B Map 4 E3
129 S 2nd St, 19106
Tel *(215) 923-8523*
W thomasbondhousebandb.com
The 1769 colonial manor offers
quality accommodations at
reasonable prices. Hosts a wine
hour every day.

**Wyndham Philadelphia
Historic District** $$
Business Map 4 E2
400 Arch St, 19106
Tel *(215) 923-8660*
W phillydowntownhotel.com
Only a block from Market Street,
the Wyndham has comfortable
rooms and large conference halls.

**Best Western Plus Independence
Park Hotel**
Business Map 4 E3
235 Chestnut St, 19106
Tel *(215) 922-4443*
W independenceparkhotel.com
A national historic landmark, the
hotel has well-appointed rooms.
Courteous staff.

**Kimpton Hotel Monaco
Philadelphia** $$$
Luxury Map 4 D3
433 Chestnut St, 19106
Tel *(215) 925-2111*
W monaco-philadelphia.com
Housed in the Lafayette Building,
Monaco combines old-world
charm with modern amenities.
Offers complimentary bicycles.

Society Hill and Penn's
Landing

**Hilton Philadelphia at
Penn's Landing** $$
Business Map 4 F3
201 S Columbus Blvd, 19106
Tel *(215) 521-6500*
W hiltonpennslanding.com
The elegantly designed rooms of
this high-rise hotel have scenic
views of the Delaware River.

DK Choice

Morris House Hotel $$
Luxury Map 3 C3
225 S 8th St, 19106
Tel *(215) 922-2466*
W morrishousehotel.com
Combining the opulence of a
boutique hotel with the intimacy
of a B&B, this refurbished 18th-
century house has a colonial-
style reading room and lovely
gardens. Stylishly simple rooms.

Sheraton Society Hill Hotel $$
Luxury Map 4 E4
1 Dock St, 19106
Tel *(215) 238-6000*
W sheratonphiladelphiasociety
hill.com
This wonderfully located hotel
has the usual Sheraton comforts,
including an indoor pool.

Center City

La Reserve Center City B&B $
B&B Map 2 D5
1804 Pine St, 19103
Tel *(215) 735-1137*
W laservebandb.com
Featuring elegant period furniture,
La Reserve is a lovely 1850s town
house near Rittenhouse Square.

Price Guide
Prices are based on one night's stay in
high season for a standard double room,
inclusive of service charges and taxes.

$	up to $120
$$	$120 to $250
$$$	over $250

Alexander Inn $$
Inn Map 3 B3
12th & Spruce Sts, 19107
Tel *(215) 923-3535*
W alexanderinn.com
Near the Theater District, this hotel
has warm decor and cozy rooms.

Club Quarters $$
Business Map 3 A2
1628 Chestnut St, 19103
Tel *(215) 282-5000*
W clubquarters.com/philadelphia
Opposite Liberty Place, this hotel
offers a range of accommodations,
from basic rooms to apartments.

Days Inn $$
Business Map 3 B1
1227 Race St, 19107
Tel *(215) 564-2888*
W daysinn.com
Comfortable lodging conveniently
located near many historic sites.

**Hampton Inn
Convention Center** $$
Business Map 3 B1
1301 Race St, 19107
Tel *(215) 665-9100*
W philadelphiacc.hamptoninn.com
Pleasant lodgings close to major
business and cultural hubs.

**Hilton Garden Inn Philadelphia
Center City** $$
Business Map 3 C2
1100 Arch St, 19107
Tel *(215) 923-0100*
W hiltongardenphilly.com
Characteristically fashionable,
centrally located, with stunning
views from its rooftop restaurant.

An intimate guest room at the historic
Morris House Hotel

DK Choice

Sofitel Philadelphia $$
Business   Map 2 E4
120 S 17th St, 19103
Tel *(215) 569-8300*
W sofitel-philadelphia.com
Sofitel's distinctive design
exquisitely combines French
elegance with American
functionality. Situated close to
Rittenhouse Row, this four-
diamond hotel has spacious
rooms with stylish decor. Houses
a wonderful French restaurant.

The Independent Hotel $$
Luxury   Map 3 B3
1234 Locust St, 19107
Tel *(215) 772-1440*
W theindependenthotel.com
A lovely Georgian Revival building
houses this boutique hotel in the
trendy Midtown Village.

Hyatt at the Bellevue $$$
Luxury   Map 2 E5
200 S Broad St, 19102
Tel *(215) 893-1234*
W philadelphiabellevue.hyatt.com
The magnificent 1904 Bellevue
building offers panoramic views of
the city. Upscale shops onsite.

Kimpton Hotel Palomar $$$
Luxury   Map 2 E4
117 S 17th St, 19103
Tel *(215) 563-5006*
W hotelpalomar-philadelphia.com
A chic, eco-friendly boutique
hotel with an excellent restaurant
and a hip lobby bar.

Philadelphia Marriott
Downtown $$$
Business   Map 3 B2
1201 Market St, 19107
Tel *(215) 625-2900*
W marriott.com
Connected to the Convention
Center and the Reading Terminal
Market, the hotel has beautifully
designed rooms.

Sonesta Philadelphia
Rittenhouse Square $$$
Luxury   Map 2 E4
1800 Market St, 19103
Tel *(215) 561-7500*
W sonesta.com
Comfortable rooms, modern ameni-
ties, and a rooftop pool. It offers
excellent views of the city's skyline.

The Rittenhouse $$$
Luxury   Map 2 D5
210 W Rittenhouse Sq, 19103
Tel *(215) 546-9000*
W rittenhousehotel.com
A five-diamond hotel with lavish
rooms, indulgent spa, and two
award-winning restaurants.

A view of Kimpton Hotel Monaco in the 1907 Lafayette Building

The Ritz–Carlton Hotel $$$
Luxury   Map 2 F4
10 S Broad St, 19102
Tel *(215) 523-8000*
W ritzcarlton.com
The hotel's columned façade is
stunning. Rooms are plush and
have splendid views of City Hall.

The Westin Philadelphia $$$
Business   Map 2 E4
99 S 17th St, 19103
Tel *(215) 563-1600*
W starwoodhotels.com
Connected to Liberty Place, Westin
has opulent lounge areas and
good dining and drinking options.

Warwick Rittenhouse Square $$$
Business   Map 2 E5
220 S 17th St, 19103
Tel *(215) 735-6000*
W warwickrittenhouse.com
A majestic English Renaissance
style hotel with an excellent,
upscale steakhouse, The Prime Rib.

Logan Square and Parkway Museums District

Embassy Suites by Hilton
Philadelphia Center City $$
Business   Map 2 E3
1776 Benjamin Franklin Pkwy, 19103
Tel *(215) 561-1776*
W embassysuites3.hilton.com
The hotel's landmark cylindrical
building, opposite Logan Square,
features spacious suites with
living rooms and balconies.

Sheraton Philadelphia
Downtown $$
Business   Map 2 E3
201 N 17th St, 19103
Tel *(215) 448-2000*
W sheratonphiladelphia
downtown.com
Close to the Convention Center,
with upscale, comfortable rooms
and a superb seafood restaurant.

The Windsor Suites $$
Business   Map 2 E3
1700 Benjamin Franklin Pkwy, 19103
Tel *(215) 981-5678*
W thewindsorsuites.com
The studio and one-bedroom
suites on offer here have fully
equipped kitchens and lovely
private balconies.

Le Méridien Philadelphia $$$
Luxury   Map 2 F3
1421 Arch St, 19102
Tel *(215) 422-8200*
W starwoodhotels.com
Le Méridien Philadelphia's
Georgian Revival-style structure
features a striking atrium and
sleek decor with red accents.

Farther Afield

HI Chamounix Mansion $
Hostel
*3250 Chamounix Dr, Philadelphia,
PA, 19131*
Tel *(215) 878-3676*
W philahostel.org
Situated in the idyllic Fairmount
Park, HI Chamounix Mansion
offers lovely accommodations in
a mansion and carriage house.

Howard Johnson Express Inn
Bellmawr $
Motel
*341 B South Black Horse Pike,
Bellmawr, NJ, 08031*
Tel *(856) 931-0700*
W hojo.com
This budget hotel is just off the
New Jersey Turnpike, 10 miles
(16 km) south of central Philly.

Chestnut Hill Hotel $$
Inn
*8229 Germantown Ave, Philadelphia,
PA, 19118*
Tel *(215) 242-4900*
W chestnuthillhotel.com
A historic 1891 hotel with modern
facilities. Located near Fairmount
Park's Wissahickon Gorge.

For more information on types of hotels *see page 135*

The charming University Suite on the second floor of Cornerstone Bed & Breakfast

Cornerstone Bed & Breakfast $$
B&B **Map** 1 A2
3300 Baring St, Philadelphia, PA, 19104
Tel *(215) 387-6065*
W cornerstonebandb.com
A beautifully restored Victorian-era building with a wraparound porch and stained-glass windows.

Holiday Inn Philadelphia Stadium $$
Business
900 Packer Ave, Philadelphia, PA, 19148
Tel *(215) 755-9500*
W hiphilly.com
Close to the major sports venues (across the street from Citizens Bank Park, home of the Philadelphia Phillies, and close to Lincoln Financial Field, base of the Philadelphia Eagles), this is an ideal hotel for sports fans. The comfortable rooms offer a full range of amenities.

Homewood Suites by Hilton $$
Business
4109 Walnut St, Philadelphia, PA, 19104
Tel *(215) 382-1111*
W homewoodunivcity.com
Spacious, modern suites with kitchens in University City. Offers breakfast daily and weekday dinner and drinks on the house.

Manayunk Terrace $$
B&B
3937 Terrace St, Philadelphia, PA, 19128
Tel *(215) 483-0109*
W manayunkterracecityhouse hotel.com
This cozy, comfortable B&B offers sweeping hilltop views and easy access to the city by train.

Philadelphia Bella Vista B&B $$
B&B **Map** 3 B5
752 S 10th St Philadelphia, PA, 19147
Tel *(215) 238-1270*
W philadelphiabellavistabnb.com
Just a short stroll from Center City and major historic sites, Bella Vista has colorful, well-tended rooms.

South Bridge Bed & Breakfast $$
B&B **Map** 1 B5
2628 South St, Philadelphia, PA, 19146
Tel *(215) 219-2682*
Small, intimate house with just two rooms near the Schuylkill Park. Serves great breakfast.

The Conwell Inn $$
Inn
1331 Polett Walk, Philadelphia, PA, 19122
Tel *(215) 235-6200*
W conwellinn.com
Situated on Temple University's campus, this deluxe inn provides 22 tastefully decorated rooms.

The Gables B&B $$
B&B
4520 Chester Ave, Philadelphia, PA, 19143
Tel *(215) 662-1918*
W gablesbb.com
Provides a hearty breakfast and comfortable rooms in the friendly University City area.

The Hotel ML $$
Business
915 Rte 73, Mount Laurel, NJ, 08054
Tel *(856) 234-7300*
W thehotelml.com
Good suburban hotel with a fine restaurant and bar; tennis courts, game room, and a water park too.

Philadelphia Airport Marriott $$$
Business
1 Arrivals Rd, Philadelphia, PA, 19153
Tel *(215) 492-9000*
W marriott.com
Connected to the airport via a sky bridge, Marriott offers terrific dining at its Aviation Grill.

Sheraton Philadelphia University City Hotel $$$
Business
3549 Chestnut St, Philadelphia, PA, 19104
Tel *(215) 387-8000*
W philadelphiasheraton.com
Lavish rooms, an outdoor pool, and a convenient location make this a good spot on the campus.

Beyond Philadelphia

Atlantic City

The Inn at the Irish Pub $
Inn
164 St James Place, Atlantic City, NJ, 08401
Tel *(609) 344-9063*
W theirishpub.com
This convivial Irish pub offers its guests basic, comfortable European-style rooms. The bar serves great food.

Caesars Atlantic City Hotel Casino $$$
Luxury
2100 Pacific Ave, Atlantic City, NJ, 08401
Tel *(609) 348-4411*
W caesars.com/caesars-ac/
A luxurious casino and hotel on the Boardwalk. Houses multiple fine-dining restaurants.

Brandywine Valley

Brandywine River Hotel $$
Luxury
1609 Baltimore Pike, Chadds Ford, PA, 19317
Tel *(610) 388-1200*
W brandywineriverhotel.com
An elegant European-style hotel with fireplaces and Jacuzzis. It is quite close to popular attractions.

Cape May

Cape Harbor Motor Inn $$
Motel
715 Pittsburgh Ave, Cape May, NJ, 08204
Tel *(609) 884-0018*
W capeharbormotorinn.com
A brightly decorated motel that offers some of the best bargain deals during the high season as well as the off season. Modern and well-equipped rooms. The motel has a pool, though the beach is just seven blocks away.

DK Choice

Queen Victoria $$
B&B
102 Ocean St, Cape May, NJ, 08204
Tel *(609) 884-8702*
W queenvictoria.com
Housed in renovated 19th-century buildings amid lush grounds, the inn is beautifully decorated with period furnishings. Located near the beach and close to several gourmet restaurants. Free bicycles are provided to guests to tour the area.

Doylestown

Old Hargrave House $$
B&B
*50 South Main St, Doylestown,
PA, 18901*
Tel *(215) 348-3334*
Ⓦ hargravehouse.net
Decorated with 19th-century
furnishings, the bright, spacious
rooms of this 200-year-old
house afford guests great views
over the Doylestown Historical
Society Park.

Gettysburg

**Brickhouse Inn Bed
& Breakfast** $$
B&B
*452 Baltimore St, Gettysburg,
PA, 17325*
Tel *(717) 338-9337*
Ⓦ brickhouseinn.com
Justly popular, this charming
B&B comprises two lovely old
Victorian properties. Both feature
period rooms for an all-around
old-world feel.

DK Choice

Doubleday Inn $$
B&B
*104 Doubleday Ave, Gettysburg,
PA, 17325*
Tel *(717) 334-9119*
Ⓦ doubledayinn.com
Actually situated on the battle-
field, Doubleday is a delightful
place that houses extensive
war memorabilia and books.
The rooms are comfortable,
with period furnishings, but
there are no televisions or
phones. The gourmet breakfasts
are superb, and daily variations
are offered.

Farnsworth House Inn $$
B&B
*401 Baltimore St, Gettysburg,
PA, 17325*
Tel *(717) 334-8838*
Ⓦ farnsworthhouseinn.com
The historic Farnsworth House
Inn offers lovely Victorian rooms
and gives its guests a dining
experience reminiscent of the
Civil War era.

Harrisburg

Hilton Harrisburg $$
Business
1 N 2nd St, Harrisburg, PA, 17101
Tel *(717) 233-6000*
Ⓦ harrisburg.hilton.com
Conveniently located a mere
two blocks away from the State
Capitol, the Hilton has a fully
equipped business center and
plush rooms.

Hershey

The Inn at Westwynd Farm $
B&B
*1620 Sandbeach Rd, Hummelstown,
PA, 17036*
Tel *(717) 533-6764*
Ⓦ westwyndfarminn.com
Situated on a working farm, this
rambling, rustic house has a
wide selection of rooms available
to choose from.

New Hope

Pineapple Hill Inn $$
B&B
1324 River Rd, New Hope, PA, 18938
Tel *(888) 866-8404*
Ⓦ pineapplehill.com
This wonderfully restored
colonial manor house was built
in 1790. Its rooms are decorated
in period style and feature gas-
burning fireplaces.

Pennsylvania Dutch Country

Amish Lanterns Motel $
Motel
*290 N Decator St, Strasburg,
PA, 17579*
Tel *(717) 687-7839*
Ⓦ amishmotel.com
Close to all the major tourist
attractions, this motel offers basic,
decent-sized rooms in a pleasant
rural location.

**Best Western Plus Revere Inn
& Suites** $
Inn
*3063 Lincoln Highway, Paradise,
PA, 17562*
Tel *(717) 687-8601*
Ⓦ reveretavern.com
Accommodations here are
spread over three buildings
based around the Historic Revere
Tavern restaurant.

AmishView Inn & Suites $$
Inn
*3125 Old Philadelphia Pike, Bird-in-
Hand, PA, 17505*
Tel *(717) 768-1162*
Ⓦ amishviewinn.com
Here you'll find comfortable rooms
and suites with kitchenettes
amid the rolling cornfields of the
Plain and Fancy Farm.

Cameron Estate Inn $$
Inn
*1855 Mansion Lane, Mount Joy,
PA, 17552*
Tel *(717) 492-0111*
Ⓦ cameronestateinn.com
Upscale, artistically designed
rooms are offered in a grand
1805 mansion. There is also a
good gourmet restaurant on-site.

**The Inn & Spa at Intercourse
Village** $$
Luxury
*3542 Old Philadelphia Pike,
Intercourse, PA, 17534*
Tel *(717) 768-2626*
Ⓦ inn-spa.com
This romantic, beautifully
restored 1909 building features
beamed ceilings and traditional
fireplaces throughout.

Valley Forge

**Crowne Plaza Philadelphia–
King of Prussia** $$
Business
*260 Mall Blvd, King of Prussia,
PA, 19406*
Tel *(610) 265-7500*
Ⓦ cpvalleyforge.com
Opposite King of Prussia Mall,
the Crowne Plaza hotel has well-
appointed rooms and a large
conference center.

Wayne Hotel $$
Luxury
*139 E Lancaster Ave, Wayne,
PA, 19087*
Tel *(610) 687-5000*
Ⓦ waynehotel.com
Lavishly appointed with ornate
chandeliers and bright-orange
furniture, the Wayne Hotel is
a historic landmark on the
Main Line.

Wilmington

Hotel du Pont $$
Luxury
*11th & Market Sts, Wilmington,
DE, 19801*
Tel *(302) 594-3100*
Ⓦ hoteldupont.com
Close to Brandywine Valley, Hotel
du Pont has opulent rooms that
include sleek mahogany furniture
and brass bathroom fittings.
There is also a vast on-site
shopping arcade.

The beautiful exterior of Queen Victoria
inn, Cape May

For more information on types of hotels *see page 135*

WHERE TO EAT AND DRINK

Though the city is perhaps traditionally best known for the Philadelphia cheesesteak, its culinary repertoire has expanded widely and it is today home to some of the country's top-rated restaurants. In addition to superb traditional American fare, some of the city's best dining rooms specialize in trendy contemporary American cuisine, where farm-to-table principles are adhered to and menus are more creative. Excellent bistros, seafood restaurants, and steakhouses feature styles from Southern home cooking to colonial fare. There are ethnic restaurants aplenty: French, Italian, Chinese, Mexican, Thai, Moroccan, and many more, as well as venues offering fusion cuisine or international menus.

Park-side alfresco dining at Rouge in Rittenhouse Square *(see p147)*

Numerous restaurants in popular outdoor areas, such as Rittenhouse Square, Manayunk, and Chestnut Hill are stylish with upscale bistros and cafés. There are more than 200 restaurants here offering outdoor dining. Many are small, cosy spots serving cocktails and trendsetting dishes in an ambience reminiscent of a Parisian café. Several restaurants and comfortable neighborhood bars are also located along Fairmount Avenue, close to the Museum of Art.

Philly Fare

For breakfast, the locals love to order grilled pork rolls along with eggs and hash browns. At noon, cheesesteaks and lunchmeat-filled "hoagies" or "grinders" are favorites, found at the many food courts, pizzerias, and sandwich shops dotting the city. Hoagies are Italian rolls filled with meats and cheeses, as well as lettuce, tomatoes, and onions, sprinkled with oregano on top. Philly cheesesteaks consist of finely-sliced grilled beef with onions, topped with cheese sauce and served in a foot-long roll.

In Pennsylvania Dutch Country, meals are influenced by the traditional cooking of the Amish and Mennonites *(see p117)*. Family-style restaurants usually offer a good selection of this distinctive food, while staple and favorite treats are available at local farmers' markets *(see p142)*.

Restaurants, Bistros, and Cafés

Many of Philadelphia's best restaurants are in Center City. Fine dining rooms can also be found near the theater district, home to the Kimmel Center and other performing arts venues. In Old City, head to the area around Market and Chestnut Streets, between Front and 4th Streets, where some popular establishments can be found. Chinatown is home to several excellent restaurants, while some of the best family-owned trattorias are located in the Italian Market in south Philadelphia.

Hours and Prices

Luncheonettes and coffee shops open early for breakfast and may stay open through lunch only. Finer restaurants open for lunch and dinner, with lunch served from 11:30am to 2:30pm or 3pm, and dinner from 5:30pm until 10pm or 10:30pm, and often later on weekends. Late-night restaurants that are also nightclubs stay open until 2am, but may stop serving food earlier.

Cuba Libre in Old City recreates 1940s Havana *(see p144)*

The modest bar with chalkboard menu at Percy Street Barbeque *(see p147)*

Breakfast at diners and eateries can cost anywhere between $10 and $15 with a tip, while hotel buffet breakfasts can cost $15–$20. Sunday brunches at upscale restaurants can start at $20–$35 or more per person.

A typical lunch ranges from sandwiches and sodas, for about $5–$9, to sit-down meals costing $15–$25 with a tip. Dinner is usually the big meal of the day. Starters and salads cost $5–$10. Entrées can run from $12 to $40, even up to $50 or more at high-end steakhouses and restaurants. Desserts and wine by the glass generally cost $5–$12.

Some ethnic restaurants offer generous portions of quality food at reasonable prices, with meals costing up to $15 or more per person.

Eateries and Fast Food

Good pizza, sandwiches, and salads abound in Philadelphia. Many pizza shops sell individual slices, as well as hoagies and cheesesteaks. *Taquerias* near the Italian Market offer authentic Mexican dishes at low prices. The Reading Terminal Market, at 11th and Arch Streets, offers a variety of affordable international food.

Alcohol and Smoking

Many restaurants serve wine by the glass or bottle. Simple eateries and fast-food spots generally do not serve alcohol. Philadelphia is known for its "BYOB" restaurants that do not sell alcohol but allow patrons to "Bring Your Own Bottle" at no extra charge. Few BYOB places do sell liquor but impose daunting "corkage" fees for the privilege.

Restaurants and bars in Pennsylvania and New Jersey stop serving alcohol by 2am. The legal drinking age is 21 and ID is often required when entering a bar. All restaurants and bars are non-smoking.

Reservations and Dress

Reservations at upscale restaurants are recommended, and are often required on weekend nights. Nonetheless, some popular spots may not reserve tables, and use waiting lists. Even if you have reservations, you might have to wait for up to an hour on busy days.

Casual wear is accepted at most places, although some fine dining establishments expect patrons to wear smart-casual styles or business attire. Check while booking to be certain.

Tipping

At most restaurants, your wait-person will bring your bill. A 15 per cent tip is considered a minimum, with up to 20 percent for superior service.

Children

Children are usually welcome in restaurants. It is not recommended, however, to bring young children to establishments that have late-night crowds and a bar area, as anyone under 21 may not be allowed inside.

Recommended Restaurants

Restaurants in Philadelphia offer an amazing array of cuisines – from traditional American and colonial dishes to Southern-style and New American fare. A classic American menu is largely meat-based, but vegetarian options are also accommodated. New American blends traditional American dishes with recipes from other parts of the world. The innovative menus feature farm-fresh, seasonal products. Establishments serving colonial cuisine represent the old-school culinary traditions of the 13 British colonies in North America. Down-home Southern fare is characterized by wholesome, farm-style cooking and hearty portions. Cajun and Creole cuisines originating in Louisiana typify Southern comfort food. The city also boasts a considerable number of restaurants offering ethnic cuisines such as Greek, Chinese, Indian, Mexican, Italian, and Middle Eastern.

The restaurants featured in this guide have been selected across a wide price range for their value, good food, atmosphere, and location. From no-frills snack shacks to pricey gastronomic venues, these restaurants run the gamut of price levels and cuisine types. For the best of the best, look out for restaurants featured as "DK Choice." These establishments have been highlighted for an exceptional quality – a celebrity chef, exquisite food, or an inviting ambience. Most of these venues are popular among locals and visitors alike, so inquire about reservations or you may face a lengthy wait for a table.

Delectable food on offer at Spasso Italian Grill *(see p145)*

Flavors of the Pennsylvania Dutch Country

Philadelphians savor the broad range of American and ethnic tastes from the many cultures that call the city home. Nearby Pennsylvania Dutch Country has its own unique flavors, comprising basic, hearty foods prepared from simple recipes. Amish and Mennonite cooks take advantage of the plentiful harvests to prepare dishes often characterized as good home cooking. To preserve the excess from the harvests, fresh country produce is both canned and jarred in homes and small shops, with much of it turned into tangy relishes and sweet jellies. Such treats are available at various farmers' markets.

Corn on the cob

Fresh produce at a farmer's market in Lancaster County

Bountiful Harvests

Amish and Mennonite food stems from the cultural tastes that the settlers brought from their home countries of Germany and Switzerland – recipes later adapted to the available crops that could be cultivated in the New World. Throughout the generations, the Amish have continued to nurture their gardens and fields through traditional methods with horse-drawn farming equipment. They grow all manner of fresh vegetables, including corn, string beans, carrots, beets, onions, tomatoes, peppers, lettuce, potatoes, sweet potatoes, cauliflower, and more. Fruits include apples, cherries, plums, peaches, and sweet watermelon, with many used as ingredients for the delicious desserts that have made the Pennsylvania Dutch Country famous.

Meats and Delis

Amish delis and restaurants feature a wide variety of cheeses, meats, and poultry, including fresh country sausages, sweet bologna, bacon, ham, dried beef and jerky, and smoked turkey. Cuts of fresh beef, pork, and chicken are favorites among the locals, who serve them up as part of tasty recipes such as scrapple, a dish that is made of pork, onions, cornmeal, and spices.

Whoopie pie   Molasses cookies   Mincemeat cookies   Apple pie   Shoofly pie

A selection of Pennsylvania Dutch Country cakes and desserts

Local Dishes and Specialties

Pennsylvania Dutch restaurants are known for their family-style buffets with meat dishes such as golden fried chicken, roast beef, chicken pot pie, and spicy sausage. Staples include mashed potatoes, homemade noodles and breads, and a choice of vegetables. Popular jellies and relishes include smooth apple butter, and Chow Chow, a mixture of sweet pickled vegetables. Amish recipes are handed down from mother to daughter to granddaughter, making for unique tastes. Dishes include Amish bean soup, corn fritters, spare ribs and sauerkraut, baking powder biscuits, cornmeal mush, and "Schnitz and Knepp," made with dried apples and ham. Popular desserts include whoopie pies – creamy filling sandwiched between two cake-like cookies – and shoofly pie, which has a coffee cake-like topping with a thick molasses bottom.

Fresh green apples

Chicken pot pie comprises tender chicken pieces with vegetables and noodles, cooked in a pot of broth.

Where to Eat and Drink

Philadelphia

Old City

Aqua Malaysian & Thai Restaurant $
Asian **Map** 4 D3
705 Chestnut St, 19106
Tel *(215) 928-2838* **Closed** *Sun*
Classic Thai curries and noodles are highlights of this BYOB restaurant, as are the Malaysian Beef *Rendang* (spicy meat dish) and *Kari Ayam* (chicken curry). Try the *Roti Canai* – thin bread served with curry sauce. Good vegetarian choices.

Ariana Restaurant $
Afghan **Map** 4 E3
134 Chestnut St, 19106
Tel *(215) 922-1535*
Enjoy authentic Afghan cuisine such as Kabuli *pulao* (rice with vegetables and meat) and marinated lamb kebabs. The cosy interior is decorated with ethnic photographs and Afghan-style bay windows. Guests can bring their own wine.

Café Ole $
Café **Map** 4 E2
147 N 3rd St, 19106
Tel *(215) 627-2140*
Welcoming breakfast and lunch spot offering a wide choice of snacks, especially from the Mediterranean region, such as *shakshuka* (poached eggs in spicy tomato sauce) and baklava, complemented by non-alcoholic beverages.

Chlöe $
New American **Map** 4 E2
232 Arch St, 19106
Tel *(215) 629-2337* **Closed** *Sun–Tue*
With an emphasis on sourcing seasonal ingredients from local farmers, the couple who run this tiny BYOB restaurant lovingly turn out a range of dishes from saucy ribs with mac-and-cheese to skewered lamb with minted couscous.

El Fuego $
Mexican **Map** 3 C3
723 Walnut St, 19106
Tel *(215) 592-1901* **Closed** *Sun*
A lively California-style burrito house where patrons can enjoy hearty versions of the signature dish or slightly lighter but equally tasty tacos and quesadillas. Bright, cheerful interior.

Franklin Fountain $
Desserts **Map** 4 E3
116 Market St, 19106
Tel *(215) 627-1899*
This parlor treats guests with home-made ice creams, sodas, plus other desserts. Try one of their excellent sundaes (especially hot fudge). Old-fashioned decor recalls a bygone era.

Kisso Sushi Bar $
Japanese **Map** 4 E2
205 N 4th St, 19106
Tel *(215) 922-1770*
Offers a wide selection of sushi, sashimi, and maki rolls, along with salads and simple desserts. Bright, pleasant interior. It does not sell alcohol, but diners can bring their own bottle.

Mrs. K's Coffee Shop $
Café **Map** 4 E3
325 Chestnut St, 19106
Tel *(215) 627-7991*
Popular place serving a standard variety of sandwiches, breakfast combos and sides, wraps, burgers, and steaks. The menu includes beverages and ice creams.

Race Street Café $
International **Map** 4 E2
208 Race St, 19106
Tel *(215) 267-6181*
This lively bar-restaurant offers cuisines from all across the world. Enjoy savory dishes such as shrimp quesadilla, Moroccan-style lamb burger, shrimp *pad Thai*, and *petit filet Dianne*. Good selection of beers.

Sonny's Cheesesteaks $
Classic American **Map** 4 E3
228 Market St, 19106
Tel *(215) 629-5760*
Famous no-frills eatery selling the signature Philly cheesesteaks. Patrons can choose from a bewildering array of fillings for

Neatly laid out tables in the elegant dining room at City Tavern

Price Guide
Prices are for a three-course meal per person, including a glass of house wine, and other charges such as service and tax.

$	under $35
$$	$35–$60
$$$	over $60

sandwiches and add side dishes such as onion rings, chicken fingers, and fries.

The Bourse $
International **Map** 4 D3
111 S Independence Mall East, 19106
Tel *(215) 625-0300*
Closed *Nov–Feb: Sun*
The former lobby of the 19th-century commodities exchange building now houses a food court with upscale cafes and food stalls. It's an ideal lunch spot near Independence National Historic Park.

DK Choice

Amada $$
Spanish **Map** 4 E3
217–219 Chestnut St, 19106
Tel *(215) 625-2450*
Authentic tapas based on earthy Mediterranean flavors is the prime attraction at Amada. Founder and executive chef Jose Garces has long been passionate about the tapas tradition. The impressive menu of inspired creations gives guests the opportunity to mix and share multiple dishes. Signature tapas include octopus, garlic shrimps, and tortillas. Good list of Spanish wines.

Bistro 7 $$
French **Map** 4 E3
7 N 3rd St, 19106
Tel *(215) 931-1560* **Closed** *Sun & Mon*
Elegant bistro presenting a modern twist to classic French dishes such as fennel and black pepper seared *coulotte* (beef) steak. Also try the wonderful ten-course tasting menu. Patrons can bring in their own wine.

City Tavern $$
American-Colonial **Map** 4 E3
138 S 2nd St, 19106
Tel *(215) 413-1443*
Classic colonial-style cuisine, such as West Indies pepperpot soup and roasted duckling, accompanied with colonial ales. The restaurant is a historically accurate reconstruction of the original 1773 tavern, with staff serving in period costume.

For more information on types of restaurants *see page 141*

Impressively high ceilings match the culinary offerings and beers at La Peg

Cuba Libre Restaurant and Rum Bar $$

Cuban Map 4 E3
10 S 2nd St, 19106
Tel *(215) 627-0666*
Four dining rooms and two bars serve modern Cuban and inventive Latin cuisine, as well as rums and Cuban cocktails. The bright colors and vintage decor evoke memories of 1940s Havana.

DiNardo's Famous Crabs $$

Seafood Map 4 E2
312 Race St, 19106
Tel *(215) 925-5115*
A local favorite since 1976, this seafood restaurant prepares excellent crabs. Specialties include steamed Louisiana crabs served Baltimore-style, jumbo shrimp, and stuffed flounder. Casual and friendly atmosphere.

Eulogy Belgian Tavern $$

Belgian Map 4 E3
136 Chestnut St, 19106
Tel *(215) 413-1918*
Cosy pub and restaurant featuring a huge selection of international and Belgian beers. Traditional Belgian fare, including fish, meatballs, fries, and mussels prepared in five different sauces.

Farmicia $$

New American Map 4 E3
15 S 3rd St, 19106
Tel *(215) 627-6274* **Closed** *Mon*
Stylish place that, as the name suggests, concentrates on locally farmed organic produce. The must-try dishes include Dijon grilled pork and duck confit.

Han Dynasty $$

Chinese Map 4 E3
123 Chestnut St, 19106
Tel *(215) 922-1888*
Traditional Sichuan Chinese food, featuring the famous combina-

tion of chili heat and peppercorn tingle. Spicy Dan Dan noodles with ground pork, wontons in chili oil, and fish in dry pot stand out.

Jones $$

Classic American Map 4 D3
700 Chestnut St, 19106
Tel *(215) 223-5663*
Upscale versions of old-fashioned American comfort food complemented by fancy cocktails served in a fun, retro setting. Indulge in mac-and-cheese or chicken and waffles. Lively pop music entertains guests.

Kabul Afghan Cuisine Restaurant $$

Afghan Map 4 E3
106 Chestnut St, 19106
Tel *(215) 922-3676*
Welcoming restaurant with traditional Afghan decor. The menu focuses on meat kebabs and vegetarian specialties cooked with exotic spices. Book ahead to dine in classic Afghan style on a platform with rugs and pillows.

La Peg $$

French Map 4 F3
140 N Columbus Blvd, 19106
Tel *(215) 375-7744*
Housed in a former pumping station with high ceilings and large arched windows. Choose from a well-curated list of beers to wash down French delights such as lamb shoulder and lemon-braised rabbit. Extensive selection of wines.

La Veranda Restaurant $$

Italian Map 4 F4
Pier 3, 30 N Columbus Blvd, 19106
Tel *(215) 351-1898*
Enjoy breathtaking views of the Delaware River while dining on fresh fish and meats cut to order and cooked on a woodburning

grill. Veal stuffed with mozzarella cheese and tuna steak grilled with capers are two of the highlights.

Panorama $$

Italian Map 4 E3
14 N Front St, 19106
Tel *(215) 922-7800*
Enjoy home-made pasta and the finest veal at this busy trattoria in Penn's View Hotel. The bar has a 120-bottle wine keeper – the world's largest wine dispensing system. Florentine tiles and hand-painted murals grace the interior.

Serrano-Tin Angel $$

International Map 4 E3
20 S 2nd St, 19106
Tel *(215) 928-0770* **Closed** *Mon*
Stylish restaurant set in an 1820s town house with the popular folk music café, Tin Angel, on the second level. House specialties include Malaysian pork chop, vegetable *kung pao*, and calamari. Vibrant, eclectic interior.

The Continental Restaurant and Martini Bar $$

Asian Map 4 E3
138 Market St, 19106
Tel *(215) 923-6069*
With its imaginative interior, the Continental is one of the hippest haunts in the Old City's nightlife district. Offers contemporary cuisine with pan-Asian flair. Extensive martini, champagne, and wine list. Live Latin and lounge music.

The Plough & The Stars $$

Irish Map 4 E3
123 Chestnut St, 19106
Tel *(215) 733-0300*
Housed in the Corn Exchange Building, this trendy pub dishes up gourmet and creative food. Guinness casserole and Irish-style chicken curry are some of the highlights. Traditional Irish music is played on Sundays. Outdoor seating in the warmer months.

Wedge + Fig $$

International Map 4 E2
160 N 3rd St, Philadelphia, PA, 19106
Tel *(267) 603-3090* **Closed** *Mon*
Describing itself as a cheese bistro, this BYOB establishment offers a range of fine cheeses in various forms – main courses to desserts – as well as other dishes such as roast chicken and braised pork.

Buddakan $$$

Fusion Map 4 E3
325 Chestnut St, 19106
Tel *(215) 574-9440*
Modern Asian cuisine is the focus here resulting in imaginative

dishes such as soy bean ravioli, wasabi tuna pizza, and miso-glazed black cod. Sleek decor with a giant Buddha statue gazing over an illuminated communal table.

Common Wealth $$$
Southern   **Map** 4 E3
319 Market St, 19106
Tel *(215) 372-7581*
This elegant bar-restaurant offers favorites from South Carolina and the rest of the Low Country, such oysters Bienville, rich gumbo, and shellfish with grits, as well as craft beers and whiskey cocktails.

Fork $$$
New American   **Map** 4 E3
306 Market St, 19106
Tel *(215) 625-9425*
Offering a mix of plush urban style and casual sophistication, Fork prepares modern American, bistro-style cuisine with an international flavor. Delicately printed velvet curtains and chandeliers surround a unique central bar.

Morimoto $$$
Japanese   **Map** 4 D3
723 Chestnut St, 19106
Tel *(215) 413-9070*
Morimoto, the eponymous chef, brings contemporary Japanese cuisine to the diner's table through the artful blending of a Western twist with traditional Japanese cooking. The elegant dining room features chic, modern decor.

Spasso Italian Grill $$$
Italian   **Map** 4 E3
34 S Front St, 19106
Tel *(215) 592-7661*
This trattoria serves traditional Italian fare with dishes from both southern and northern Italy. Home-made pastas, fresh seafood, veal, and chicken are popular choices. Good-value fixed menus.

Society Hill and Penn's Landing

Cavanaugh's Headhouse $
Classic American   **Map** 4 E4
421 S 2nd St, 19147
Tel *(215) 928-9307*
A popular local hangout with six bars that doubles up as a restaurant. Serves hearty pub fare, such as lamb chops and crab-stuffed mushrooms. Colonial inn-style decor with dozens of TVs to watch sports while dining.

Famous 4th Street Delicatessen $
Jewish/Deli   **Map** 4 D5
700 S 4th St, 19147
Tel *(215) 922-3274*
This traditional Jewish corner deli, established in 1923, has a menu that features all the mouthwatering classics you'd expect – from hot pastrami sandwiches, to knishes and whitefish salad.

Jim's Steaks $
Classic American   **Map** 4 D4
400 South St, 19147
Tel *(215) 928-1911*
With its distinctive Art Deco storefront, Jim's is one of Philadelphia's favorite eateries. Visitors and locals alike flock here for authentic Philly cheesesteaks or excellent hoagies.

South Street Diner $
Classic American   **Map** 4 E5
140 South St, 19147
Tel *(215) 627-5258*
This classic diner has somewhat achieved the status of an institution. The extensive menu includes breakfast combos, huge burgers, sandwiches, wraps, and Mexican dishes such as quesadillas. Offers round-the-clock service.

South Street Souvlaki $
Greek   **Map** 4 D4
509 South St, 19147
Tel *(215) 925-3026*   **Closed** *Mon*
Iconic South Street restaurant serving traditional Greek and Mediterranean cuisine. Lamb *fricassé*, seafood, and baked vegetables are house specialties. Take-out available.

Tattooed Mom $
Classic American   **Map** 4 D4
530 South St, 19147
Tel *(215) 238-9880*
Fun, trendy eatery offering a good choice of sandwiches, buffalo wings, nachos and *tater tots* (deep-fried grated potatoes), plus great beers and cocktails. The quirky decor inside makes use of cartoons and graffiti.

DK Choice

Bistro Romano $$
Italian   **Map** 4 E4
120 Lombard St, 19147
Tel *(215) 925-8880*
Housed in a converted 18th-century granary with wood and brick decor, Bistro Romano makes quality pasta dishes and mains such as grouper *asparagi* or crispy roasted half duckling. The unique wine cellar, located under the street, is a part of the former network of underground tunnels in Society Hill. The restaurant organizes mystery dinner theaters on Fridays or Saturdays where guests can participate as well.

Bridget Foy's $$
Classic American   **Map** 4 E5
200 South St, 19147
Tel *(215) 922-1813*
Sample good old American standards such as steaks, fresh fish, burgers, and sand-wiches. The outdoor café is a great spot to break for lunch while watching the bustling South Street.

Marrakesh $$
Moroccan   **Map** 4 D5
517 S Leithgow St, 19147
Tel *(215) 925-5929*
Lounge on cushioned pillows and enjoy an authentic seven-course Moroccan feast beginning with ritual hand-washing and ending with a tea ceremony. Private dining rooms and belly dancers are available upon request at this BYOB restaurant.

The Art Deco frontage of the ever-popular restaurant Jim's Steaks

For more information on types of restaurants *see page 141*

Pizzeria Stella $$
Italian   **Map** 4 E4
420 S 2nd St, 19147
Tel *(215) 320-8000*
Neapolitan-style pizzas with
creative toppings are the focus
here. The traditional dome-
shaped wood-burning oven
bakes crisp pizzas in minutes.
A few starters, salads, and great
gelato round off the menu.

The Twisted Tail $$
Southern   **Map** 4 E4
509 S 2nd St, 19147
Tel *(215) 558-2471*
Occupying a fine, vibrantly painted
town house, this place serves
Southern-style comfort food with
dishes such as lamb pappardelle,
Florida shrimp and grits, and
brown butter skate wing.

Xochitl $$
Mexican   **Map** 4 E4
408 S 2nd St, 19147
Tel *(215) 238-7280*
Relish contemporary Mexican
cuisine based on recipes from
Puebla. Savory ceviches, creative
tacos, and enticing snacks are
prepared with a degree of sophis-
tication. First-rate margaritas.

Bistrot La Minette $$$
French   **Map** 4 D5
623 S 6th St, 19147
Tel *(215) 925-8000*
Authentic French restaurant with
appropriately chic decor. Start
with grilled quail before moving
on to mustard-braised rabbit and
finish with chocolate mousse
cake. Cap that with a fine cognac.

Chart House $$$
Seafood   **Map** 4 E4
555 S Columbus Blvd, 19147
Tel *(215) 625-8383*
Part of a well-known nationwide
chain, serving everything from

creamy clam chowder and crab
cakes to a mighty, mixed seafood
grill. There are ample options for
vegetarians, plus a good wine list.

La Famiglia Ristorante $$$
Italian   **Map** 4 E3
8 S Front St, 19106
Tel *(215) 922-2803*   **Closed** *Sun*
First-class, delicious Italian fare
presented with a creative touch.
Fried calamari, pan-seared sole,
and veal with cheese topping
are among the standouts. Warm,
homely atmosphere.

Moshulu $$$
New American   **Map** 4 F4
401 S Columbus Blvd, 19106
Tel *(215) 923-2500*
Lovely fine-dining restaurant
aboard a restored, century-old
ship, ablaze with lights at night.
Splash out on the filet mignon or
boneless rib eye. Superb views
from indoor dining rooms or from
atop the deck in warmer months.

Southwark $$$
New American   **Map** 4 D5
701 S 4th St, 19147
Tel *(215) 238-1888*   **Closed** *Mon*
Maintaining long-standing
relationships with local farms,
Southwark serves only the freshest
seasonal products. Vibrant flavors
testify to the virtues of taking the
farm-to-table movement seriously.
Great cocktails too.

Vernick Food & Drink $$$
New American   **Map** 2 D4
2031 Walnut St, 19103
Tel *(267) 639-6644*
People come here for creative
fare served in an elegant
Rittenhouse brownstone. Sample
delights such as *fromage blanc*
and plum chutney on toast, small
plates of red curry shrimp, and
warm Parmesan custard.

Zahav $$$
Israeli   **Map** 4 E3
237 St James Pl, 19106
Tel *(215) 625-8800*
Israeli street food is served here –
albeit with a gourmet spin.
Modern cooking techniques and
fresh ingredients add a creative
touch to the menu's traditional
kebabs, snacks, and salads.
Sample the chef's good-value
tasting menu.

Center City

Mama's Vegetarian $
Middle Eastern   **Map** 2 D4
18 S 20th St, 19103
Tel *(215) 751-0477*   **Closed** *Sat*
Interesting vegetarian restaurant
that uses strictly kosher
ingredients. Tasty falafels,
eggplant sandwiches, and a
mighty salad platter are among
the highlights.

Nan Zhou Hand Drawn
Noodle House $
Chinese   **Map** 3 C1
1022 Race St, 19107
Tel *(215) 923-1550*
As the name suggests, hand-
pulled noodles – either as
steaming bowls of soup or dry
dishes – is what draws in guests
to this BYOB spot. Good choice
of dumplings, rice dishes, and
other appetizers.

Ocean City $
Chinese   **Map** 3 C1
234 N 9th St, 19107
Tel *(215) 829-0688*
A huge, open dining hall known
for dim sums – its house specialty.
Serves good seafood as well. The
drinks menu includes beer and
wine. Modest interior with
minimal decor.

Penang $
Asian   **Map** 3 C2
117 N 10th St, 19107
Tel *(215) 413-2531*
Trendy restaurant in the
heart of Chinatown with a
predominantly Malaysian menu,
featuring spicy curries and
seafood dishes, plus some
Thai, Indian, and Indonesian
specialties thrown in.

Rangoon $
Burmese   **Map** 3 C2
112 N 9th St, 19107
Tel *(215) 829-8939*
Sample unusual Burmese
delights such as coconut *galanga*
soup, spicy papaya salad, and
pork in mango-pickled curry at
this colorful little place. Also try
the traditional Burmese tea, hot
or cold.

Welcoming interior of Zahav with hand-carved wooden tables and open kitchen

Key to Price Guide *see page 143*

Reading Terminal Market $
International   Map 3 B2
12th & Arch Sts, 19107
Tel *(215) 922-2317*
Part farmers' market and part food court, the RTM offers everything from fresh produce to prepared meals. Highlights are DiNic's roast pork sandwich and traditional Amish fare. The ethnic food stands are a good bet as well.

Sakura Mandarin $
Chinese   Map 3 C2
1038 Race St, 19107
Tel *(215) 873-8338*
Serves specialties of Shanghai, such as *xiao long bao* (soup dumplings) and "lion's head" (pork meatballs), joined by Szechuan and Cantonese favorites. Try the thin scallion pancake. Good sushi and other Japanese dishes.

Schleisinger's Restaurant & Deli $
Deli   Map 3 A3
1521 Locust St, 19107
Tel *(215) 735-7305*
Relish home-style comfort food – from juicy wraps or savory sandwiches to hearty meals such as tender turkey with gravy and fries or boneless beef short ribs.

Alma de Cuba $$
Cuban   Map 3 A3
1623 Walnut St, 19103
Tel *(215) 988-1799*
Enjoy excellent Cuban fare such as sugarcane tuna, or dishes with an ethnic twist, as in the delicious Thai young coconut ceviche. Sleek, mirror-decorated interior.

Caribou Café $$
French   Map 3 B3
1126 Walnut St, 19107
Tel *(215) 625-9535*
This French bistro offers dishes from 15 regions of France, such as *salade Niçoise, quiche Lorraine,* and *crêpes Normandes.* The prix fixe menu is good value.

Devon Seafood Grill $$
Seafood   Map 2 D5
225 S 18th St, 19103
Tel *(215) 546-5940*
Great place for fresh fish specialties, such as Maryland crab cakes, pan-roasted Alaskan halibut, Maine lobsters, and Block Island swordfish. Eat in the dining room or on the sidewalk seating facing Rittenhouse Square.

El Vez $$
Mexican   Map 2 F2
121 S 13th St, 19107
Tel *(215) 928-9800*
Dine on delicious, contemporary versions of Mexican classics

Flashy red decor in the bar area of Alma de Cuba, which serves Cuban fusion food

at the stylish El Vez. The fresh guacamole and *mahi-mahi* (dolphinfish) tacos are highly recommended, as is the wonderful pomegranate margarita.

Fogo de Chão $$
Steakhouse   Map 3 B3
1337 Chestnut St, 19107
Tel *(215) 636-9700*
Located in the historic Caldwell's Jewelry Building, this branch of the steakhouse chain is a carnivore's delight. Serve yourself at the salad bar, then tuck into chunks of roasted meat brought to your plate straight from the grill.

Percy Street Barbecue $$
Barbecue   Map 3 C4
900 South St, 19147
Tel *(215) 625-8510*
A Texas-style barbecue joint with a roadhouse vibe. The highlight is beef brisket – moist and tender with an assertive smoke flavor. Also on offer are pork ribs, chicken, and fantastic desserts.

Rouge $$
International   Map 2 D5
205 S 18th St, 19103
Tel *(215) 732-6622*
Rouge is a hip bistro and popular late-night spot with outdoor seating facing Rittenhouse Square. The impressive menu lists a cross between Continental, American, and French fare with contemporary seafood, poultry, and beef dishes. Exquisite vintage wines.

Talula's Garden $$
American   Map 2 D5
210 W Washington Sq, 19106
Tel *(215) 592-7787*
Seasonal farm-to-table cuisine is served in a spacious, rustic-chic dining room festooned with vines and featuring its own cheese bar (and tempting cheese menu).

Dishes range from caramelized cauliflower soup to honey-glazed lamb belly.

The Black Sheep Irish Pub $$
Irish   Map 2 E5
247 S 17th St, 19103
Tel *(215) 545-9473*
Spread over three floors of a colonial town house, the Black Sheep dishes up hearty Irish stews and other favorites such as shepherd's pie and crab cakes. The antique bars feature drinks from around the world.

Zavino $$
Italian   Map 3 B3
112 S 13th St, 19107
Tel *(215) 732-2400*
Casual wine bar serving signature Neapolitan-style pizza. The domed oven creates a puffy crust topped with high-quality ingredients. Fine salads, pastas, and daily specials, plus a decent wine selection.

Zinc $$
French   Map 3 B3
246 S 11th Street, 19107
Tel *(215) 351-9901*   **Closed** *Mon*
Stylish Parisian restaurant with wall shelves full of quality wines that create a suitably Gallic ambience. Order the house specialty – *canard à la presse* (pressed duck) – and witness the preparation of this famous French dish.

Amuse $$$
French   Map 2 F3
1421 Arch St, 19102
Tel *(215) 422-8222*
Located in the Le Méridien hotel, this classy restaurant focuses on Gallic cuisine with delights such as truffled *foie gras torchon* (*foie gras* wrapped in towel and slow cooked) and lobster *bouillabaisse.* Extensive wine list.

For more information on types of restaurants *see page 141*

Alla Spina $$
Italian
1410 Mt Vernon St, Philadelphia,
PA, 19130
Tel *(215) 600-0017*   **Closed** *Mon*
An Italian gastropub that
combines a wider range of
options than can be found
in either genre alone. Fried
oysters with bacon horseradish
mayonnaise typifies the
chef's creativity. Local and
imported brews.

Cantina dos Segundos $$
Mexican
931 N 2nd St, Philadelphia,
PA, 19123
Tel *(215) 629-0500*
Authentic and typically colorful
Mexican eatery churning out
national favorites – from crispy
tacos to creamy quesadillas –
along with some offbeat
offerings such as the vegan
cheesesteak burrito.

Chickie's and Pete's Café $$
Seafood
1526 Packer Ave, Philadelphia,
PA, 19145
Tel *(215) 218-0500*
This popular meeting place for
locals bills itself as a crab house
and sports bar. Apart from the
signature crab fries, seasoned
fried mussels and lobster pie
are other enduring favorites.

City Tap House $$
New American
3925 Walnut St, 2nd Floor, 19103
Tel *(215) 662-0105*
Sleek, modern gastropub
offering a great combination
of enjoyable ales and tasty
pub fare. Good-value pizzas
and burgers are available,
alongside pricier dishes such
as rabbit bolognese.

In Riva $$
Italian
4116 Ridge Ave, Philadelphia,
PA, 19129
Tel *(215) 438-4848*   **Closed** *Mon*
Feast on the house specialty
Neapolitan-style pizza cooked
in a wood oven, with a wide
choice of toppings. Decent
wine selection. Alfresco seating
in warmer months.

Jake's and Cooper's Wine Bar $$
New American
4365 Main St, Manayunk, Philadelphia,
PA, 19127
Tel *(215) 483-0444*
Choose between Jake's, the
pioneering fine-dining
restaurant, or the casual and
less expensive Cooper's. Menu
highlights include pizza,
gourmet cheeses, stuffed quail,
and grilled calves' liver. Patrons
can bring their own wine.

La Collina $$
Italian
37–41 Ashland Ave, Bala Cynwyd,
PA, 19004
Tel *(610) 668-1780*
Elegant, friendly establishment
serving up classic Italian fare
by the Schuylkill River and the
adjacent expressway. Live music
thrice a week. Excellent service.

Noord Eetcafe $$
Northern European/Dutch
1046 Tasker St, Philadelphia,
PA, 19148
Tel *(267) 909-9704*
This lively Dutch-influenced
BYOB restaurant in South Philly,
offers such delicacies as *snert*
(Dutch split-pea soup),
bitterballen (fried pork meatballs),
Amsterdam-style mussels, and
Icelandic pollock.

Guests enjoying drinks at Standard Tap,
a popular gastropub

Ralph's Italian Restaurant $$
Italian
760 S 9th St, Philadelphia,
PA, 19147
Tel *(215) 627-6011*
Cosy yet classy restaurant run
by four generations of a family
since 1900. Serves up classic
red sauce pastas, veal, poultry,
seafood, and meat dishes, such
as pork chops *pizzaiola*.

Ristorante Pesto $$
Italian
1915 S Broad St, Philadelphia,
PA, 19148
Tel *(215) 336-8380*
This classic South Philly Italian
diner has a cult following for its
tasty plates of home-made pasta
and seafood. The house specialty
is the *portobello alla parmigiana*
(portobello mushrooms topped
with cheese and crab meat).

Standard Tap $$
International
901 N 2nd St, Philadelphia,
PA, 19123
Tel *(215) 238-0630*
An original Philadelphia
gastropub, Standard Tap has
great draft beer. The food is
artfully prepared and the menu
is chalked out on a blackboard.
Their burgers are legendary and
the duck confit salad beats most
French restaurants.

White Dog Café $$
New American
3420 Sansom St, Philadelphia,
PA, 19104
Tel *(215) 386-9224*
Housed in three adjacent Victorian
brownstones, this eclectic café
presents an unusual blend of
contemporary American cuisine
using fresh ingredients from local
farmers. Music in the piano parlor
entertains guests.

The chic and brightly lit dining room at White Dog Café

Reading Terminal Market $
International   Map 3 B2
12th & Arch Sts, 19107
Tel *(215) 922-2317*
Part farmers' market and part food court, the RTM offers everything from fresh produce to prepared meals. Highlights are DiNic's roast pork sandwich and traditional Amish fare. The ethnic food stands are a good bet as well.

Sakura Mandarin $
Chinese   Map 3 C2
1038 Race St, 19107
Tel *(215) 873-8338*
Serves specialties of Shanghai, such as *xiao long bao* (soup dumplings) and "lion's head" (pork meatballs), joined by Szechuan and Cantonese favorites. Try the thin scallion pancake. Good sushi and other Japanese dishes.

Schleisinger's Restaurant & Deli $
Deli   Map 3 A3
1521 Locust St, 19107
Tel *(215) 735-7305*
Relish home-style comfort food – from juicy wraps or savory sandwiches to hearty meals such as tender turkey with gravy and fries or boneless beef short ribs.

Alma de Cuba $$
Cuban   Map 3 A3
1623 Walnut St, 19103
Tel *(215) 988-1799*
Enjoy excellent Cuban fare such as sugarcane tuna, or dishes with an ethnic twist, as in the delicious Thai young coconut ceviche. Sleek, mirror-decorated interior.

Caribou Café $$
French   Map 3 B3
1126 Walnut St, 19107
Tel *(215) 625-9535*
This French bistro offers dishes from 15 regions of France, such as *salade Niçoise, quiche Lorraine*, and *crêpes Normandes*. The prix fixe menu is good value.

Devon Seafood Grill $$
Seafood   Map 2 D5
225 S 18th St, 19103
Tel *(215) 546-5940*
Great place for fresh fish specialties, such as Maryland crab cakes, pan-roasted Alaskan halibut, Maine lobsters, and Block Island swordfish. Eat in the dining room or on the sidewalk seating facing Rittenhouse Square.

El Vez $$
Mexican   Map 2 F2
121 S 13th St, 19107
Tel *(215) 928-9800*
Dine on delicious, contemporary versions of Mexican classics

Flashy red decor in the bar area of Alma de Cuba, which serves Cuban fusion food

at the stylish El Vez. The fresh guacamole and *mahi-mahi* (dolphinfish) tacos are highly recommended, as is the wonderful pomegranate margarita.

Fogo de Chão $$
Steakhouse   Map 3 B3
1337 Chestnut St, 19107
Tel *(215) 636-9700*
Located in the historic Caldwell's Jewelry Building, this branch of the steakhouse chain is a carnivore's delight. Serve yourself at the salad bar, then tuck into chunks of roasted meat brought to your plate straight from the grill.

Percy Street Barbecue $$
Barbecue   Map 3 C4
900 South St, 19147
Tel *(215) 625-8510*
A Texas-style barbecue joint with a roadhouse vibe. The highlight is beef brisket – moist and tender with an assertive smoke flavor. Also on offer are pork ribs, chicken, and fantastic desserts.

Rouge $$
International   Map 2 D5
205 S 18th St, 19103
Tel *(215) 732-6622*
Rouge is a hip bistro and popular late-night spot with outdoor seating facing Rittenhouse Square. The impressive menu lists a cross between Continental, American, and French fare with contemporary seafood, poultry, and beef dishes. Exquisite vintage wines.

Talula's Garden $$
American   Map 2 D5
210 W Washington Sq, 19106
Tel *(215) 592-7787*
Seasonal farm-to-table cuisine is served in a spacious, rustic-chic dining room festooned with vines and featuring its own cheese bar (and tempting cheese menu).

Dishes range from caramelized cauliflower soup to honey-glazed lamb belly.

The Black Sheep Irish Pub $$
Irish   Map 2 E5
247 S 17th St, 19103
Tel *(215) 545-9473*
Spread over three floors of a colonial town house, the Black Sheep dishes up hearty Irish stews and other favorites such as shepherd's pie and crab cakes. The antique bars feature drinks from around the world.

Zavino $$
Italian   Map 3 B3
112 S 13th St, 19107
Tel *(215) 732-2400*
Casual wine bar serving signature Neapolitan-style pizza. The domed oven creates a puffy crust topped with high-quality ingredients. Fine salads, pastas, and daily specials, plus a decent wine selection.

Zinc $$
French   Map 3 B3
246 S 11th Street, 19107
Tel *(215) 351-9901*   **Closed** *Mon*
Stylish Parisian restaurant with wall shelves full of quality wines that create a suitably Gallic ambience. Order the house specialty – *canard à la presse* (pressed duck) – and witness the preparation of this famous French dish.

Amuse $$$
French   Map 2 F3
1421 Arch St, 19102
Tel *(215) 422-8222*
Located in the Le Méridien hotel, this classy restaurant focuses on Gallic cuisine with delights such as truffled *foie gras torchon* (*foie gras* wrapped in towel and slow cooked) and lobster *bouillabaisse*. Extensive wine list.

For more information on types of restaurants *see page 141*

An elegant plate of food at Lacroix at the Rittenhouse

Chops Restaurant & Bar $$$
Steakhouse **Map** 2 E4
1701 John F Kennedy Blvd, 19103
Tel *(215) 567-7111* **Closed** *Sun*
Boasting an ultramodernist interior, Chops delivers old-time quality with its succulent steaks and other meat or fish dishes. Plenty of choice of salads, starters, and drinks as well.

DK Choice

**Lacroix at the
Rittenhouse** $$$
Fusion **Map** 2 D5
210 W Rittenhouse Square, 19103
Tel *(215) 790-2533*
Stylish restaurant on the second floor of the Rittenhouse Hotel, offering stunning views of Rittenhouse Square. Decorated with a minimalist and Asian theme, Lacroix serves outstanding French-American cuisine of three, four or five courses. Guests can also create their own menus. Enjoy complimentary dessert from the chef.

**McCormick and Schmick's
Seafood & Steaks** $$$
Seafood/Steakhouse **Map** 2 F4
1 S Broad St, 19102
Tel *(215) 568-6888*
This upscale chain restaurant offers over 40 varieties of fresh fish, flown in from both the Atlantic and Pacific. The dark wood-paneled dining room has a stained-glass ceiling and mosaic flooring.

Oyster House $$$
Seafood **Map** 3 A3
1516 Sansom St, 19102
Tel *(215) 567-7683* **Closed** *Sun*
Modern versions of old favorites such as clam chowder, snapper (turtle) soup, lobster rolls, and crab cakes on offer. But the main attraction is the broad selection of fresh oysters, expertly shucked to order.

Parc $$$
French **Map** 2 D5
227 S 18th St, 19103
Tel *(215) 545-2262*
Chic French bistro offering classics such as onion soup and *escargots* (snails) in hazelnut butter, as well as meat and fish platters, and a choice of baguettes.

Pumpkin $$$
New American **Map** 3 A4
1713 South St, 19146
Tel *(215) 545-4448* **Closed** *Mon*
This BYOB restaurant features a daily changing seasonal menu prepared from fresh, local produce. Rainbow trout and Berkshire pork loin are top choices. Relaxed atmosphere.

The Prime Rib $$$
Steakhouse **Map** 2 E5
1701 Locust St, 19103
Tel *(215) 772-1701*
This upscale steakhouse in the Warwick Hotel is one of the city's best. Its specialties are aged prime rib, blue-ribbon steaks, extra-thick chops and fresh seafood. The decor is reminiscent of a 1940s Manhattan supper club.

Tinto $$$
Spanish **Map** 2 D4
114 S 20th St, 19103
Tel *(215) 665-9150*
Tapas-style dining with a Basque flavor from chef Jose Garces. Serves tasty *pintxos* (snacks) that are more elegant than the ones found at bars in northern Spain, but still retain a rustic essence. Well-chosen wine list.

Verti Ristorante $$$
Italian **Map** 3 B3
1312 Spruce St, 19107
Tel *(215) 732-3478*
The only dining option here is the pricey, chef's tasting menu, which can be customized to suit dietary requirements. Some of the highlights include Nantucket Bay scallop and Texas antelope.

Logan Square and Parkway Museums District

Pizzeria Vetri $
Pizzeria **Map** 2 D2
1939 Callowhill St, 19130
Tel *(215) 600-2629*
Apart from the usual range of savory pizzas and a sprinkling of salads, Pizzeria Vetri also serves a decent selection of beer, wine, and cocktails. The dessert menu includes Nutella pizza topped with marshmallow.

Bridgid's $$
Italian **Map** 1 C1
726 N 24th St, 19130
Tel *(215) 232-3232*
Welcoming family eatery offering an intimate environment to enjoy some of the chef's recommendations such as bucatini pasta with clams and bacon, pan-seared salmon, or grilled lamb chops with arugula.

Fare $$
New American **Map** 2 D1
2028 Fairmount Ave, 19130
Tel *(267) 639-3063*
Locally sourced, sustainable cuisine is served here, right across from the Eastern State Penitentiary, with plenty of gluten-free, organic options. Try the lobster grilled cheese.

Hickory Lane $$
New American **Map** 2 D1
2025 Fairmount Ave, 19130
Tel *(215) 769-2420*
This hidden gem offers excellent dining in a relaxed atmosphere. Expect to find anything from classic burgers to more creative dishes like beer braised mussels. Early-evening fixed menu during weekdays.

Jack's Firehouse $$
Southern **Map** 2 D1
2130 Fairmount Ave, 19130
Tel *(215) 232-9000*
Located in a 19th-century firehouse, Jack's dishes up down-home fare made from local ingredients. The building retains some of its original features such as a sliding pole, accentuating the old-world feel.

DK Choice

London Grill $$
New American **Map** 2 D1
2301 Fairmount Ave, 19130
Tel *(215) 978-4545*
Trendy and comfortable, this restaurant combines the cosiness of a neighborhood pub with the elegance of fine dining. The menu changes daily, featuring dishes such as roasted chicken with garlic mashed potato cake, broccoli rosemary jus, and honey-glazed grilled salmon. The co-owned Paris wine bar next door stocks a handsome selection of wines and plays live music.

Luigi's Pizza Fresca $$
Italian/Pizza **Map** 1 C1
2401 Fairmount Ave, 19130
Tel *(215) 769-8888*
Part of a mini-chain, this local
pizza joint specializes in inventive
takes on portobello, margherita
and Mexican pizzas, as well as
pasta, sandwiches, calzones, and
chicken Parmesan.

McCrossen's Tavern $$
Classic American **Map** 2 D2
529 N 20th St, 19130
Tel *(215) 854-0923*
Bare-brick walls and subtle decor
create just the right ambience to
sit and tuck into a hearty meatloaf
sandwich or some calamari and
chorizo pasta. A great range of
beers and cocktails to choose from.

Rembrandt's $$
New American **Map** 2 D1
741 N 23rd St, 19130
Tel *(215) 763-2228*
Elegant, fine-dining restaurant
affording fabulous views of
the skyline. Specialties include
creative seafood, meat, pasta,
and vegetarian dishes. Eight
draught beers on tap.

Rose Tattoo Café $$
International **Map** 2 E2
1847 Callowhill St, 19130
Tel *(215) 569-8939*
Dine amid a multitude of hanging
and potted plants that create a
cheerful ambience. The menu
offers dishes from all over the
world, from mushroom bisque
and pulled pork tacos to filet
mignon steaks.

Sabrina's Café $$
Classic American **Map** 2 E2
1804 Callowhill St, 19130
Tel *(215) 636-9061*
Part of a small chain of four
quaint BYOB restaurants; guests
can find anything from granola

or egg breakfasts to chunky
Angus beefburgers, plus some
interesting salads and sides.

The Belgian Café $$
International **Map** 2 D2
21st & Green Sts, 19130
Tel *(215) 235-3500*
A fine selection of Belgian beers
on tap or bottled is the main
draw here. The food features
tastes from a wide range of
countries, including a delicious
line of mussels.

Zorba's Tavern $$
Greek **Map** 2 D1
2230 Fairmount Ave, 19130
Tel *(215) 978-5990* **Closed** *Mon*
Start with popular appetizers
such as *tzatziki* (yogurt cucumber
dip), *skordalia* (potato garlic
puree), *dolmades* (stuffed grape
leaves), and calamari, before
feasting on mains such as lamb
shank braised with red wine at
this neighborhood family spot.

Osteria $$$
Italian
640 N Broad St, 19130
Tel *(215) 763-0920*
Award-winning restaurant that
follows a farm-to-table policy,
guaranteeing the freshest local
produce. The creative mains
include rabbit with pancetta
and dry aged rib eye. Wonderful
wine selection.

Urban Farmer $$$
Steakhouse **Map** 2 E3
1 Logan Sq, 19103
Tel *(855) 439-2515*
Set inside the posh Logan hotel
and rated as one of the best
restaurants of the city, Urban
Farmer serves high-quality steaks
and local seasonal produce. The
rustic-chic dining room
showcases contemporary artwork
and views of the Swann Fountain.

Farther Afield

Fatty's Bar & Grill $
Pub
*812 E Willow Grove Ave, Wyndmoor,
PA, 19038*
Tel *(215) 233-5909*
Friendly sports bar serves pub
fare such as wings, burgers, and
cheesesteaks to be washed
down with US or imported ales.
Lots of TVs add to the lively feel.

Geno's Steaks $
Classic American
1219 S 9th St, Philadelphia, PA, 19147
Tel *(215) 389-0659*
Try the signature big fat cheese-
steak with all the works or tasty
fries at one of the city's cheese-
steak giants. Colorful decor with
brash neon lighting.

Maria's Ristorante on Summit $
Italian
8100 Ridge Ave, Philadelphia, PA, 19128
Tel *(215) 508-5600*
Casual BYOB eatery that offers
pizzas loaded with toppings, plus
pasta dishes and salads.

McCloskey's Tavern $
Pub
17 Cricket Ave, Ardmore, PA, 19003
Tel *(610) 642-9280*
Convivial Irish pub presenting
a decent choice of sandwiches,
burgers, and Italian dishes, as
well as a good selection of beers.

Pat's King of Steaks $
Classic American
*1237 Passyunk Ave, Philadelphia,
PA, 19147*
Tel *(215) 468-1546*
This close rival to Geno's *(see p149)*
serves classic Philly cheesesteaks
that have made it an institution
since 1930. Housed in an attrac-
tive wooden building right across
the street from the former.

Rocket Cat Café $
Café
*2001 Frankford Ave, Philadelphia,
PA, 19125*
Tel *(215) 739-4526*
Hip, little café offering a fine line
in gourmet coffees and snacks,
with savory items emphasizing
vegan and vegetarian options.
Plenty of choice in sweet pastries.

Thornton's Soul Food Restaurant $
Southern
*4401 Lancaster Ave, Philadelphia,
PA, 19104*
Tel *(215) 452-5146* **Closed** *Mon*
Authentic flavors and true soul
food are the order of the day at
this modest, down-home eatery.
Sample crabs and butterfly
shrimps, or tuck into a chunky
catfish sandwich.

Geno's Steaks, one of the most popular destinations for cheesesteaks in the city

For more information on types of restaurants *see page 141*

Alla Spina $$
Italian
1410 Mt Vernon St, Philadelphia,
PA, 19130
Tel *(215) 600-0017*   **Closed** *Mon*
An Italian gastropub that combines a wider range of options than can be found in either genre alone. Fried oysters with bacon horseradish mayonnaise typifies the chef's creativity. Local and imported brews.

Cantina dos Segundos $$
Mexican
931 N 2nd St, Philadelphia,
PA, 19123
Tel *(215) 629-0500*
Authentic and typically colorful Mexican eatery churning out national favorites – from crispy tacos to creamy quesadillas – along with some offbeat offerings such as the vegan cheesesteak burrito.

Chickie's and Pete's Café $$
Seafood
1526 Packer Ave, Philadelphia,
PA, 19145
Tel *(215) 218-0500*
This popular meeting place for locals bills itself as a crab house and sports bar. Apart from the signature crab fries, seasoned fried mussels and lobster pie are other enduring favorites.

City Tap House $$
New American
3925 Walnut St, 2nd Floor, 19103
Tel *(215) 662-0105*
Sleek, modern gastropub offering a great combination of enjoyable ales and tasty pub fare. Good-value pizzas and burgers are available, alongside pricier dishes such as rabbit bolognese.

In Riva $$
Italian
4116 Ridge Ave, Philadelphia,
PA, 19129
Tel *(215) 438-4848*   **Closed** *Mon*
Feast on the house specialty Neapolitan-style pizza cooked in a wood oven, with a wide choice of toppings. Decent wine selection. Alfresco seating in warmer months.

Jake's and Cooper's Wine Bar $$
New American
4365 Main St, Manayunk, Philadelphia,
PA, 19127
Tel *(215) 483-0444*
Choose between Jake's, the pioneering fine-dining restaurant, or the casual and less expensive Cooper's. Menu highlights include pizza, gourmet cheeses, stuffed quail, and grilled calves' liver. Patrons can bring their own wine.

La Collina $$
Italian
37–41 Ashland Ave, Bala Cynwyd,
PA, 19004
Tel *(610) 668-1780*
Elegant, friendly establishment serving up classic Italian fare by the Schuylkill River and the adjacent expressway. Live music thrice a week. Excellent service.

Noord Eetcafe $$
Northern European/Dutch
1046 Tasker St, Philadelphia,
PA, 19148
Tel *(267) 909-9704*
This lively Dutch-influenced BYOB restaurant in South Philly, offers such delicacies as *snert* (Dutch split-pea soup), *bitterballen* (fried pork meatballs), Amsterdam-style mussels, and Icelandic pollock.

Guests enjoying drinks at Standard Tap, a popular gastropub

Ralph's Italian Restaurant $$
Italian
760 S 9th St, Philadelphia,
PA, 19147
Tel *(215) 627-6011*
Cosy yet classy restaurant run by four generations of a family since 1900. Serves up classic red sauce pastas, veal, poultry, seafood, and meat dishes, such as pork chops *pizzaiola*.

Ristorante Pesto $$
Italian
1915 S Broad St, Philadelphia,
PA, 19148
Tel *(215) 336-8380*
This classic South Philly Italian diner has a cult following for its tasty plates of home-made pasta and seafood. The house specialty is the *portobello alla parmigiana* (portobello mushrooms topped with cheese and crab meat).

Standard Tap $$
International
901 N 2nd St, Philadelphia,
PA, 19123
Tel *(215) 238-0630*
An original Philadelphia gastropub, Standard Tap has great draft beer. The food is artfully prepared and the menu is chalked out on a blackboard. Their burgers are legendary and the duck confit salad beats most French restaurants.

White Dog Café $$
New American
3420 Sansom St, Philadelphia,
PA, 19104
Tel *(215) 386-9224*
Housed in three adjacent Victorian brownstones, this eclectic café presents an unusual blend of contemporary American cuisine using fresh ingredients from local farmers. Music in the piano parlor entertains guests.

The chic and brightly lit dining room at White Dog Café

Marigold Kitchen $$$
New American
501 S 45th St, Philadelphia, PA, 19104
Tel *(215) 222-3699*
Closed *Sun & Mon*
Highly rated BYOB venue, with four-, five-, and six-course tasting menus. Daily changing choices include venison or tofu curry.

Mica Restaurant $$$
International
8609 Germantown Ave, Philadelphia, PA, 19118
Tel *(267) 335-3912*
The chef employs recipes from all over the world in this dignified, maple wood-furnished dining room. From Moroccan squash soup to ricotta doughnuts, everything on the à la carte or fixed menus is first-rate.

Paramour $$$
New American
139 E Lancaster Ave, Wayne, PA, 19087
Tel *(610) 977-0600*
Upscale establishment serving exceptional cuisine with nods to different part of the globe. Samples include chicken liver mousse and wild boar bolognese. Consider the interesting tasting menus.

DK Choice

Pod $$$
Asian
3636 Sansom St, Philadelphia, PA, 19104
Tel *(215) 387-1803*
Excellent recipes influenced by various Asian cuisines and reliably good sushi are served in a fun, futuristic setting. Japanese, Thai, and Chinese flavors predominate, with elaborate sushi platters and favorites such as wasabi-crusted filet mignon. Color-changing seating pods and a screen projecting Japanese cartoons set the scene for contemporary food.

The Capital Grille $$$
Steakhouse
2000 Route 28, Cherry Hill, NJ, 08002
Tel *(856) 665-5252*
This branch of the renowned national chain is just a few miles across the Delaware River. Tender meat and fresh seafood can be enjoyed with a choice of starters.

Victor Cafe $$$
Italian
1303 Dickinson St, Philadelphia, PA, 19147
Tel *(215) 468-3040*
Photographs and operatic memorabilia still cover the walls at this old-fashioned Italian restaurant in what was once

DiStefano's Gramophone Shop. The waiters perform live opera every evening.

Beyond Philadelphia

Atlantic City

Los Amigos $
Mexican
1926 Atlantic Ave, Atlantic City, NJ, 08401
Tel *(609) 344-2293*
This simple but colorfully decorated eatery churns out heaps of salsa and chips to go with tasty tacos, burritos, and quesadillas. Convenient location near the bus station.

White House Sub Shop $
Classic American
2301 Arctic Ave, Atlantic City, NJ, 08401
Tel *(609) 345-8599*
A favorite since 1946, it's worth the wait for classic submarine sandwiches. Try the legendary "Special" – a large portion of various Italian cold cuts. Their cheesesteaks may even surpass those of Philadelphia.

Capriccio $$$
Italian
Resorts Casino Hotel, 1133 Boardwalk, Atlantic City, NJ, 08401
Tel *(609) 340-6789*
One of Atlantic City's most popular restaurants, Capriccio has a lavish dining room with ocean views and serves sumptuous plates of pasta, seafood, and veal. There is also an extensive wine list.

Izakaya $$$
Japanese
1 Borgata Way, Atlantic City, NJ, 08401
Tel *(609) 317-1000* **Closed** *Wed, Thu*
Ornately decorated restaurant in the Borgata Hotel Casino & Spa, with a menu inspired by the casual drinking and snacking culture of Japan. Try the gourmet dumplings, sushi rolls, or Kobe sirloin.

Brandywine Valley

Charcoal Pit $
Classic American
2600 Concord Pike, Rte-202, Wilmington, DE, 19803
Tel *(302) 478-2165*
A local landmark, around since 1956, this authentic burger outlet also serves soups, salads, sandwiches, and steaks. Round it off with one of their many tempting sundaes.

Buckley's Tavern $$
International
5812 Kennett Pike, Wilmington, DE, 19807
Tel *(302) 656-9776*
Much-loved meeting place for Brandywine Valley locals, Buckley's

serves a variety of fine food, from Maryland crab cakes to Vietnamese shrimp salad. The outdoor dining patio is very popular.

Four Dogs Tavern $$
French
1300 W Strasburg Rd, West Chester, PA, 19382
Tel *(610) 692-4367*
A converted stable that now serves a range of delights from fondues, charcuterie boards, and Burgundy snails to crab nachos and slow-cooked pork.

Cape May

Mad Batter $$
Seafood
19 Jackson St, Cape May, NJ, 08204
Tel *(609) 884-5970*
Visit at any time of day to enjoy a range of dishes – from filling breakfasts, through lunchtime snacks to fried fish and other delights at dinner. Art exhibitions in the dining room and live music in the bar.

The Black Duck on Sunset Restaurant $$
New American
1 Sunset Blvd, West Cape May, NJ, 08204
Tel *(609) 898-0100*
An array of seafood, much of it local, dominates the menu at this pleasant BYOB restaurant. Plenty of other choices, including roast duck. Good-value fixed price early-bird menu.

La Verandah $$$
French
107 Grant St, Cape May, NJ, 08204
Tel *(609) 884-5868*
Closed *Mon & mid-Sep–late May*
Upscale restaurant set in the plush Hotel Alcott. The emphasis is on seafood such as pan-seared grouper or grilled halibut, but patrons can also enjoy veal chops or roast rack of lamb. Fine wine list too.

Futuristic decor at Pod with neon lighting and quirky seating arrangement

For more information on types of restaurants *see page 141*

The Lobster House $$$
Seafood
*Fisherman's Wharf, Cape May
Harbor, NJ, 08204*
Tel *(609) 884-8296*
Feast on the region's freshest
seafood in a picturesque dining
room overlooking Cape May
harbor. Many of the ingredients
arrive in the kitchen on the
restaurant's own boat.

Doylestown

Hickory Kitchen $$
Southern
9 W Court St, Doylestown, PA, 18901
Tel *(215) 348-5170*
Down-home comfort food
aplenty is to be relished at this
homely BYOB establishment.
Lots of BBQ items supplemented
by soups, salads, and some
vegetarian options.

Honey $$
Fusion
42 Shewell Ave, Doylestown, PA, 18901
Tel *(215) 489-4200*
Trendy and welcoming, Honey
offers diners a seasonally changing
menu. Expect to find imaginative
items such as oxtail dumplings or
sturgeon melt. Bare-brick interior
with modern furnishings.

Gettysburg

Thai Classic IV $
Thai
*51 Chambersburg St, Gettysburg,
PA, 17325*
Tel *(717) 334-6736*
Pleasantly decorated and laid-
back Thai restaurant where guests
can enjoy meats or seafood cooked
in a variety of delicious and often
spicy sauces. Try the *kapow* (stir-
fried meat in spicy sauce) or the
pad prik king (Thai curry).

Blue Parrot Bistro $$
International
*35 Chambersburg St, Gettysburg,
PA, 17325*
Tel *(717) 337 3739* **Closed** *Sun & Mon*
Occupying the ground floor of
a pretty, mock-Tudor house, Blue
Parrot offers a wide range of
cuisines from North and Latin
America, the Mediterranean, and
parts of Asia.

Dobbin House Tavern $$
American-Colonial
89 Steinwehr Ave, Gettysburg, PA, 17325
Tel *(717) 334-2100*
An imposing mansion dating
from 1776 houses two separate
restaurants – the casual, pub-style
Springhouse Tavern and the colonial
Alexander Dobbin Dining Rooms.
Excellent traditional dishes at both.

Herr Tavern $$$
New American
*900 Chambersburg Rd, Gettysburg,
PA, 17325*
Tel *(717) 334-4332*
This 1815 country inn is now a
B&B with five elegantly decorated
dining rooms. The menu offers
carefully prepared meat and
seafood dinners served with
flavorful garnishes and sauces.

Harrisburg

**Appalachian Brewing
Company** $
Pub
50 N Cameron St, Harrisburg, PA, 17010
Tel *(717) 221-1080*
The first brewpub in Pennsylvania's
state capital is located in an
impressive, historic brick-and-
timber building. A large selection
of handcrafted ales and lagers, complemented by an innovative menu.

Char's at Tracy Mansion $$$
French
1829 N Front St, Harrisburg, PA, 17102
Tel *(717) 213-4002*
Housed in a beautiful mansion
overlooking the Susquehanna
River; people flock from miles
around to enjoy fine dining here.
Try the trout almodine or honey-
pepper glazed duck breast.

Hershey

The Bear's Den $
Classic American
*W Chocolate Ave & University Dr,
Hershey, PA, 17033*
Tel *(717) 533-3311*
This massive diner, designed like
a hockey rink, is located in the
Hershey Lodge complex. Sample
favorites like burgers, fries, and
ice cream while watching sports
events on huge screens.

Impressive interior of Char's at Tracy
Mansion with artfully decorated ceiling

Tröegs Brewing Company $$
New American
*200 E Hershey Park Dr, Hershey,
PA, 17033*
Tel *(717) 534-1297*
Modern snack bar set inside a
brewery that makes a fine selection of ale and lager. Offers some
surprisingly creative bar food such
as crispy pork belly, mad elf fondue,
and beef short rib pot roast.

King of Prussia

Desi Village $
Indian
145 S Gulph Rd, King of Prussia, PA, 19406
Tel *(610) 265-8500* **Closed** *Mon*
Rustles up a variety of traditional
Indian delights, including lamb,
goat, seafood, and lots of vege-
tarian options. Specializes in
tandoori dishes. Family-friendly
BYOB spot.

Legal Sea Foods $$
Seafood
*680 W Dekalb Pike, King of Prussia,
PA, 19406*
Tel *(610) 265-5566*
This Boston-based chain restaurant
is a good venue to dine at while
shopping in the huge local mall.
Impressive range of seafood from
fish sandwiches to king crab
ravioli and lobster, plus a full bar.

New Hope

Havana $
International
105 S Main St, New Hope, PA, 18938
Tel *(215) 862-9897*
Serves savory recipes from Latin
America and other parts of the
globe. There is also a convivial
bar where guests can watch
live music performances while
sipping beer or a cocktail. Well-
chosen wine list too.

Logan Inn Restaurant $$
Mediterranean
10 W Ferry St, New Hope, PA, 18938
Tel *(215) 862-2300*
Fine-dining restaurant in a
historic 18th-century inn, one
of the five oldest in the US. Enjoy
delicately cooked duck, seafood,
beef, and pastas, while sitting
inside or on the lovely porch.

The Landing $$
American
22 N Main St, New Hope, PA, 18938
Tel *(215) 862-5711*
Elegant dining venue overlooking
the Delaware River. Simple snacks,
salads, and sandwiches are as
tastefully and efficiently prepared
as the more sophisticated pastas,
steaks, and seafood dishes. Dine
on the deck in summers.

Pennsylvania Dutch Country

Bird-in-Hand Family Restaurant & Smorgasbord $
Classic American
2760 Old Philadelphia Pike, Bird-in-Hand, PA, 17505
Tel *(717) 768-1550* **Closed** *Sun*
Considered among the best places for Amish cooking. Load your plate with ham, beef, fried or roast chicken, and vegetables; then settle at a communal table. Great desserts too.

Historic Revere Tavern $
Classic American
3063 Lincoln Hwy E, Paradise, PA, 17562
Tel *(717) 455-7663*
Built in 1740, this tavern was once owned by the 15th US president, James Buchanan. Casual dining in a colonial atmosphere with fireplaces is the prime attraction here. Seafood and steaks stand out.

Kling House Restaurant $
Classic American
3529 Old Philadelphia Pike, Intercourse, PA, 17534
Tel *(717) 768-8261* **Closed** *Sun*
Amish and standard American fare, with home-made jellies and relishes prepared at the adjoining Kitchen Kettle Village. House specials include meatloaf and the coconut cream pie.

Miller's Smorgasbord $
Classic American
2811 Lincoln Hwy E (Rt 30), Ronks, PA, 17572
Tel *(717) 687-6621*
Feast on the smorgasbord buffet with unlimited meat, seafood, vegetables, salad, and dessert; or take the lighter route with soup, salad, and bread. A more limited à la carte menu on offer as well.

DK Choice

Plain and Fancy Farm Restaurant $
Classic American
3121 Old Philadelphia Pike, Bird-in-Hand, PA, 17505
Tel *(717) 768-4400*
Closed *Jan, Feb & few days in Mar (call ahead for March timings)*
Popular family-style restaurant that recalls Grandma's home cooking. Friendly pass-the-platter dining with roast beef, fried chicken, baked Lancaster County sausage, mashed potatoes, shoofly pie, and more. One of the most preferred venues to sample a filling, traditional Amish meal.

The pretty front porch and entrance to the Kling House Restaurant

General Sutter Dining Room $$
New American
14 E Main St, Lititz, PA, 17543
Tel *(717) 626-2115*
Colonial decor adds to the charm of this elegant dining room inside the landmark 18th-century General Sutter Inn. Black Angus beef, oversized chops, seafood, fowl, and pasta are the top draws.

John J. Jeffries $$
New American
Lancaster Arts Hotel, 300 Harrisburg Ave, Lancaster, PA, 17603
Tel *(717) 431-3307*
Seasonal, sustainable, farm-to-table fine dining is offered here, utilizing local organic meats and vegetables in dishes such as crayfish and grits, beef and pork meatballs, and soft tacos filled with braised beef.

Lancaster Brewing Co. $$
International
302 N Plum St, Lancaster, PA, 17602
Tel *(717) 391-6258*
Excellent brewhouse restaurant producing hoppy ales and crisp lagers on the premises. The menu highlights here include Asian duck tacos, *pierogi* (Polish dumplings), white chili soup, Greek salad, and artisan pork and apple sausage.

Trenton

Rozmaryn Restaurant $
International
925 N Olden Ave, Trenton, NJ, 08638
Tel *(609) 656-1600* **Closed** *Mon & Tue*
Enjoy Polish classics such as *pierogi*, stuffed cabbage, *borscht* (beetroot soup), and much more in a homely atmosphere. There is also a selection of American standards and tempting desserts. Patrons are allowed to bring their own wine.

Settimo Cielo $$
Italian
17 E Front St, Trenton, NJ, 08608
Tel *(609) 656-8877* **Closed** *Sat & Sun*
The "Seventh Heaven" specializes in northern Italian cuisine. Some of the less usual items include baked little neck clams, chicken liver in balsamic vinegar, and a fine mixed seafood stew. Handsome selection of wines.

Washington Crossing

Washington Crossing Inn $$$
New American
1295 Washington Memorial Rd, Washington Crossing, PA, 18977
Tel *(215) 493-3634*
Dating back to 1817, this restaurant is located close to where General Washington crossed the Delaware River in 1776. Modern American cuisine is served in a colonial ambience. Chops, steaks, seafood and arugula are well prepared.

Wilmington

Harry's Seafood Grill $$
American/Seafood
101 S Market St, Wilmington, DE
Tel *(302) 777-1500*
Buzzing restaurant specializes in fresh fish, oysters, and riverfront views, knocking out huge pots of clam chowder, jumbo shrimp cocktails, sushi, ceviche, and roasted trout, salmon, halibut, and bronzino.

Washington Street Ale House $$
New American
1206 Washington St, Wilmington, DE
Tel *(302) 658-2537*
Friendly pub with a warm wood-and-brick interior. St Louis pork ribs in lager BBQ sauce and candied pork belly are among the star items on the innovative menu. Handcrafted beers on tap.

For more information on types of restaurants *see page 141*

SHOPS AND MARKETS

The Philadelphia area is a stronghold for shopping, with stores and outlets ranging from specialty boutiques, grand shopping centers, and malls to discount retailers and factory stores. Key shopping areas mentioned on the following pages include Center City's boutiques and shops on Market and Walnut Streets, and the shops and galleries in Old City and in the chic

district of South Street. Situated in downtown Philadelphia are Antique Row and Jewelers' Row, while a variety of upscale and trendy shops are the highlights on the main streets of Manayunk and Chestnut Hill. The King of Prussia Mall is one of the nation's largest retail shopping complexes, while the cities of Reading and Lancaster have a large number of factory outlet stores.

Shopping Hours

Most retailers in central Philadelphia are open seven days a week, from 10am to 6pm on Mondays through Saturdays with some varying hours, and from noon until 5pm or 6pm on Sundays. Many Center City stores are open for an extra hour or two on Wednesday nights and sometimes on Friday nights.

Outside the city, individual retail stores usually have similar hours from 10am to 6pm. Malls, however, are often open until 9pm or 9:30pm Monday through Saturday, and noon until 6pm or 7pm on Sundays. Some specialty stores have reduced hours on weekends, or may close one or two days during the week.

Storefronts on a street in Chestnut Hill, Philadelphia

The popular VF Outlet Center in Reading, Pennsylvania

Taxes

There is no sales tax on clothing and shoes in Pennsylvania. For all other items, there is a 6 percent state sales tax and an additional 2 percent tax within Philadelphia, adding up to an 8 percent sales tax when shopping in the city. However, no sales tax is levied if your purchases are shipped to an address outside Pennsylvania, but additional shipping fees may apply. Foreign visitors may have to pay duties on larger purchases they wish to take home.

Sales

Finding a sale in the US is as easy as picking up a local newspaper – especially on weekends. Most large retailers compete on a daily basis, with many regularly slashing prices. Smaller stores may have clearance racks with reduced items, while sales are often more limited in trendy shops

and high-end boutiques. The nation's "biggest shopping day of the year" occurs on the day after Thanksgiving and is called "Black Friday," when prices are cut by 70 percent or more. Similar sales take place after Christmas.

Payment

Except for the smallest stores, major credit cards are accepted at most shops, boutiques, and retail outlets. In fact, department stores usually issue their own credit cards for return shoppers, though these are often issued at higher interest rates. In the US, the major credit cards accepted are Visa, Master Card, American Express, Discover Card, and Diners Club.

Cash is always accepted, and identification is necessary when using traveler's checks. Personal checks are discouraged, unless drawn from a local or well-known US bank. Stores do not accept foreign currency.

Returning Merchandise

Most shops and stores will willingly issue refunds and credits for returns, providing the merchandise is in good condition and not used or damaged. Sales receipts must accompany goods. Time limits for returns vary from store to store, with most allowing between 10 to 30 days. Be aware, however, that certain items purchased during special sales or promotions are nonreturnable, and that some stores will issue in-store-credit returns only and not cash.

Department Stores

There is no shortage of world-class department stores in the Philadelphia area, with most concentrated in the **King of Prussia Mall** *(see p156)*, Center City, and a few other area malls.

The historic Wanamaker Building *(see p72)* at 13th and Market Streets was named after Pennsylvanian John Wanamaker, a businessman who is considered to be the father of

American merchant John Wanamaker

the department store. This Italian Renaissance-style building has housed many of the best department stores since its completion in 1910. Today, **Macy's** Center City occupies this impressive space. This flagship store features high-end designers and affordable brand names. It also has a full-service Visitors' Center where shoppers can make dinner reservations and get information on the city's attractions. Another upmarket retail giant in Center City is **Barney's New York** and in the King of Prussia Mall, the high-end department store **Neiman Marcus** offers the ultimate shopping experience with some of the best names in fashion in women's apparel, accessories, shoes, and jewelry. The same is true for children's and men's clothing. The store also offers quality bed and bath items, novelty rugs, and furniture. The King of Prussia Mall also has another branch of Macy's.

Nordstrom, another leading fashion specialty store, offers

high-quality gifts, apparel, shoes, and beauty products from several hundred brand names. High fashion, stylish accessories, and the latest fragrances can be found at **Lord and Taylor** and at **Bloomingdale's**, which also stocks a wide range of house gifts, luggage, and more. **JCPenney** has a broad range of apparel, shoes, and gifts for men, women, and children. **Sears**, in northeast Philadelphia, is also one of the nation's best-known department stores, known for its large appliances, tools, lawn and garden gear, automobile repair services, and household services.

DIRECTORY

Center City

Barney's New York
1811 Walnut St.
Tel (215) 563-5333.
Map 2 D5.
W barneys.com

Macy's
1300 Market St.
Map 3 B2.
Tel (215) 214-9000.
W macys.com

King of Prussia Mall

Bloomingdale's
Tel (610) 337-6300.
W bloomingdales.com

JCPenney
Tel (610) 992-1096.
W jcpenney.com

Lord and Taylor
Tel (610) 992-0333.
W lordandtaylor.com

Macy's
Tel (610) 337-9350.
W macys.com

Neiman Marcus
Tel (610) 354-0500.
W neimanmarcus.com

Nordstrom
Tel (610) 265-6111.
W nordstrom.com

Sears
Great Northeast Plaza,
7300 Bustleton Ave,
Philadelphia, PA, 19152.
Tel (215) 697-8888.
W sears.com

Interior of King of Prussia Mall, a retail shopping complex

Interior of Shops at Liberty Place, a shopping mall in Center City

Malls

There are several indoor malls in and around Philadelphia, allowing people to enjoy and indulge in year-round shopping, dining, and entertainment.

Fashion Outlets Philadelphia, the city's largest mall, is located in Center City along Market Street between 8th and 12th Streets. The four-level mall connects with both the Pennsylvania Convention Center and Jefferson Station. It reopened in 2017 following a major renovation and houses 125 upscale stores offering all sorts of goods, ranging from sunglasses and artworks to household wares and much more.

The **King of Prussia Mall**, located in a suburb to the northwest of the city, is accessible via the Schuylkill Expressway and is a 30-minute drive from Center City. With six major department stores *(see p155)* and vast parking lots and garages, it is one of the nation's largest retail shopping complexes formerly comprising two separate sections that are now linked: The Plaza and The Court. Expansive buildings with elaborate glass-ceiling atriums house more than 360 specialty shops, and an array of 40 restaurants and eateries. Encircling the mall, Mall Boulevard has a good selection of retail and whole-sale stores, and a multiscreen movie complex. North of the city, along Route 1 in Bensalem, is the **Neshaminy Mall**, which includes 125 stores, restaurants, and a colossal 24-screen cinema complex.

Specialty Shopping Centers

Groups of specialty shops are housed in large central Philadelphia buildings, offering visitors and office workers easy access to shopping – especially during the lunch hour or after work.

With offices and the luxury Park Hyatt hotel above it, the century-old **Bellevue Building** in Center City has a host of upscale boutiques, world-class restaurants, a spa, a food court with the classic American steakhouse, The Palm, and more to offer. Also in Center City, the **Shops at Liberty Place** features 60 shops that sell fine apparel, shoes, jewelry, specialty foods, and beauty products. An impressive glass dome sits atop a circular rotunda – all part of the complex that makes up Liberty Place *(see p81)*.

The **Bourse Food Court and Specialty Shops** is in the heart of Independence Mall, directly across from the Liberty Bell Center. The Bourse offers tourists in Old City a break from sightseeing itineraries with gift and souvenir shops and an upscale food court.

Shopping Districts

Clusters of shops and restaurants in popular neighborhoods are known as shopping districts. One of Center City's most chic areas, **Rittenhouse Row**, includes upscale establishments along Walnut Street leading up to Rittenhouse Square *(see p80)*. Several restaurants have storefronts facing the square, with outdoor seating in summer.

Shop sign at Manayunk

Anchored by New Market and Head House Square, **South Street** *(see pp68–9)* offers a diversity of stores, shops, restaurants, eateries, and bars. Many of these cater to the avant-garde and eclectic trends of the younger crowds that often cram the area along South Street from Front to 11th Streets. **Main Street Manayunk** *(see p99)* is very popular on weekends for its many restaurants, pubs, and nightlife. Clothes and shoe shops, salons, antique shops,

Shops and boutique windows at Main Street Manayunk

and a host of boutiques and galleries also line Main Street.

In **Chestnut Hill** (see pp98–9), more than 100 boutiques, galleries, antiques stores, restaurants, and cafés take up nearly a dozen blocks along Germantown Avenue. **Jewelers' Row** and **Antique Row** span several blocks in Center City.

Markets

The city's central farmers' market is the popular **Reading Terminal Market** (see p75), where vendors sell farm-fresh produce, meats, poultry and seafood, flowers, pastries, and baked goods. Amish specialties and ethnic dishes representing the city's diverse population are particularly popular.

The nation's oldest and largest outdoor market, the **Italian Market** (see p101), features several blocks of vendors who sell seafood, fresh produce, meats, Italian specialties, and desserts. The area is home to some of the city's best Italian restaurants.

To savor some delicious, home-style cooking of the

Vendors at the Italian Market, one of the city's oldest outdoor markets

Pennsylvania Dutch Country, take some time to drive out to the small villages of Bird-In-Hand and Intercourse. **The Old Country Store** (see p120), for instance, offers authentic local food as well as handicrafts and souvenirs.

Discount and Outlet Malls

Located in an area northeast of Philadelphia is the **Philadelphia Mills Mall**, home to more than 200 retail and factory stores such as Last Call, H&M, Bed Bath & Beyond, and Burlington Coat Factory. Its outlets include those for Sears, Saks Fifth Avenue, Polo Ralph Lauren, JCPenney, and many others.

A complex of restored old factory buildings, **VF Outlet Center** in Reading is one of the county's largest groupings of factory store outlets. Several multistory buildings house discounted clothing, shoes, and household wares from Vanity Fair, Wrangler, Lee, Adidas, Timberland, Nautica, and Reebok.

Tanger Outlets, The Walk, in Atlantic City, New Jersey, has merchandise from manufacturers, including Van Heusen, Guess, Abercrombie & Fitch, Kenneth Cole, and Brooks Brothers, at reduced prices.

DIRECTORY

Malls

Fashion Outlets Philadelphia
Market St between 9th & 11th Sts. **Map** 3 C2.
Tel (215) 625-4962.

King of Prussia Mall
160 N Gulph Rd, King of Prussia. **Tel** (610) 245-5794.

Neshaminy Mall
Rte 1 & Bristol Rd, Bensalem.
Tel (215) 357-6100.

Specialty Shopping Centers

The Bourse Food Court and Specialty Shops
111 S Independence Mall East. **Map** 4 D3.
Tel (215) 625-0300.

The Shops at the Bellevue
200 S Broad St. **Map** 2 F5.
Tel (215) 875-8350.

Shops at Liberty Place
16th & Chestnut Sts.
Map 2 E4.
Tel (215) 851-9055.

Shopping Districts

Antique Row
Pine St between 9th & 17th Sts. **Map** 3 B4.

Chestnut Hill
7600–8700 Germantown Ave, Chestnut Hill.
Tel (215) 247-6696.

Jewelers' Row
Sansom St between 7th & 8th Sts; and 8th St from Chestnut to Walnut Sts.
Map 3 C3.
Tel (215) 278-2903.

Main Street Manayunk
Main St, Manayunk.
Tel (215) 482-9565.

Rittenhouse Row
Area around Rittenhouse Sq. **Map** 2 D5.
Tel (215) 972-0101.

South Street
South St from Front to 11th Sts. **Map** 3 B4.
Tel (215) 413-3713.

Markets

Italian Market
9th St between Christian & Wharton Sts.
Map 3 C5. **Tel** (215) 922-5557.

The Old Country Store
3510 Old Philadelphia Pike, Rte 340, Bird-in-Hand, PA.
Tel (717) 768-7101.

Reading Terminal Market
12th & Arch Sts.
Map 3 C2.
Tel (215) 922-2317.

Discount and Outlet Malls

Philadelphia Mills Mall
1455 Franklin Mills Circle, PA.
Tel (215) 262-4386.

Tanger Outlets, The Walk
2014 Baltic Ave, Atlantic City, NJ.
Tel (609) 872-7002.

VF Outlet Center
801 Hill Ave, Reading, PA.
Tel (610) 378-0408.

Fashion and Accessories

Center City is Philadelphia's main shopping district, with more than 2,100 retail stores. Many offer the finest in clothes, shoes, accessories, and jewelry. Key fashion shops and boutiques are located along Walnut Street on Rittenhouse Row. Designer clothing stores are also found at the Fashion Outlets Philadelphia mall, as well as within the small shopping centers at the Bellevue Building and Liberty Place. When looking for the latest in high fashion, do not forget the department stores and specialty stores at the King of Prussia Mall.

Entrance to the upmarket shops in Liberty Place

Women's Fashion

With so many stores and boutiques to choose from, women will be delighted with a shopping spree in Center City. Located just one block from Rittenhouse Square on Chestnut Street, **Joan Shepp** has been a trusted source for fashionable, designer women's clothing, shoes, and accessories for more than 40 years.. Nearby, the **Knit Wit** boutique carries a variety of elegant black cocktail dresses as well as cruisewear. **Ann Taylor**, on the same block, has upbeat and high-fashion designs for both business and pleasure. **LOFT**, **Express**, and lingerie store **Victoria's Secret** are also at Liberty Place.

The number of women's apparel stores in the King of Prussia Mall is extensive and you will need plenty of time to get round them all. In addition to Victoria's Secret

and Ann Taylor, there are upscale stores from top international designers, the latest classic and trendy fashions from **New York & Company** and **Lane Bryant**, and **Eileen Fisher**.

Main Street Manayunk features several women's clothing boutiques. Nicole Miller and **Paula Hian Designs** stock upscale evening wear for women.

Men's Fashion

Men looking for the perfect suit or designer clothing will not leave the city empty-handed. **Boyds Philadelphia** has been around for over 60 years and is one of Center City's premier stores. One of the most elegant shops at the Bellevue, **Polo Ralph Lauren** has a full line of clothing from the world-renowned designer. Men will also find a variety of stores at the Shops at Liberty Place, including **Jos. A. Bank**, **Les Richards Menswear**, and LR2.

In the King of Prussia Mall, **Hugo Boss Store** features the label's clothing, sportswear, and accessories. Other popular men's stores include **Brooks Brothers**, a high-end businesswear retailer, and **Tommy Bahama**, which features casual clothing and sportswear inspired by coastal living.

Men's and Women's Fashion

With shops in the Bellevue Building and Manayunk, **Nicole Miller** features men's and women's formalwear, as well as accessories. A line of both casual and dressy apparel can be found at **J. Crew** and **Express** at the Shops at Liberty Place, while casual wear is the highlight of **Old Navy** on Chestnut Street. **Finish Line**, at Macy's (1300 Market St), features athletic footwear. **Eddie Bauer** features winter clothes, while **Banana Republic** offers casual jeans and dressy jackets. Other popular outlets include **Abercrombie & Fitch**, and the hip styles of **Diesel**.

Casual sneakers

Shoes and Accessories

Featuring a line of fur, shearling, leather, and cloth, **Jacques Ferber** on Walnut Street offers unique outerwear. **Fire & Ice**, located at the Shops at Liberty Place, specializes in handcrafted jewelry and accessories as well as unique items for the home.

For men's shoes, **Sherman Brothers** offers a wide selection of top brands and hard-to-find sizes. Both men's and women's choices for shoes abound in the King of Prussia Mall, with stores including **Aldo**, **Skechers**, **Rockport**, **Timberland**, **Bostonian**, and **Johnston & Murphy**.

Window-shopping at one of Center City's numerous upscale boutiques

Jewelry

Philadelphia's Jewelers' Row was established in 1851, and is the nation's oldest and one of the largest diamond districts. Stores on the Row include a seemingly unlimited selection of diamonds, rubies, sapphires, and emeralds. Owned by the same family for four generations, **Barsky Diamonds** specializes in diamonds. **Safian & Rudolph Jewelers**, in business for over 60 years, deals in precious stones, while **Tiffany & Co.**, in Center City, has offered the finest in jewelry, crystal, and accessories for more than 150 years. Other prominent Center City jewelers include **Govberg Jewelers** and **LAGOS The Store**.

DIRECTORY

Women's Fashion

Ann Taylor
1713 Walnut St. **Map** 2 E5.
Tel (215) 977-9336.
King of Prussia Mall.
Tel (610) 354-9380.

Century 21
821 Market St.
Map 3 C2.
Tel (215) 952-2121.

Eileen Fisher
King of Prussia Mall.
Tel (610) 768-7150.

Joan Shepp
1811 Chestnut St. **Map** 2 E4. **Tel** (215) 735–2666.

Knit Wit
1729 Walnut St. **Map** 2 E5.
Tel (215) 564-4760.

Lane Bryant
King of Prussia Mall.
Tel (610) 265-6106.

LOFT
Liberty Place. **Map** 2 E4.
Tel (215) 557-9181.
King of Prussia Mall.
Tel (610) 337-1550.

New York & Company
King of Prussia Mall.
Tel (610) 354-0560.

Paula Hian Designs
106 Gay St, Manayunk.
Tel (215) 487-2762.

Victoria's Secret
Liberty Place. **Map** 2 E4.
Tel (215) 564-1142.
King of Prussia Mall.
Tel (610) 337-0788.

Men's Fashion

LR2
1625 Chestnut St.
Map 2 E4.
Tel (215) 851-9661.

Boyds Philadelphia
1818 Chestnut St.
Map 2 D4.
Tel (215) 564-9000.

Brooks Brothers
1513 Walnut St. **Map** 2 E5.
Tel (215) 564-4100.
King of Prussia Mall.
Tel (610) 337-9888.

Hugo Boss Store
King of Prussia Mall.
Tel (610) 992-1400.

Jos. A. Bank
Liberty Place. **Map** 2 E4.
Tel (215) 563-5990.
King of Prussia Mall.
Tel (610) 337-2131.

Les Richards Menswear
1625 Chestnut St.
Map 2 E4.
Tel (215) 751-1155.

Polo Ralph Lauren
200 S Broad St. **Map** 2 F5.
Tel (215) 985-2800.

Tommy Bahama
King of Prussia Mall.
Tel (484) 688-8042.

Men's and Women's Fashion

Abercrombie & Fitch
King of Prussia Mall.
Tel (610) 265-5650.

Banana Republic
1401 Walnut St. **Map** 2 F5.
Tel (215) 751-0292.
King of Prussia Mall.
Tel (610) 768-9007.

Diesel
King of Prussia Mall.
Tel (610) 768-5855.

Eddie Bauer
King of Prussia Mall.
Tel (610) 233-0086.

Express
Liberty Place. **Map** 2 E4.
Tel (215) 851-0699.
King of Prussia Mall.
Tel (610) 337-8912.

Finish Line
1300 Market St.
Map 3 C2.
Tel (215) 241-9000.

J. Crew
Liberty Place. **Map** 2 E4.
Tel (215) 977-7335.

Nicole Miller
200 S Broad St.
Map 2 F5. **Tel** (215) 546-5007. 4249 Main Street, Manayunk.
Tel (215) 930-0307.

Old Navy
1618 Chestnut St.
Map 2 E5.
Tel (215) 665-8757.
Philadelphia Mills.
Tel (215) 281-1670.

Shoes and Accessories

Aldo
King of Prussia Mall.
Tel (610) 337-4086.

Bostonian
King of Prussia Mall.
Tel (610) 265-4323.

Fire & Ice
1625 Chestnut St.
Map 3 A2.
Tel (215) 564-2871.

Jacques Ferber
1708 Walnut St.
Map 2 E5.
Tel (215) 735-4173.

Johnston & Murphy
King of Prussia Mall.
Tel (610) 265-0165.

Nine West
Liberty Place. **Map** 2 E4.
Tel (215) 851-8570.

Rockport
King of Prussia Mall.
Tel (610) 265-5800.

Sherman Brothers Shoes
1520 Sansom St.
Map 2 E4. **Tel** (215) 561-4550.

Skechers
King of Prussia Mall.
Tel (610) 337-7366.

Timberland
King of Prussia Mall.
Tel (610) 265-2193.

Jewelry

Barsky Diamonds
724 Sansom St.
Map 4 D3.
Tel (215) 925-8639.

Govberg Jewelers
1521 Walnut St.
Map 2 E5.
Tel (215) 546-6505.

LAGOS The Store
1735 Walnut St.
Map 2 E4.
Tel (215) 567-0770.

Safian & Rudolph Jewelers
701 Sansom St.
Map 4 D3.
Tel (215) 627-1834.

Tiffany & Co.
1414 Walnut St.
Map 2 E5.
Tel (215) 735-1919.

Specialty Shops

With shopping districts, upscale shops, and one-of-a-kind stores, central Philadelphia has a wide range of merchandise that would satisfy even the hard-to-please shopper. Many specialty shops and gift stores specialize in finding the perfect gift or souvenir. Antique Row has numerous stores along an eight-block stretch in Center City, while in Old City sits a large cluster of art galleries. Other key shopping areas with unique crafts, books, and flower stores include Manayunk and Chestnut Hill. The colossal King of Prussia Mall has a seemingly unending choice of everything, from home furnishings and electronics to sporting goods.

Shops located in the Chestnut Hill market area

Antiques

Spread over eight blocks on Pine Street between 7th and 11th Streets, Antique Row *(see p157)* features boutiques and shops offering a selection of fine furniture, period antiques, collectibles, estate jewelry, and vintage clothing. One such store is **M. Finkel & Daughter**, which sells period furniture, 17th- to 19th-century needlework, and decorative accessories. The nearby **Classic Antiques** offers a large selection of country French furniture, mirrors, and accessories as well as 18th- and 19th-century European antiques. The **Philly Flea** is the seasonal flea market, with numerous dealers selling pieces from vintage Victorian to modern, including estate jewelry, furniture, pottery, and accessories.

Art Galleries

The Old City Arts Association has 50 members, including art galleries, which are open until 9pm on the first Friday of every month – an event that is appropriately called "First Friday." The **Moderne Gallery** features contemporary furniture, pottery, fine arts, and metalwork. The gallery also specializes in the American Craft Movement and is the world's leading dealer for pieces by woodworker George Nakashima.

Seraphin Gallery, on Antique Row, has art from international contemporary painters, sculptors, and photographers, including 18th- through 20th-century works by artists from America and Europe.

In Center City, **Newman Galleries** specializes in 19th-century American and European paintings, and early 20th-century American art from the New Hope School.

Established in 1974, **The Clay Studio** in Old City exhibits works by emerging and established artists and also offers a range of classes.

Books

An excellent choice for mainstream books and magazines is **Barnes & Noble** at Rittenhouse Square. Also in that square is the independent **Joseph Fox Bookshop**, established in 1951, with a huge range of literature, architecture, music, and poetry books, and books for children..

For hard-to-find books, the **Philadelphia Rare Books and Manuscript Company** features early printed books dating from the 16th century, and manuscripts, old Bibles, and other books from around the world that cover a wide realm of topics. Located behind the Free Library of Philadelphia, **The Book Corner** has an excellent collection of used books, well-organized and available at a reasonable price.

Food and Cookery

Within the Italian Market are specialty food stores. Family owned since 1939, **DiBruno Bros. House of Cheese** sells more than 400 types of cheese and gourmet foods. **Termini Brothers Gold Medal Pastry Bakery** is a local favorite with handmade Italian confections made from recipes that date to the 1800s. Serving chefs and home cooks since 1906, **Fante's Kitchen Wares Shop** offers an extensive selection of cooking wares and utensils.

Gourmet cheese

Gifts, Crafts, and Souvenirs

As a result of its varied traditions and its status as one of America's oldest cities, Philadelphia offers a range of gifts and mementos. **Xenos Candy'n Gifts** has classic souvenirs showcasing Old City sights, including replicas of Liberty Bell, flags, and other collectibles. Similar items are found in **The Bourse** nearby, while the **Pennsylvania General Store** has locally-made foods and crafts. **Scarlett Alley** offers art, furnishings, jewelry, leather goods, books, and children's items. **Little Apple** features fine gifts for personal care as well as for homes. Fine-rolled, handmade cigars can be bought at the **Black Cat Cigar Company** and **Holt's Cigar Company** in Center City.

Florists

A wide-ranging choice of flowers is available from Philadelphia's florists. Some, such as **Nature's Gallery Florist** in Center City, are also able to assist with the floral side of party planning. **Ten Pennies Florist**, a staple in Philadelphia for more than 30 years, offers exquisite arrangements for any occasion.

Vinyl at Philadelphia Record Exchange

Music

For a wide range of music and recordings, visit **Repo Records** on South Street to thumb through their selection of import singles, and rows of used records and CDs. First opened in 1986 in the small town of Wayne, PA, Repo relocated here in 1998. **Philadelphia Record Exchange** is the city's spot to find second-hand vinyl and CDs.

Sporting Goods

The nation's largest family-owned sports goods chain, **Modell's Sporting Goods**, has stores in Philadelphia Mills Mall and King of Prussia Mall, and also sells home-team apparel and footwear. For camping gear, kayaks, and other outdoor items, visit **Eastern Mountain Sports**, also at King of Prussia Mall.

DIRECTORY

Antiques

Classic Antiques
922 Pine St.
Map 3 C4.
Tel (215) 629-0211.

M. Finkel & Daughter
936 Pine St.
Map 3 C4.
Tel (215) 627-7797.

Philly Flea
Various locations (see website for details).
Tel (215) 625-3532.
w philafleamarkets.org

Art Galleries

The Clay Studio
139 N 2nd St.
Map 4 E2.
Tel (215) 925-3453.

Moderne Gallery
111 N 3rd St.
Map 4 E2.
Tel (215) 923-8536.

Newman Galleries
1625 Walnut St.
Map 2 E5.
Tel (215) 563-1779.

Seraphin Gallery
1108 Pine St.
Map 3 B4.
Tel (215) 923-7000.

Books

Barnes & Noble
1805 Walnut St.
Map 2 D4.
Tel (215) 665-0716.

Joseph Fox Bookshop
1724 Sansom St.
Map 3 A2.
Tel (215) 563-4184.

Philadelphia Rare Books and Manuscript Company
2375 Bridge St.
Tel (215) 744-6734.

The Book Corner
311 N 20th St.
Map 2 D2.
Tel (215) 567-0527.

Food and Cookery

DiBruno Bros. House of Cheese
Italian Market,
930 S 9th St.
Map 3 C5.
Tel (215) 922-2876.
109 S 18th St.
Map 2 E4.
Tel (215) 665-9220.

Fante's Kitchen Wares Shop
Italian Market,
1006 S 9th St.
Map 3 C5.
Tel (215) 922-5557.

Termini Brothers Gold Medal Pastry Bakery
1523 S 8th St.
Tel (215) 334-1816.

Gifts, Crafts, and Souvenirs

Black Cat Cigar Company
46 W Germantown Pike,
East Norriton, PA.
Tel (800) 220-9850.

The Bourse
5th between Market & Chestnut Sts.
Map 4 D3.
Tel (215) 625-0300.

Holt's Cigar Company
1522 Walnut St.
Map 2 E3.
Tel (215) 732-8500.

Little Apple
4353 Main St, Manayunk.
Tel (267) 335-4968.

Pennsylvania General Store
Reading Terminal Market.
Map 3 C2.
Tel (215) 592-0455.

Scarlett Alley
241 Race St.
Map 4 E2.
Tel (215) 592-7898.

Xenos Candy'n Gifts
231 Chestnut St.
Map 4 E3.
Tel (215) 922-1445.

Florists

Nature's Gallery Florist
2124 Walnut St.
Map 2 D4.
Tel (215) 563-5554.

Ten Pennies Florist
1921 S Broad St. **Map** 3 B2. **Tel** (215) 336-3557.

Music

Philadelphia Record Exchange
1524 Frankford Ave.
Map 4 D4.
Tel (215) 425-4389.

Repo Records
538 South St. **Map** 4 D4.
Tel (215) 627-3775.

Sporting Goods

Eastern Mountain Sports
King of Prussia Mall.
Tel (610) 337-4210.

Modell's Sporting Goods
Philadelphia Mills Mall.
Tel (215) 824-3900.
King of Prussia Mall.
Tel (610) 337-4522.

ENTERTAINMENT IN PHILADELPHIA

Stretching along the "Avenue of the Arts," Broad Street is home to a plethora of renowned performing arts facilities. Heading the list are the Kimmel Center for the Performing Arts and the Academy of Music, home to the world-class Philly POPS, Philadelphia Orchestra, Opera Philadelphia, and the Pennsylvania Ballet. Numerous other venues feature live chamber music, theater productions and musicals, rock, hip-hop and jazz-fusion concerts, and varied programs of gospel. Universities also put on several music, theater, and dance shows. Nightclubs hosting live bands abound in Old City and South Street, while a drive or train ride of an hour or so brings you to Atlantic City's glittering casinos on the New Jersey shoreline.

Visitors wait for a show at Kimmel Center for the Performing Arts

Information

There are several websites and newspapers that carry the latest information on musical concerts, theatrical performances, nightlife, and other entertainment options in and around the city.

The *Weekend* section of the *Philadelphia Inquirer*, published every Friday, details the goings-on in town, from the latest movies to gallery exhibitions to extensive listings of live performances, including ballet, chamber and classical music, opera, theater, and jazz. The art district has its own website, **Avenue of the Arts**.

The *Philadelphia Weekly* also showcases arts, music, and cinema listings. It also has extended information on daily nightclub acts and performances. This weekly publication (issued on Wednesdays) is available free at many cafés, pubs, and bookstores throughout the city. It also has a website with up-to-date listings.

Philadelphia's most comprehensive news website is **www.phillyfunguide.com**. It has information on all types of activities in the city and also has a number of saver deals.

Tickets

Seats for most of the major symphony, opera, chamber music, ballet, and pop performances in Philadelphia can be booked through **Ticket Philadelphia**. The main box office is in the **Kimmel Center for the Performing Arts**. Tickets can be bought in person, on the phone, or online. Tickets for various events and theatrical performances can also be bought at the box office of each venue, or over the phone, online or in person via **Ticketmaster**. Be aware, however, that ticketing services often add a fee to the total cost. Ticketmaster is one of the world's largest e-commerce sites, in addition to having more than 3,300 retail outlets and 19 worldwide telephone call centers. It acts as the exclusive ticketing service for various performing arts venues and theaters.

Some hotels may also sell show tickets, especially those in Center City or near the theater district. Check with the concierge in your hotel for the best ticketing options.

The Philadelphia Orchestra at Verizon Hall in the Kimmel Center

"Avenue of the Arts" lights up for a night of theater and culture

Entertainment Districts

The hub of Philadelphia's performing arts and theater district is the so-called **Avenue of the Arts**, which extends south of City Hall on South Broad Street. This two-block area is anchored by the Kimmel Center for the Performing Arts and the world-renowned **Academy of Music** (see p78). Also located in this area is the Merriam Theater, hosting professional touring productions, as well as the 300-seat Wilma Theater (see p164), whose productions address current political and social issues. Three blocks east of the area is the Forrest Theatre (see p164), while the Prince Music Theater is on Chestnut Street.

Besides theater and cultural activities, Philadelphia has a thriving nightlife with scores of restaurants, nightclubs, smaller theater venues, and comedy clubs concentrated along South Street. A vibrant nightlife scene also abounds in the Old City area around Chestnut, Market, Front, and 2nd Streets with a wide variety of restaurants, cozy pubs, and martini bars.

Along the Delaware River, Columbus Avenue is home to some of Philadelphia's up-and-coming night spots north and south of Penn's Landing – some on piers stretching into the river, while others are seasonal outdoor clubs. Much of the city's lesbian and gay nightlife is centered in the neighborhood between Pine and Chestnut Streets north to south and Broad and 11th Streets west to east.

Across the Delaware, meanwhile, the BB&T Pavilion at the Camden Waterfront (see p103) hosts concerts throughout the year, drawing big-name musical acts, as does the Wells Fargo Center, which is in south Philadelphia (see p166).

Going beyond Philadelphia, Atlantic City (see p129) is just a short drive or train ride from Center City, and an entertainment destination in itself, with more than a dozen sprawling casino hotels and resorts, most of which have popular nightclubs, concert venues, and pulsing and glitzy discos.

South Street – an entertainment hub for the younger crowd

Disabled Access

Most of the major concert halls and theaters in Philadelphia accommodate disabled patrons and wheelchairs. The **Kimmel Center for the Performing Arts and the Academy of Music** have accessible wheelchair seating locations for performances, captioning for the hearing impaired, and assisted listening devices available on a first-come, first-served basis. Call ahead for details.

Some smaller venues and clubs may be less than adequate in accommodating disabled patrons. Check with the venue or the **Mayor's Commission on People with Disabilities** for more information. The commission provides a forum for the disabled to express opinions on programs and services in Philadelphia.

DIRECTORY

Ticketing

Ticket Philadelphia
Tel (215) 893-1999.
W ticketphiladelphia.org

Ticketmaster
Various outlets.
Tel (215) 574-3550.
W ticketmaster.com

Disabled Access

Kimmel Center for the Performing Arts and Academy of Music
Department of Audience & Visitor Services.
Map 2 E5.
Tel (215) 670-2327.
W kimmelcenter.org

Mayor's Commission on People with Disabilities
1401 JFK Blvd.
Map 2 F4.
Tel (215) 686-2798.
W phila.gov/mcpd

Useful Websites

Avenue of the Arts
W avenueofthearts.org

Philadelphia Fun Guide
W phillyfunguide.com

Philadelphia Weekly Online
W philadelphiaweekly.com

Philly.com (*Philadelphia Inquirer*)
W philly.com

The Arts in Philadelphia

A cultural Mecca for the performing arts, Philadelphia has world-class venues that host excellent chamber and symphony music, and some of the finest performances in opera, ballet, and theater. Topping the list are concerts by the renowned Philadelphia Orchestra and Philly POPS, which are performed in the city's premier venue, the multitheater Kimmel Center for the Performing Arts. Chamber music ensembles play before smaller crowds, while grand opera and ballet productions take the stage in the Victorian-era Academy of Music. Several theaters in and around Center City host performances that range from Broadway productions and musicals to African-American theater. Entertainment is also provided by choral groups and the area's top music schools, which hold classical concerts and dance performances by students.

Forrest Theatre, host to touring dance and theater companies

Classical Music and Symphony

One of the city's best, the **Philadelphia Orchestra** has shared the stage with some of the world's most influential classical musicians for more than 100 years. The orchestra's home was the **Academy of Music**, but it now performs at the Verizon Hall in the **Kimmel Center for the Performing Arts**.

Also performing at Verizon Hall is **the Philly POPS**, one of the nation's most-renowned POPS orchestras playing big band, classics, Broadway hits, and rock'n' roll tunes. In summer, both orchestras perform at an outdoor venue, **The Mann Center**, also home

to jazz, dance, opera, and musical theater programs.

Chamber music can be enjoyed on Sunday afternoons and Monday evenings at the Kimmel Center's Perelman Theater. The **Chamber Orchestra of Philadelphia** performs here, playing a musical repertoire from the 18th century to the present day. The **Philadelphia Chamber Music Society** presents more than 60 chamber music, piano, vocal, and choral concerts a year, which are performed by internationally known groups as well as emerging artists. Presenting a unique classical experience is the **Philomel Baroque Orchestra** – a small ensemble of accomplished musicians who play early classical and Baroque music on period instruments.

Theaters and Theater Companies

Stage productions run the gamut from national touring shows to politically inspired acts produced locally. The **Philadelphia Theatre Company** is the city's leading

Academy of Music, oldest opera house in the US still used for its original purpose

producer of contemporary American theater, while the **Arden Theatre Company** brings to life dramatic and theatrical stories by the greatest storytellers of all time.

The **Forrest Theatre** hosts Broadway shows and is the city's premier theatrical arts venue. The **Walnut Street Theatre** – America's oldest – is home to musicals and plays.

The **Wilma Theater** has productions with contemporary themes, while the **Society Hill Playhouse** features offbeat and "off-Broad Street" productions. The **Freedom Theatre**, located on the northern stretch of the Avenue of the Arts, is one of the country's leading venues for African-American performances.

Pennsylvania Ballet dancer performing *Swan Lake*

Opera and Ballet

Local lovers of grand opera have been enjoying performances by **Opera Philadelphia** since 1975. The **Pennylvania Ballet**, which has been thrilling audiences since it was established in 1963, performs at the Academy of Music and the Merriam Theater. Its season has six productions, including the old Yuletide favorite *The Nutcracker (see p37)*, which has become an annual Philadelphia tradition.

Vocal Arts and Choirs

There are several choral groups in the city such as the renowned **Philadelphia Boys Choir and Chorale**. The 100-member choir performs patriotic music and Broadway show tunes. The group holds more than 40 performances each year, and travels on international tours.

A 100-voice symphonic chorus, the **Choral Arts Philadelphia** also appears often with the Philadelphia Orchestra. Founded in 1982 and under the artistic direction of Matthew Glandorf since 2007, Philadelphia's premier chamber chorus works with The Bach Festival of Philadelphia to perform Bach @ Seven, a midweek early evening Bach cantata series. The **Academy of Vocal Arts**, around since 1934, produces operas with the **Chamber Orchestra of Philadelphia**. The academy's resident artists also hold recitals and concerts.

Music Schools' Performances

Often considered one of the most prestigious conservatories, the **Curtis Institute of Music** trains some of the best young musicians from around the world. The students hold free public recitals and concerts in the institute's Field Concert Hall located opposite Rittenhouse Square, and play in various venues around the city when they are not touring.

Local musicians and students training in classical, jazz, dance, and theater arts also hold recitals and concerts at the **University of the Arts**, Temple University's **Boyer College of Music and Dance**, and through **PENN Presents** at the University of Pennsylvania's Annenberg Center for the Performing Arts.

DIRECTORY

Classical Music and Symphony

Academy of Music
1420 Locust St. **Map** 2 E5. **Tel** (215) 790-5800; box office: (215) 893-1999.

Chamber Orchestra of Philadelphia
Perelman Theater, Kimmel Center. **Map** 2 E5. **Tel** (215) 545-5451; box office: (215) 893-1709.

Kimmel Center for the Performing Arts
300 S Broad St. **Map** 3 A3. **Tel** (215) 790-5800; box office: (215) 893-1999.

The Mann Center
5201 Parkside Ave. **Tel** (215) 546-7900; box office: (215) 893-1999.

Philadelphia Chamber Music Society
Various venues. **Tel** (215) 569-8587; box office: (215) 569-8080.

Philadelphia Orchestra
Verizon Hall, Kimmel Center. **Map** 2 E5. **Tel** (215) 893-1900; box office: (215) 893-1999.

The Philly POPS
Verizon Hall, Kimmel Center. **Map** 2 E5. **Tel** (215) 546-6400; box office: (215) 893-1999.

Philomel Baroque Orchestra
Various venues. **Tel** (215) 487–2344; box office: (215) 569-9700.

Theaters and Theater Companies

Arden Theatre Company
40 N 2nd St. **Map** 4 E2. **Tel** (215) 922-8900.

Forrest Theatre
1114 Walnut St. **Map** 3 B3. **Tel** (215) 923-1515.

Freedom Theatre
1346 N Broad St. **Tel** (215) 765-2793.

Philadelphia Theatre Company
480 S Broad St. **Map** 2 E5. **Tel** (215) 985-1400; box office: (215) 985-0420.

Society Hill Playhouse
Tel (215) 923-0210.

Walnut Street Theatre
825 Walnut St. **Map** 3 C3. **Tel** (215) 574-3550.

Wilma Theater
265 S Broad St. **Map** 2 E5. **Tel** box office: (215) 546-7824.

Opera and Ballet

Opera Philadelphia
Academy of Music. **Map** 2 E5. **Tel** (215) 893-3600; box office: (215) 732-8400.

Pennsylvania Ballet
Merriam Theater, Academy of Music. **Map** 2 E5. **Tel** (215) 551-7000.

Vocal Arts and Choirs

Academy of Vocal Arts
Various venues. **Tel** (215) 735-1387.

Boyer College of Music and Dance
Temple University, 1715 N Broad St. **Tel** (215) 204-8301.

Choral Arts Philadelphia
Various venues. **Tel** box office: (215) 545-8634.

Philadelphia Boys Choir and Chorale
225 N 32nd St. **Map** 1 B1. **Tel** (215) 222-3500.

Music Schools' Performances

Curtis Institute of Music
Field Concert Hall & various venues. 1726 Locust St. **Map** 2 E5. **Tel** (215) 893-7902; box office: (215) 893-1999.

PENN Presents
Annenberg Center for the Performing Arts, University of Pennsylvania. **Tel** (215) 898-6701; box office: (215) 898-3900.

University of the Arts
Broad & Pine Sts. **Map** 2 E5. **Tel** (215) 545-1664.

Music and Nightlife

Philadelphia fills its after-dark hours with the latest sounds in rock, folk, pop, jazz-fusion, hip-hop, and salsa. These rhythms can be heard at venues offering live music, sometimes seven days a week. Many are clustered within the prominent entertainment districts of South Street, Old City, Main Street Manayunk, and the areas along the Delaware Avenue waterfront. Philadelphia is often a regular stop for major bands and musical acts on world tours, including top rock, jazz, hip-hop, and country and pop musicians. Those opting for a less energized night out can enjoy conversation and cocktails at friendly neighborhood taverns and bars located throughout the city.

Rock and Folk Music

For the top touring rock bands, check listings in local newspapers *(see p162)* for concerts at the **Wells Fargo Complex** and other major venues, including the **Tower Theater, Keswick Theatre**, and the **BB&T Pavilion**, located on the waterfront. Also check listings for concerts held in Atlantic City.

For a taste of local rock music, **Khyber Pass Pub** in Old City has shows several nights a week and is a mainstay for Philadelphia's rock scene. Live performances by local rock groups also take place at the **Manayunk Brewing Company** in Manayunk.

Folk musicians and fans frequent the **Tin Angel** in Old City. One of the region's best venues for folk artists, gospel choirs, and alternative rock acts is **World Café Live**, located on the campus in University City.

Blues, Jazz, and World Music

Blues and jazz clubs range from upbeat night spots and restaurants, where top artists perform, to smaller and cozier

Alma de Cuba, famous for its Cuban cuisine and live music

lounges. **Warmdaddy's** is a popular southern blues club and restaurant offering live jazz. Its 100-seat dining room overlooks the main stage where artists perform nightly; Tuesdays are reserved for open jam sessions made up of local musicians. **Ortlieb's Lounge** is another hot venue that offers world-class jazz music seven nights a week. **Chris' Jazz Café**, on Samson Street, has become something of an institution amongst the city's jazz lovers. The line-up includes a good mix of up-and-coming and established talent. Some clubs offer a range of international music, such as

Performers at the popular Chris' Jazz Café

salsa, flamenco, and more. For instance, musicians at **Alma de Cuba** belt out live Cuban music performances every week.

Nightclubs and Discos

Philadelphia offers a wide range of late-night venues to suit all musical persuasions. The city's younger crowd parties late into the night with clubs churning out music until 2am. **The 700** in the trendy Northern Liberties neighborhood is a local bar by day and a lively nightclub when the sun goes down. On Delaware Avenue, restaurant and nightclub **Cavanaugh's River Deck** features concerts and DJs in an all-outdoors venue along the Delaware River, with views of the Benjamin Franklin Bridge.

A trendy night spot for the city's chic elite is the **Infusion Lounge** in Old City. It includes a hookah bar and a lush VIP lounge with European bottle service. Diner club and lounge bar, **Silk City** is also one of the city's hottest night spots. For classic funk to old-school hip-hop and reggae, to the latest DJ mixes, **Bleu Martini** in Old City is the place to be seen in Philadelphia.

Bars and Taverns

Many Center City hotels and restaurants have comfortable bars that are ideal for relaxing and for conversation. Philadelphia also has a number of neighborhood bars and pubs that play live music. **Monk's Café** in south Philadelphia is a bistro with more than 200 beer brands from around the world and 20 Belgian draft ales. If you are not sure what to go for, their *Beer Bible* gives a description of each beer available.

Draft Guinness

Irish pubs with great food and Guinness beer on tap include **Fergie's Pub**, which has live music most evenings and a traditional Irish menu, and the **Irish Pub** that serves Irish-American food in a casual dining ambience. **McGillin's Olde Ale House** is the oldest operating tavern in the city, offering a great selection of beer. The **Bishop's Collar** has a friendly atmosphere with a selection of microbrews, and creative but inexpensive pub fare. It is a great place to unwind after visiting the Museum of Art or Boathouse Row.

LGBT Clubs and Bars

Several nightclubs and bars are centered in the city's main gay and lesbian district, located between Broad and 11th Streets, and Chestnut to Pine Streets. **Woody's** is a popular gay lounge serving food and cocktails seven days a week. With three floors of energizing house music, disco, and hip-hop, **Voyeur Nightclub** has a bit

of everything and is worth a visit. **Stir Lounge**, just off the ritzy Rittenhouse Square, has a dive-bar feel. For more information, visit the Greater Philadelphia Tourism and Marketing Corporation's website *(see p135)* or look at the Philadelphia Convention and Visitors Bureau's *Navigaytour Travel Guide*, available online at the bureau's website.

Voyeur Nightclub, a prominent gay night spot

Comedy Clubs

Many clubs in town and across the river in New Jersey feature stand-up comedy acts. The city's "Original Comedy Club," the **Laff**

House on Collins Street, brings in comedians from all over the country, with open-mic nights, and main acts on Friday and Saturday nights. The **Helium Comedy Club** draws the nation's top acts to this 250-seat theater. Two lounges inside the club offer food and specialty drinks. Punters buying a drink before 7pm on Wednesdays can see that night's show for free.

DIRECTORY

Rock and Folk Music

BB&T Pavilion
1 Harbour Blvd,
Camden Waterfront, NJ.
Tel (856) 365-1300.
W livenation.com

Keswick Theatre
291 N Keswick Ave,
Glenside, PA.
Tel (215) 572-7650.
W keswicktheatre.com

Khyber Pass Pub
56 S 2nd St. **Map** 4 E3.
Tel (215) 238-5888.

Manayunk Brewing Company
4120 Main St. **Tel** (215) 482-8220. W manayunk brewery.com

Tin Angel
20 S 2nd St. **Map** 4 E3.
Tel (215) 928-0978.
W tinangel.com

Tower Theater
69th & Ludlow Sts,
Upper Darby, PA.
Tel (215) 568-3222.
W tower-theater.com

Wells Fargo Center
3601 S Broad St at
Pattison Ave.
Tel (215) 336-3600.
W wellsfargocenter philly.com

World Café Live
3025 Walnut St.
Tel (215) 222-1400.
W worldcafelive.com

Blues, Jazz, and World Music

Alma de Cuba
1623 Walnut St.
Map 2 E4.
Tel (215) 988-1799.

Chris' Jazz Café
1421 Samson St.
Map 3 A3.
Tel (215) 568-3131.
W chrisjazzcafe.com

Ortlieb's Lounge
847 N 3rd St.
Tel (215) 922-1035.
W ortliebslounge.com

Warmdaddy's
1400 Colombus Blvd.
Map 4 E5.
Tel (215) 462-2000.
W warmdaddys.com

Nightclubs and Discos

The 700
700 N 2nd St. **Map** 4 E1.
Tel (215) 413-3181.
W the700.org

Bleu Martini
245 2nd St. **Map** 4 E2. **Tel** (215) 940-7900. W bleu martiniphilly.com

Cavanaugh's River Deck
417 N Columbus Blvd.
Map 4 F1.
Tel (215) 629-7400.
W theriverdeck.com

Infusion Lounge
16 S 2nd St. **Map** 4 E4. **Tel** (215) 908-4009.
W infusionphilly.com

Silk City
435 Spring Garden St. **Map** 1 A2. **Tel** (215) 592-8838.
W silkcityphilly.com

Bars and Taverns

Bishop's Collar
2349 Fairmount Ave. **Map** 2 D1. **Tel** (215) 765-1616.

Fergie's Pub
1214 Sansom St. **Map** 2 F5.
Tel (215) 928-8118.
W fergies.com

Irish Pub
2007 Walnut St. **Map** 1 C4.
Tel (215) 568-5603.

McGillins Olde Ale House
1310 Drury St. **Map** 3 B2.
Tel (215) 735-5562.

Monk's Café
264 S 16th St. **Map** 2 E5.
Tel (215) 545-7005.
W monkscafe.com

LGBT Clubs and Bars

Stir Lounge
1705 Chancellor St. **Map** 2 E5. **Tel** (215) 732-2700.

Voyeur Nightclub
1221 St James Pl. **Map** 2 F5. **Tel** (215) 735-5772.

Woody's
202 S 13th St. **Map** 2 F4.
Tel (215) 545-1893.

Comedy Clubs

Helium Comedy Club
2031 Sansom St. **Map** 2 D4.
Tel (215) 496-9001.
W philadelphia.helium comedy.com

Laff House
3320 Collins St.
Tel (443) 485-0271.

Outdoor Activities and Sports

Whether you are an active participant or simply a spectator, there is no shortage of sporting activities in Philadelphia all year round. In the warmer months, the region's many recreational areas and parks are packed with hikers, bicyclists, joggers, and golfers. In the winter months, outdoor enthusiasts opt for iceskating or head for the nearby ski slopes in the Pocono Mountains. Local sports fans are passionate about their many professional home teams that play throughout the year. They flock to the city's stadiums and arenas to watch baseball, football, basketball, and hockey. The area's colleges and universities compete in the above sports and others such as volleyball, swimming, and gymnastics.

Bicycling, Jogging, and Skating

Philadelphia has an extensive greenbelt running through it with miles of walking and biking trails, most of which are found in Fairmount Park *(see p99)*. On warmer days of the year, hundreds of enthusiasts take to the city's most popular trail, the 8.4-mile (13.5-km) paved inline skating, walking, and biking path that runs parallel to Kelly Drive and Martin Luther King Jr Boulevard *(see p100)* along both sides of the Schuylkill River. The **Bicycle Club of Philadelphia**

has information about the various bike paths within the area, and schedules bike rides each weekend for cyclists of all experience levels.

Other popular hiking and biking trails can be found along Wissahickon Gorge in Fairmount Park. There are also 6 miles (9.6 km) of trails within **Valley Forge National Historic Park** *(see p131)*. Valley Forge is a starting point for the 22-mile (35-km) bike path ending in Fairmount Park. The path runs on a former railroad track route along the Schuylkill River.

Golf and Tennis

The Philadelphia area has numerous 18-hole golf courses that challenge players at all levels. Courses situated in the city include the **Cobbs Creek Golf Club** and the **Walnut Lane Golf Club**, located within Wissahickon Valley Park. The professionally ranked **Broad Run Golfers Club** sits in scenic West Chester countryside, while **Makefield Highlands Golf Club** is the only true links-style golf course in the Tri-State area.

Public tennis courts in many parks are free on a first-come, first-served basis. Local tennis clubs that charge a fee include **Friends of Chamounix Tennis** situated in Fairmount Park and **Philadelphia Tennis Court**.

Winter Activities

As Christmas approaches, many outdoor enthusiasts bundle up and trade their inline blades for ice skates. Philadelphia and its surrounding areas have several ice-skating rinks, but the most popular is the **Blue Cross RiverRink** at Penn's Landing, where skaters enjoy an Olympic-sized rink with views of the Ben Franklin Bridge and the Delaware River.

Skiers head to the Pocono Mountains. This usually involves a day trip, and most ski slopes are within a two-hour drive. The **Pocono Mountains Visitors Bureau** has information about ski slopes and snow conditions.

Professional Spectator Sports

South Philadelphia's modern stadiums are the venue for most professional sports competitions held in the city. The **Philadelphia Phillies** play throughout the summer season at the Citizens Bank Park. The 43,000-seat stadium is one of the most fan-friendly ballparks to host major league baseball games. Rough-and-tumble football action kicks off in August as the **Philadelphia**

Paved walking and biking path in Fairmount Park *(see p99)*

Eagles start their season with games at Lincoln Financial Field, a 68,000-seat stadium.

During the cold winter months, sports fans head back indoors to watch basketball played by the **Philadelphia 76ers** at the Wells Fargo Center, which seats 21,000. Hockey fans flock to the Wells Fargo Center as well for spirited games on ice with the **Philadelphia Flyers**. The area's popular college baseball team, the **Rutgers–Camden Scarlet Raptors**, plays ball at Campbell's Field at the Camden Waterfront. Other popular home teams play soccer and lacrosse.

For horse-racing fans, the **Parx Casino and Racing** has live thoroughbred racing all year round every Saturday through Tuesday. The racetrack is home to the GII Pennsylvania Derby on Labor Day.

Philadelphia 76ers under attack from the New York Knicks at the Wells Fargo Center

College Sports

Over a dozen colleges and universities in the Philadelphia area take part in intercollegiate sports programs and competitions, a tradition that dates back more than 200 years. Some of the nation's best college basketball is played by what is called the Big Five – **St. Joseph's University**, **University of Pennsylvania**, **Temple University**, **Villanova University**, and **LaSalle University**. Schools in the area have both men's and women's activities in a full range of other sports, and competitions in football, soccer, field hockey, volleyball, swimming, gymnastics, and more are held regularly.

DIRECTORY

Bicycling, Jogging, and Skating

Bicycle Club of Philadelphia
Tel (215) 735-2453.
W phillybikeclub.org

Valley Forge National Historic Park
1400 N Outer Line Drive.
Tel (610) 783-1099.
W nps.gov/vafo

Golf and Tennis

Broad Run Golfer's Club
1520 Tattersall Way, West Chester, PA.
Tel (610) 738-4410.
W broadrungc.com

Cobbs Creek Golf Club
72nd & Lansdowne Aves.
Tel (215) 877-8707.
W cobbscreek.golf philly.org

Friends of Chamounix Tennis
50 Chamounix Dr, Fairmount Park.
Tel (215) 877-6845.
W friendsofchamounix tennis.org

Makefield Highlands Golf Club
1418 Woodside Rd, Yardley, PA.
Tel (215) 321-7000.
W makefield highlandsgolf.com

Philadelphia Tennis Court
4700 Spruce St.
Tel (215) 683-3639.

Walnut Lane Golf Club
800 Walnut Lane.
Tel (215) 482-3370.
W walnutlanegolf.com

Winter Activities

Blue Cross RiverRink
Penn's Landing.
Map 4 F3.
Tel (215) 925-7465.
W delawareriver waterfront.com

Pocono Mountains Visitors Bureau
1004 Main St, Stroudsburg, PA 18360.
Tel (800) 762-6667.
W poconomountains. com

Professional Spectator Sports

Parx Casino and Racing
3001 Street Rd, Bensalem.
Tel (215) 639-9000, (800) 523-6886.
W parxracing.com

Philadelphia 76ers
Wells Fargo Center, 3601 S Broad St. Tel (215) 339-7600. W nba.com/ sixers

Philadelphia Eagles
Lincoln Financial Field, 1020 Pattison Ave.
Tel (267) 570-4510.
W philadelphia eagles.com

Philadelphia Flyers
Wells Fargo Center, 3601 S Broad St. Tel (215) 465-4500. W nhl.com/flyers

Philadelphia Phillies
Citizens Bank Park, 1 Citizen Bank Way.
Tel (215) 463-1000.
W phillies.com

College Sports

LaSalle University
1900 W Olney Ave.
Tel (215) 951-1000.
W lasalle.edu

Rutgers–Camden Scarlet Raptors
Campbell's Field, 401 N Delaware Ave, Camden.
Tel (856) 963-2600.
W scarletraptors.com

St. Joseph's University
5600 City Ave.
Tel (610) 660-1712.
W sju.edu

Temple University
801 N Broad St.
Map 2 F1.
Tel (215) 204-8499.
W temple.edu

University of Pennsylvania
3451 Walnut St.
Map 1 A4.
Tel (215) 898-6151.
W upenn.edu

Villanova University
Tel (610) 519-4500.
W villanova.edu

CHILDREN'S PHILADELPHIA

Parents will find a plethora of activities that will keep their children amused when in Philadelphia and the surrounding area. Museums, such as the Franklin and the Academy of Natural Sciences, thrill kids with hands-on exhibits and workshops, while the Adventure Aquarium and the Philadelphia Zoo entertain with an array of sea creatures and animals. Educational tours can be taken at historic buildings, where actors dress up as colonial figures and perform skits. In the Dutch Country, kids can enjoy Amish-style buggy rides and much more at the Dutch Wonderland Family Amusement Park in Lancaster.

Interior of the National Constitution Center, on Independence Mall

Historic Sights and Tours

Tour guides at key historic buildings provide informative tours to young and old alike; however, some sights will interest children more than others. The **National Constitution Center** *(see pp50–51)* features interactive exhibits explaining the US Constitution, where for example, children, might try on a judge's robe at a replica of the Supreme Court bench, or cast their ballot for their all-time favorite president. Independence National Historical Park *(see pp50–51)* –

Historic Lights of Liberty show at Independence Hall

comprising the Liberty Bell Center, Independence Hall, and the Independence Visitor Center – features several interactive exhibits geared toward kids. In the summer, the park offers ranger-led walking tours around the park based on themes such as Benjamin Franklin and the Underground Railroad.

Kids also enjoy the multimedia **Lights of Liberty Show** *(see p187)*, a brisk walking tour through Old Town at dusk. Participants don headphones and watch images – which tell the story of the American Revolution – projected on historic buildings. For younger children, ask for a special version for ages 6 to 12.

Museums

Philadelphia's premier museum for children is the **Please Touch Museum**. Aimed at kids aged under eight, it has several exhibits that enhance a child's ability to learn discovery and play. For instance, the Alice's Adventures in Wonderland exhibit is based on the popular classic story and includes many settings from the book to encourage problem solving and language skills. The SuperMarket has checkouts, shopping carts, and toy food items, while Barnyard Babies teaches about life on a farm. Other activities include interactive theater performances with musicians, dancers, and storytellers. The museum is located in Memorial Hall in the Fairmount Park District.

The Franklin Institute *(see p87)* has hands-on exhibits, with some such as Electricity Hall reflecting Benjamin Franklin's inventions. Children learn about the human heart and bioscience at the Giant Walk-Through Heart. Other exhibits include the Train Factory, which has an actual 350-ton (770,000-lb) locomotive, and the Franklin Air Show, which has a flight simulator. The Fels Planetarium features virtual tours through space. At the **Academy of Natural Sciences** *(see p87)*, children can see the fossils of a Tyrannosaurus rex and other species in Dinosaur Hall. Youngsters can also check out the Live Animal Center, which houses over 100 animals, and live butterflies stored in a tropical rainforest habitat that has been replicated at the museum. In addition to model

Banner at the Academy of Natural Sciences

boats and deep-sea diving apparatus, kids enjoy squeezing through the small hatches and passageways of the submarine *Becuna* at the **Independence Seaport Museum** *(see pp66–7)*. Boys, in particular, enjoy the old fire engines and pumpers at **Fireman's Hall Museum** *(see p53)*. At the **Fairmount Water Works** *(see p90)*, interactive exhibits challenge children to learn about city water resources. The center also has a virtual helicopter tour of the watershed.

The **National Liberty Museum** *(see p55)* takes a more serious approach to entertaining children by helping combat violence and bigotry through interactive exhibits, glass artworks, and more. One display is Kids Vote, which asks youngsters to take a stand on such issues as handgun law and the death penalty. Another exhibit, Jellybean People, features two life-sized models made of multicolored jellybeans to show that people are the same inside, regardless of skin color.

For children with an artistic flair, the **Philadelphia Museum of Art** *(see pp92–5)* offers drawing classes and gallery tours on Sundays. The **Pennsylvania Academy of the Fine Arts** *(see pp76–7)* has workshops on most Saturday mornings.

Beyond Philadelphia, in the Pennsylvania Dutch Country,

Philadelphia Zoo, home to many animal species

Strasburg offers kids train displays, a train museum, and rides on the **Strasburg Railroad** *(see p121)*. In Hershey, children will love the simulated chocolate factory at **Chocolate World** *(see p126)*, and the roller-coaster rides and attractions at Hershey Park.

Gardens, Zoos, and Waterfront Activities

An instant hit with children is the **Philadelphia Zoo** *(see p100)*. While close-up views of wild animals such as lions and rare tigers are a big draw, children also enjoy KidZooU, where they can pet docile sheep, rabbits, and newly hatched chicks.

Tarantula at the Insectarium

At the **Philadelphia Insectarium**, youngsters can safely observe the workings of a beehive from behind a glass partition, touch the likes of tarantulas and giant beetles,

and see thousands of other live and mounted insects. Kids can also play in a man-made spider web. The **Adventure Aquarium** at the Camden Waterfront *(see p103)* has a huge tank with hundreds of aquatic species, including sharks, sea turtles, and more than 1,000 kinds of fish. Kids can touch harmless species in the Touch-a-Shark exhibit and see seals frolic in outdoor pools. Also at the waterfront, the **Camden Children's Garden** is an interactive park with different areas, including the Butterfly Garden, Railroad Garden, Dinosaur Garden, and the Storybook Gardens. The **Sister Cities Park**, an outdoor oasis in the heart of the city, has a lovely children's garden with winding pathways, a stream, and a boat pond.

DIRECTORY

Museums

Please Touch Museum
4231 Avenue of the Republic.
Tel (215) 581-3187.
Ⓦ pleasetouchmuseum.org

Gardens, Zoos, and Waterfront Activities

Adventure Aquarium
1 Riverside Dr, Camden, NJ.
Tel (856) 365-3300.
Ⓦ adventurequarium.com

Camden Children's Garden
3 Riverside Drive, Camden, NJ.
Tel (856) 365-8733.
Ⓦ camdenchildrens garden.org

Philadelphia Insectarium
8046 Frankford Ave.
Tel (215) 335-9500.
Ⓦ myinsectarium.com

Sister Cities Park
200 N 18th St.
Tel (800) 537-7676.

Interactive exhibits inside Fairmount Water Works

SURVIVAL GUIDE

PRACTICAL INFORMATION

Philadelphia thrives on tourism thanks to its rich colonial history and culture, and its world-class museums and restaurants. An efficient infrastructure – including clearly marked signs, a state-of-the-art visitor center, and a well-planned transit system – has been created by the city authorities and the National Park Service to give visitors a memorable vacation. Most of Philadelphia's central neighborhoods can be explored on foot and many areas in the city are safe, but visitors should take sensible precautions as in any major city. The following pages include tips on a wide range of practical matters to ensure a trouble-free stay.

Visas and Passports

All visitors to the US must have a valid passport and, in some cases, a visa. The US is 1 of 36 countries, including the UK, France, and Australia, participating in the Visa Waiver Program (VWP), which permits those who qualify to enter without a visa and stay up to 90 days.

The US operates an Electronic System for Travel Authorization (ESTA) for VWP travelers. Visitors must register and pay online at https://esta.cbp.dhs.gov at least 72 hours in advance of departure; authorization will be valid for two years when issued. Alternatively, your national passport-issuing agency can provide information. VWP travelers who have not obtained approval through ESTA will be denied boarding any plane to the US.

It is always best to check the US State Department's website (www.state.gov/travel) before travel for the most up-to-date information and entry requirements.

Travel Safety Advice

Visitors can get up-to-date travel safety information from the Foreign and Commonwealth Office in the UK, the State Department in the US, and the Department of Foreign Affairs and Trade in Australia.

Tourist Information

The **Independence Visitor Center** *(see p47)*, located in the heart of Independence National Historical Park, is within walking distance of many sights in Philadelphia's central historic core. In addition to brochure

Tour guide in colonial attire leading tourists in Old City

racks and self-service information booths, visitor concierges assist with ticket sales and provide information on shopping, attractions, hotels, restaurants, and other visitor needs. The free, timed tickets which are required for entrance to Independence Hall are also available here.

Visit Philadelphia offers comprehensive information about the Philadelphia region on its website.

The **Philadelphia Convention & Visitors Bureau** provides information for tour groups, conventions, and international visitors on their website.

Smoking is prohibited in most buildings and stores, except in designated areas, and it is strictly banned from all restaurants, taverns, and pubs throughout the city.

Admission Prices

Attractions within Independence National Historical Park are free of charge, which makes Philadelphia a budget-friendly place to visit. A number of others, including the Rodin Museum, request nominal donations of $3–5. Admission fees for most major sights, such as the National Constitution Center and Franklin Institute, generally range between $10 and $16. Many offer discounts or free admission for children. The **Philadelphia CityPass** offers entry to six sights for $59 and is valid for nine consecutive days.

Opening Hours

Most museums and historic buildings open from 9 or 10am to 5pm daily, with extended summer hours. Business and banking hours are 9am–5pm Monday to Friday *(see p178)*. Central Philadelphia shops open 10am to 7pm *(see p154)*.

Public Conveniences

Free public and wheelchair-accessible restrooms can be found at the Independence Visitor Center and in the Bourse at 5th Street between Market and Chestnut Streets. In other parts of Center City, the Reading Terminal Market, the Shops at the Bellevue, department stores, and malls have facilities.

Taxes and Tipping

Pennsylvania's hotel occupancy taxes are 6 percent (7 percent in Philadelphia), and car rental taxes and hotel fees can add 20 percent or more to quoted prices.

It is usual to tip wait staff 15 percent of the final bill, and 20 percent or more for great service; for bar staff $1 per drink. Tip hotel or airport porters $1 per bag, at least as much for the room maid per night ($2 at upscale hotels), and up to $10 or more for a helpful concierge. Valet parking attendants expect $1–2; cab drivers 10–15 percent of the fare.

Travelers with Special Needs

Most city buildings and sidewalks accommodate disabled persons as required by US law, but some historic colonial structures do not have adequate provisions. SEPTA buses *(see p186)* are equipped with lifts, while **SEPTA CCT** and **ADA Paratransit** offer transportation for passengers unable to use standard services. The **Mayor's Commission on People with Disabilities** has information for disabled visitors to Philadelphia.

International Student Identity Card

Students and Senior Travelers

The Philadelphia area has numerous colleges and universities, so an **International Student Identification Card (ISIC)** or **Student Advantage Card** is recommended as these are accepted for discounts. Senior citizens also receive discounts, including reduced admission to many sights.

LGBT Travelers

Philadelphia is a gay-friendly destination known for its lively LGBT scene. Midtown Village (between 11th and Broad Streets and Chestnut and Pine Streets) is nicknamed "the Gayborhood" for its many gay-owned and gay-friendly shops, restaurants, accommodations, and clubs. The **William Way LGBT Community Center** hosts tours, activities, and programs geared toward the gay community. The weekly *Philadelphia Gay News* lists events, as does www.visitphilly.com.

Responsible Tourism

Greenworks Philadelphia, an initiative focusing on expanding environmentally friendly policies and programs, has had a major effect on the city's commitment to sustainability.

There are now several neighborhood farmers' markets from May through November. One of the most popular is the Saturday-morning market at Head House Square in the Society Hill district. The **Clark Park Farmers' Market** in the University City area operates year-round (May–Oct: Thu and Sat, Dec–Apr: Sat). From Thursday to Saturday, Amish farmers bring their home-baked goods and produce to **Reading Terminal Market**, where other purveyors sell their foodstuffs all week long.

Many city restaurants build their menus around locally sourced produce.

Several Philadelphia hotels, including Kimpton Hotel Palomar *(see p137)*, have earned LEED status (Leadership in Energy and Environmental Design) for their energy-efficient design.

Locally grown, organic produce at a neighborhood farmers' market

DIRECTORY

Travel Safety Advice

UK: Foreign and Commonwealth Office
W gov.uk/foreign-travel-advice

US: US Department of State
W travel.state.gov

Australia: Department of Foreign Affairs and Trade
W dfat.gov.au
W smartraveller.gov.au

Tourist Information

Independence Visitor Center
6th & Market Sts. **Map** 4 D2. **Tel** (800) 537-7676. W **independence** visitorcenter.com

Philadelphia CityPass
W citypass.com/philadelphia

Philadelphia Convention & Visitors Bureau
1601 Market St. **Map** 2 E4.
Tel (215) 636-3300.
W discoverphl.com

Visit Philadelphia
W visitphilly.com

Travelers with Special Needs

ADA Paratransit
Tel (215) 580-7145.

Mayor's Commission on People with Disabilities
Tel (215) 686-2798.
W phila.gov/mcpd

SEPTA CCT
1234 Market St. **Map** 2 F4.
Tel (215) 580-7145.

Student Travelers

International Student Identification Card
W isic.org

Student Advantage Card
W studentadvantage.com

LGBT Travelers

William Way LGBT Community Center
1315 Spruce St. **Map** 1 C5.
Tel (215) 732-2220.
W waygay40.org

Responsible Tourism

Clark Park Farmers' Market
43rd St & Baltimore Ave.

Reading Terminal Market
12th & Arch Sts. **Map** 3 B2.

Personal Security and Health

For the most part, central Philadelphia is generally safe and the majority of visitors touring the sights do not have any problems with crime. Nonetheless, as in any big American city, taking common-sense precautions will ensure a trouble-free visit. Although major crime is rare in high-density tourist areas, it is advisable to be aware of your surroundings at all times. Public transportation and walking in much of the central area is usually safe during the day, but visitors should opt for a taxi at night or for staying in prominent nightlife areas such as those in Old City, Center City, and Society Hill and Penn's Landing.

Philadelphia police officers on bicycles

Police

The Philadelphia Police Department provides round-the-clock car patrols as well as bicycle, horseback, and foot patrols. Police presence is plentiful throughout Center City, and there is often 24-hour surveillance by police and National Park Service rangers around key sights in Independence National Historical Park. The city's public transportation service, SEPTA, has its own police force that patrols the underground transit systems. Traffic and parking enforcement officers also make rounds on foot. Most are friendly when approached and will offer directions. Park rangers are usually helpful with answering questions about city sights and attractions. In Center City, police stations are located at 8th and Race Streets (Map 4 D2), 9th and South Streets (Map 3 C4), and 1201 S 20th Street.

In an Emergency

Call 911 to report life-or-death emergency situations or matters requiring an immediate response from medical, police, or fire department personnel. Most hospital emergency rooms in and around the city are open 24 hours daily and take walk-in patients or those delivered by ambulance. Emergency rooms are busiest during weekend evenings so there might be a long wait. Hotel personnel can locate the nearest hospital, or arrange a doctor's appointment for non-life threatening medical conditions. To get specialized assistance for people with disabilities, call **Relay Services**. Philadelphia International has its own **Airport Medical Emergencies** center. The **University of Pennsylvania Dental School Clinic** is one of a number of city clinics offering emergency dental care services. Ask your hotel staff for assistance.

What to be Aware of

The popular tourist areas in Center City and around Independence National Historical Park are generally safe, but it is wise to follow basic safety precautions. Watch out for purse-snatchers and pickpockets, and do not leave personal items such as handbags or cameras unattended. Avoid wandering into dark alleys and deserted streets, especially in West Philadelphia. Local police and park rangers can offer directions and answer questions.

Do not carry a large amount of cash or wear excessive jewelry. Carry just one credit card and enough cash for the day's activities; leave other cards, traveler's checks, and your passport locked in your hotel room safe. Passports should be carried only when exchanging currency or traveler's checks. It is wise to make copies of your passport and record your credit card numbers in case of theft.

You may see homeless people on the city streets. If approached, it is best to ignore requests for a cash handout.

A 24-hour CVS pharmacy in a Philadelphia neighborhood

Police car

Police SUV

Fire engine

The legal drinking age in Pennsylvania and New Jersey is 21. Young people need to show photo ID as proof of age when ordering alcohol. Liquor and wine can be bought only at state-run stores, while beer is sold at special distribution centers or by the six-pack in bars.

Lost and Stolen Property

If your property is lost or stolen, chances of recovery are slim. Nonetheless, contact local authorities through the **Philadelphia Police (Non-Emergency)** line to file a report and keep a copy of the same for insurance purposes. It may be helpful to contact the Lost and Found in department stores, the Independence Visitor Center (see p174–5), or **Philadelphia International Airport**. Also, contact taxi companies or the public transit system in case missing items are turned in.

Call your debit or credit card company to report a lost or stolen credit card, and contact your currency exchange provider for lost traveler's checks (see p179). If your passport is lost or stolen, contact your country's consulate or embassy immediately (see p175).

Hospitals and Pharmacies

Philadelphia has excellent medical facilities should you become ill during your visit. There are a number of walk-in clinics that will treat minor ailments, while all main hospitals in the city offer accident and emergency care.

Visitors should be advised, however, that medical care can be very expensive. Even if carrying medical insurance, you may still have to pay upfront and claim reimbursement from your insurance company later, so do not forget to ask for all necessary forms and receipts. Most medical facilities in the city accept credit cards.

Pack enough prescription drugs, and it is advisable to keep two sets of the same medicines in different travel bags, in the unlikely event that one is lost or stolen. There are several pharmacies open 24 hours daily in Central and Greater Philadelphia, including **CVS** and **Rite Aid**. Some pharmacies have medical personnel for minor, non-critical health issues (such as **Jefferson at Washington Square**). Ask hotel personnel for directions.

Travel and Health Insurance

Because the cost of medical care in the US is so high, it is essential to purchase travel insurance before you visit. Packages should include medical and dental coverage, as well as trip cancelation, flight delay, lost or stolen baggage, and even death and dismemberment insurance.

DIRECTORY

Police

All Emergencies
Tel 911 for police, fire, and emergency medical attention.

Philadelphia Police (Non-Emergency)
Tel (215) 686-1776.

In an Emergency

Airport Medical Emergencies
Tel (215) 937-3111.

Dental Emergencies
Tel (215) 925-6050.

Relay Services (Special Assistance)
Tel (800) 654-5984.

University of Pennsylvania Dental School Clinic
240 S 40th St.
Tel (215) 898-8965.

Lost and Stolen Property

Philadelphia International Airport Lost and Found
Communications Center located between Terminals C and D.
Tel (215) 937-6888.

Hospitals and Pharmacies

CVS
1826 Chestnut St.
Map 2 D4.
Tel (215) 972-0909.

Finding a Doctor (Non-Emergency)
Tel (215) 563-5343.

Jefferson at Washington Square
700 Walnut St.
Map 3 C3.
Tel (215) 503-7300.

Rite Aid
2301 Walnut St.
Map 1 C4.
Tel (215) 636-9634.
5040 City Line Ave.
Tel (215) 877-2116.

Thomas Jefferson University Hospital
111 S 11th St.
Map 3 C3.
Tel (215) 966-6000.
W hospitals.jefferson.edu

Banking and Currency

There is no shortage of local and international banks in Philadelphia, especially in Center City. Cash can be easily withdrawn through the city's numerous ATMs, which accept most major credit and debit cards. Foreign notes can be exchanged for American dollars in hotels and at currency exchange offices. However, be advised that most currency exchange offices and banks are closed on Sundays and hotels charge high commission. Also, it is prudent not to carry all your money and cards at the same time.

The lobby of a PNC Bank branch with multiple ATMs

Banks and Currency Exchange

Major banks found in Philadelphia include **PNC Bank**, **Citizens Bank**, **Citibank**, and **Wells Fargo Bank**, which are usually open from 9am to 5pm weekdays (later on Fridays), and 9am until noon on Saturdays. TD Bank is open daily and most branches are open until 8pm during the week. Currency exchange services are available at airport kiosks and several banks. Hours vary, but most currency exchange offices are open from 9am to 5:30pm. Some hotels offer an exchange service, but fees are higher. It is a good idea to bring around $100 into the United States in case exchange services are not immediately available.

ATMs

Cash is easily accessible through the numerous ATMs in the Philadelphia area. They are found at bank entrances, in office complexes, at shopping malls, grocery stores, and restaurants, and even in convenience stores. Cash is distributed in $10 and $20 bills, and can be withdrawn with a debit or credit card, including Visa or MasterCard. ATMs usually charge a fee for withdrawals by non-bank members, while the user's bank might also charge a fee. Generally, fees are significantly higher, sometimes up to $4, at freestanding ATMs not attached to a bank. One exception is **Wawa**, a local

Automated teller machine (ATM) for convenient withdrawals

convenience store chain, which offers ATMs with no service fees. Check with your bank which transaction fees apply. Also, notify your credit or debit card provider of your travel plans so your card does not get blocked while you are away.

Credit Cards and Traveler's Checks

Most restaurants and shops accept major credit cards such as **Visa**, **MasterCard**, **American Express**, **Discover Card**, and **Diners Club**. Credit cards are not only safer than carrying lots of cash; some credit cards also offer insurance benefits on retail goods while providing reward points or airline miles. For travelers, credit cards are essential in the event of a medical emergency, as they are honored as payment at most US hospitals. A valid credit card is required for car rentals, and most hotels request credit card numbers to make a room reservation. Many businesses accept traveler's checks in US dollars as payment without charging a fee. You can cash them at local banks with identification such as a passport, driver's license, or student ID. Personal foreign currency checks are rarely accepted.

Wiring Money

Money can be wired internationally through **Western Union**, which has locations in supermarkets, convenience stores, travel agencies, business centers, and other locations including **Travelex Currency** in Center City. In addition to sending and receiving money within minutes, Western Union also offers overnight delivery of checks to private residences or offices as well as a three-day service whereby cash can be deposited directly into a designated bank account. The amount you may send and hours of operation vary by location. Fees generally start at about $40 and increase based on the amount being wired and expedited delivery options.

PRACTICAL INFORMATION | **179**

Coins

American coins (actual size shown) come in 1-, 5-, 10-, and 25-cent, as well as $1 denominations; 50-cent pieces are minted but rarely used. Each coin has its own name: 1-cent coins are known as pennies; 5-cent coins as nickels; 10-cent coins as dimes; and 1-dollar coins (and bills) are sometimes called "bucks."

25-cent coin (a quarter)

10-cent coin
(a dime)

5-cent coin
(a nickel)

1-cent coin (a penny)

Bills (Banknotes)

The units of currency in the United States are dollars and cents. There are 100 cents to the dollar. Bills come in the following denominations: $1, $5, $10, $20, $50, and $100. There is also a $2 bill, but it is rarely used and is more of a collector's item. Security features include subtle color hues and improved color-shifting ink in the lower right-hand corner of the face of each bill.

1-dollar bill ($1)

5-dollar bill ($5)

10-dollar bill ($10)

20-dollar bill ($20)

50-dollar bill ($50)

100-dollar bill ($100)

DIRECTORY

Banks and Currency Exchange

Citibank
1234 Market St.
Map 2 F4.

Citizens Bank
1515 Market St.
Map 2 D4.

PNC Bank
1600 Market St.
Map 2 E4.

Wells Fargo Bank
123 S Broad St.
Map 3 B3.

ATMs

Wawa
912-916 Walnut St.
Map 3 C3.

Credit Cards and Traveler's Checks

American Express
Tel (800) 528-4800.

Diners Club
Tel (800) 847-2911.

Discover Card
Tel (800) 347-2683.

MasterCard
Tel (800) 307-7309.

Visa
Tel (800) 847-2911.

Wiring money

Travelex Currency
1800 JFK Blvd. **Map** 1 B3.
Tel (215) 563-7348.

Western Union
930 Market St.
Map 2 F2. **Tel** (215) 928-1351.

Communications and Media

Like most major cities, Philadelphia has excellent communication systems. The US Postal Service is reliable and efficient, with regular pickups from mailboxes throughout the city. There are numerous local television and radio stations, as well as two major daily newspapers. Internet cafes and wireless hot spots are located throughout the city, and, for those who need them, fax services are also available. With the advent of cell phones, card- or coin-operated pay phones are less common but can be found in hotels, malls, restaurants, and on some street corners.

Cell Phones

The major cell phone services in Philadelphia are **Sprint**, **Verizon**, **AT&T**, and **T-Mobile**. The US uses a different frequency for cell services than that used overseas, so you need a quad-band phone to connect to the US network. Tri-band phones are usually compatible, too. You may also need to activate the "roaming" facility.

Alternatively, you can rent a cell phone, available at **AllCell Rental**, or buy a disposable phone at local pharmacies or convenience stores.

Public Telephones

The increase in cell phone usage has resulted in fewer coin- and credit-card-operated pay phones, but some are still available in hotel lobbies, shopping malls, restaurants, gas stations, bars, and some city streets. Pay phone rates vary by carrier but most local call charges start at about 50 cents for the first three minutes. Prices for long-distance or calls abroad can vary as different telephone companies set their own rates. Operator-assisted calls are more costly than calling direct. Prepare to have lots of dimes, nickels, and quarters on hand for coin-operated phones. Local and international phone cards can be bought from convenience stores.

Internet

Internet access is available at Internet cafés, public libraries, bookstores, and at some office supply and photocopy/fax centers, such as **FedEx Office**.

One of many cafés offering Wi-Fi to its customers

Useful Dialing Codes

- Philadelphia's area codes are **215**, **267**, and **445**. Western suburbs and surrounding areas use **610**, **484**, and **835**. The area code for the Pennsylvania Dutch Country and Gettysburg is **717**.
- For calls outside the local area but within the US and Canada, dial **1** followed by the area code and phone number.
- For local operator assistance, dial **0**.
- For local and national directory inquiries, dial **411**. Directory assistance for toll-free numbers is **1–800–555–1212**.
- Phone numbers with the codes **800**, **888**, **877**, or **866** indicate a toll-free number.
- For international direct-dial calls, dial **011** followed by the country code, city or area code, and number.
- To make an international call via the operator, dial **01** and then follow the same procedure as detailed above.
- For international directory inquiries, dial **00**.
- For more information about calling in Philadelphia, check the local *White Pages* directory, which also lists country codes for international calls.

Most hotels have business centers where guests can check their emails. These services are often charged by the minute or by 15-minute blocks, which can become costly, so check the hotel's prices before making a reservation.

Library Internet services are often free but may have time limits.

Many book stores and the **Capital One 360 Cafe** in Center City are free Wi-Fi hot spots, as are **Philadelphia Java Company** in the Society Hill neighborhood and **Old City Coffee** in the Old City arts district.

For connectivity on the go, many Amtrak trains offer Wi-Fi on some intercity routes out of Philadelphia.

Postal Services

Philadelphia's **Main Post Office** at Market and 30th Streets, directly across from the 30th Street Station, is open 8am to 9pm Monday through Saturday and noon to 6pm on Sunday. Most other branches are open weekdays from 9am to 5pm and Saturday from 9am to noon.

Letters and parcels weighing less than 16 ounces (454 g) require only stamps and can be mailed in the blue mailboxes on street corners, or in letter slots in hotels and office buildings.

Standard blue US mailbox

The cost of a stamp for first-class delivery of a standard letter is 47 cents. The US Postal Service, **FedEx**, and **DHL** offer a variety of overnight letter and parcel services, while **UPS** delivers large boxes and packages. FedEx offices are located in major office buildings in Center City and in Kinko's business services stores.

Television and Radio

Philadelphia carries the major US broadcast networks. Channel numbers vary depending on the service provider but generally you can find CBS on channel 3, ABC on channel 6, NBC on channel 10, PBS on channel 12, FOX on channel 29, CW on channel 57, and Telemundo on channel 62. Cable companies carry popular sports, news, entertainment, and movie networks, such as ESPN, HBO, and CNN.

Radio stations, on both the AM and FM frequencies, include a variety of music, talk, and news shows. Radio station KYW 1060 AM provides round-the-clock news, weather, sports, and finance reports. Some public radio stations offer commercial-free programming. WHYY-FM (90.9) focuses on call-in shows, political reports, and cultural news, while WXPN-FM (88.5) airs world, alternative, and new music. WRTI (90.1) focuses on jazz and blues as well as reporting on cultural events.

Satellite radio is available through subscription and offers dozens of channels dedicated to a particular format.

Newspapers and Magazines

The city's two main daily newspapers are the *Philadelphia Inquirer* *(see p162)* and the *Philadelphia Daily News*. Both can be found in newsstands or in news boxes on street corners. Both weekday editions are $1.50 each. The *Inquirer*'s Sunday edition is $1.50; the *Daily News* does not publish a Sunday edition.

The *Philadelphia Business Journal* is published weekly and focuses on local business news as it relates to national trends. Other special-interest publications include the *Philadelphia Tribune* focusing on the African-American community, the *Philadelphia Gay News*, and *Al Dia*, the city's Latino newspaper. Two weekly alternative publications, *Philadelphia City Paper* and the *Philadelphia Weekly*, provide political commentary and entertainment coverage. They are available for free and can be found in news boxes on street corners.

Monthly magazines *Philadelphia Magazine* and *Philadelphia Style* focus on trends, fashion, dining, and cultural activities.

Selection of local Philadelphia newspapers at a newsstand

TRAVEL INFORMATION

Whether traveling from within or outside the country, Philadelphia is easily accessible by air, train, bus, and car. Philadelphia International Airport is served by many international and regional airlines. Amtrak's 30th Street Station is a busy rail hub on the Northeast Corridor line that runs between Washington, D.C. and Boston. The station is also a stop for trains arriving from other regions of the country. A number of interstate highways, which crisscross most of the Philadelphia metropolitan area, cater to motorists and long-distance bus services. The city also has a cruise ship terminal along the Delaware River that serves as a stop on some liners' itineraries.

View of Terminal A at Philadelphia International Airport

Arriving by Air

Philadelphia is conveniently located in the middle of the US Northeast Corridor, situated about halfway between New York and Washington, D.C. Flying times are about 5 hours from the US West Coast, 1 to 3 hours from the Midwest, 3 to 5 hours from the Caribbean, and 7 to 10 hours from Europe.

Philadelphia is a hub for **American Airlines** and **Frontier Airlines**. It is also served by many other airlines, including **Air Canada**, **Spirit Airlines**, **British Airways**, **Delta Airlines**, **Southwest Airlines**, **Lufthansa**, and **United Airlines**.

Philadelphia International Airport

Philadelphia's airport is located 7 miles (11 km) south of Center City. Seven terminals accommodate more than 1,200 flights daily to and from 120 cities, with direct flights to 36 destinations in Europe, Canada, and the Caribbean, and connecting flights to Asia.

The International Terminal A-West has 13 gates and 60 ticket counters, over 20 retail shops and restaurants, and currency exchange centers.

Domestic service is located in Terminals A-East through F.

The airport also has more than 100 shops, restaurants, and fast-food stands scattered throughout the terminals, with more than 30 contained in the Philadelphia Marketplace located between Terminals B and C.

Drivers who are picking up arriving passengers can wait in the nearby Cell Phone Lot. Located 1 minute from the passenger pick-up zone, the lot has space for 150 cars and monitors that provide real-time flight arrival information.

On Arrival

Most international flights arrive at Terminal A-West. The modern terminal has plenty of US immigration booths to ensure you get through security checks as soon as possible. There are also food halls, gift shops, and currency exchange desks in the terminal. A staff member fluent in the language of the plane's country of origin meets each plane to answer questions and direct visitors to the Immigration Hall (INS).

Upon arrival at INS, staff will check the customs forms distributed during the flight. It asks questions such as name, birth date, country of citizenship, passport number, and current address. The

Arrivals Hall at Philadelphia International Airport, featuring words from the Declaration of Independence

SEPTA bus ferrying passengers to Philadelphia

customs form asks further questions, including whether you have any vegetables, fruit, or commercial merchandise in your baggage. Foreign visitors (with visas, or visa-free) are no longer required to fill out form I-94.

Non-US citizens are directed to CBP (Customs and Border Protection), where officers check passports and customs, and will also fingerprint and photograph foreign visitors.

Passengers who warrant further inspection are directed to a secondary screening area.

Once cleared, everyone may collect their baggage in the customs area; customs forms must be returned before exiting.

Upon exiting, passengers can proceed to the International Arrivals Hall.

Tickets and Fares

A little research can bring big savings on airfares. Generally, the lowest fares are available 14 to 21 days before the departure date, although reasonably priced tickets can still be bought 7 days in advance. Before booking, check the airlines' policies as changing travel arrangements can incur penalties.

While airlines and travel agents often offer good fares, it is worth examining popular travel Internet sites as well, such as **FareCompare**, **Expedia**, **Priceline**, **Travelocity**, **Kayak**, **cheapflights.com**, and **lastminute.com**. These websites often sell consolidated tickets, which are also available through travel agents.

Several airlines offer special discounts through their websites, and, while many of those offers require departures within a short time frame, the savings can be significant.

Other options include booking with smaller carriers and flying during the off-season, which can also reduce rates.

Philadelphia's high season peaks in the summer, then around Thanksgiving (late November), and the week before Christmas through New Year's Day. Book well in advance if you plan to travel during those times and don't expect to find any discounts.

Transport into the City

SEPTA's Airport Regional Rail Line operates every 30 minutes and connects all terminals with Center City and Amtrak's 30th Street Station, which has rail connections to other points in the city and beyond. Train stations for each terminal lie between the ticketing and baggage claim areas – visitors should look for the relevant signs. Tickets are $8.

SEPTA buses 37 and 108 also ferry passengers into the city for a $2.25 fare. Look for the red-white-and-blue SEPTA bus signs.

For shuttle van services, look for **Centralized Ground Transportation** counters in all baggage claim areas.

Taxis are plentiful at each terminal. They charge a flat rate of $28.50 for a trip into Center City, with an additional fee of $1 per passenger.

Major rental car companies also operate at the airport. They include **AVIS**, **Enterprise**, **Hertz**,

and **National Car Rental**. Most have information phones at all baggage claim areas. There are limo companies specializing in airport transit, too.

Arriving by Car

Several major roadways and interstate highways lead to Philadelphia from surrounding states and major cities in the northeast. Driving times to Philadelphia from some of these cities are as follows: 6 hours from Boston, 2 hours from Baltimore and New York, and 3 hours from Washington, D.C. The resort beach towns of New Jersey are about 1 to 1 hour and 30 minutes away.

The major north–south highway is I-95, which leads into the city center as it parallels the Delaware River. From the east, motorists driving on the New Jersey Turnpike should take Exit 4 and then follow signs to the Benjamin Franklin Bridge or the Walt Whitman Bridge into Philadelphia.

An alternative from the New Jersey Turnpike is taking Exit 6 to connect with the **Pennsylvania Turnpike** that runs north of the city. This is the major highway leading into Philadelphia from the west. Take the Valley Forge exit and then proceed east on I-76, the Schuylkill Expressway.

Interstate 676 cuts through the middle of Center City, connecting I-95 with I-76.

It's a good idea to carry a road atlas map and a city street map for all trips by car.

The Benjamin Franklin Bridge across the Delaware River

Philadelphia's 30th Street Station on Amtrak's Northeast Corridor, the second busiest of the Amtrak system

Arriving by Train

Philadelphia is served by **Amtrak**, the country's passenger rail service, which links the city to the entire nation and to Canada. Most trains serving the city operate along the Northeast Corridor from Boston to Washington, D.C., with stops in Baltimore, New York, and a number of locations in New Jersey, Delaware, Connecticut, and Rhode Island. Amtrak's lines also provide express services such as the premium, high-speed Acela Express that runs from Boston to Washington, D.C.

Tickets can be booked online or by calling Amtrak. It is best to reserve well in advance and be as flexible as possible to ensure good seating and prices. Note that certain discounts may apply, including those for students and senior citizens. If booked in advance, tickets can be picked up on the day of travel at either an Amtrak service window or through kiosks at train stations.

Due to increased security measures, when conductors ask to see tickets, passengers from the US, Canada, and Mexico are required to show photo identification, which may be a driver's license or passport, while other foreign visitors must show a passport.

Passenger cars are comfortable and have snack bar services as well as dining cars on longer routes. Coach class seats for most journeys are reserved, except for shorter trips. Sleeping quarters are available on trains for long-distance destinations; some of the first-class sleeping accommodations have showers and toilets in the compartments.

Philadelphia's main train hub is Amtrak's 30th Street Station – an impressive Beaux-Arts building with a columned façade and large atrium *(see p188–9)*. It is one of the busiest intercity rail stations in the US. Inside are ticket booths for both Amtrak and SEPTA regional rail lines, restaurants, fast-food eateries, gift shops, and newsstands. "Red cap" porters are available to help with luggage.

There are many taxis outside, and if you are carrying baggage, it is best to get a cab for the short hop to a central Philadelphia hotel.

Arriving by Bus

Greyhound Lines, which serves destinations across the US, operates a **bus terminal** in Center City on Filbert Street, between 10th and 11th Streets, one block north of Market Street. Buses arrive daily from New England, New York, and points south and southwest of Philadelphia. Transcontinental buses also arrive from routes through St. Louis and Chicago. Stops include Amtrak's 30th Street Station, and others in north and south Philadelphia.

Compared with other modes of transportation, such as trains or planes, Greyhound's fares are more economical. The company offers wide-ranging discounts, including those for students, senior citizens, children, military personnel, and veterans, as well as cheaper fares if tickets are bought online. While advance purchases might save you money, walk-up tickets are available at reasonable prices.

An Amtrak train – backbone of America's passenger rail system

Greyhound bus, an economical way to reach destinations across America

Greyhound's buses are modern and efficient. Much of its fleet is either equipped with elevators or other equipment to accommodate disabled passengers or those in need of help. Under certain conditions, personal care attendants may travel with disabled passengers at a reduced fare. For more information, call the **Greyhound Customers with Disabilities Travel Assistance Line** at least 48 hours before departure.

Two primary discount bus operators providing express bus services from around the East Coast and Midwest to and from Philadelphia are **BoltBus** and **Megabus**. Both companies run services to and from New York City and Washington, D.C., as well as other cities, and offer amenities such as free Wi-Fi access and plug-ins for electronic equipment. The fares start as low as $1 for a one-way ride.

BoltBus stops across the street from the western entrance to 30th Street Station and tickets for the journey can be purchased in advance online, by phone, or on the bus at the time of departure. Cities that are served by BoltBus include Baltimore, Greenbelt, Boston, and Newark.

Megabus operates in the Northeast hub of Philadelphia and stops at both the Independence Visitor Center and 30th Street Station. In addition to New York City and Washington, D.C., the other major cities in the Northeast served by Megabus include Atlantic City, Boston, Baltimore, Harrisburg, Pittsburgh, Buffalo, Syracuse, and Toronto. Note that Megabus tickets are only available online. Also, be prepared to give the driver your reservation number or show a printout of the confirmation form.

DIRECTORY

Arriving by Air

Philadelphia International Airport
Tel (215) 937-6937,
(800) 745-4283.
W phl.org

Air Canada
Tel (888) 247-2262.

American Airlines
Tel (800) 433-7300.

British Airways
Tel (800) 247-9297.

Delta Airlines
Tel (800) 221-1212.

Frontier Airlines
Tel (800) 452-2022.

Lufthansa
Tel (800) 645–3880.

Southwest Airlines
Tel (800) 435-9792.

Spirit Airlines
Tel (800) 401-2222.

United Airlines
Tel (800) 241-6522.

Tickets and Fares

Cheapflights
W cheapflights.com

Expedia
W expedia.com

FareCompare
W farecompare.com

Kayak
W kayak.com

lastminute.com
W us.lastminute.com

Priceline
W priceline.com

Travelocity
W travelocity.com

Transport into the City

Airport Parking
Tel (215) 683-9842, (215) 683-9825.

AVIS
Tel (800) 331-1212.
W avis.com

Centralized Ground Transportation
Tel (215) 937-6958.

Enterprise
Tel (800) RENT-A-CAR.
W enterprise.com

Hertz
Tel (800) 654-3131.
W hertz.com

National Car Rental
Tel (800) 227-7368.
W nationalcar.com

Arriving by Car

Pennsylvania Department of Transportation
Travel information & interstate road conditions.
Tel (717) 783-5186.
W penndot.gov

Pennsylvania Turnpike Commission
Tel (717) 939-9551.
W paturnpike.com

Arriving by Train

Amtrak
Tel (800) 872-7245.
W amtrak.com

Arriving by Bus

BoltBus
Tel (877) 265-8287.
W boltbus.com

Greyhound Customers with Disabilities Travel Assistance Line
Tel (800) 752-4841.

Greyhound Lines
Tel (800) 229-9424.
W greyhound.com

Greyhound Bus Terminal
1001 Filbert St. **Map** 3 C2.
Tel (215) 931-4000.

Megabus
Tel (877) 462-6342.
W megabus.com

Getting Around Philadelphia

Most of Philadelphia's famous sights are in Independence National Historical Park, also known as "America's most historic square mile." These sights, including Independence Hall and the Liberty Bell, are within walking distance of each other in Old City, and just a short walk from attractions in Society Hill and Penn's Landing. A quick ride or stroll from the historic area brings visitors to Center City and Parkway Museums District. The Philly Phlash bus service runs through the heart of the city during the warmer months, while buses and subways, operated by the Southeastern Pennsylvania Transit Authority (SEPTA), run year-round. Taxis are also an easy and generally affordable option.

Green Travel

Philadelphia is increasingly committed to eco-friendly initiatives, as demonstrated by its Greenworks Philadelphia plan (see p175). SEPTA has one of the largest hybrid bus fleets in the US and has been steadily replacing its diesel-powered buses with hybrid diesel/electric buses. Two car-sharing programs, **ZipCar** and **Enterprise CarShare**, have dozens of locations throughout Philadelphia that help alleviate traffic and emissions. There are also some designated bike lanes, and the core of the city is pedestrian-friendly.

Finding Your Way in Philadelphia

Thanks to the foresight of the city's founder William Penn, getting around central Philadelphia is easy with its simple grid pattern (see p20). Numbered streets begin at the city's easternmost boundary along the Delaware River at Front Street (technically "1st Street") and progress westward in an ascending order. What would be "14th Street" is called Broad Street (or Avenue of the Arts at its southern end). These streets intersect Market Street, the demarcation for whether they're preceded by "north" or "south" in the address. You'll notice that building numbers become larger the more distant they are from Market Street. Many streets running east and west are named after trees, especially in Center City.

Walking

With a compact, user-friendly downtown, the best way to explore Center City, Independence National Historical Park, and nearby sights is on foot.

Mounted on street poles throughout Center City are signs with colorful maps of the downtown area. Community service representatives in teal uniforms are also available throughout Center City to help visitors with directions.

Traveling by Subway

SEPTA operates subway routes throughout Philadelphia, making connections to regional rail lines at the Jefferson, Suburban, and 30th Street stations (see Transport Map at back). Maps are also posted in each station.

There are two lines, the Market-Frankford Line (blue line) and the Broad Street Subway (orange line).

Subway fares are $2.25, and exact change is required. Transfers cost $1 for trips that need more than one transit in the same direction. Independence passes, Family passes, and tokens are available at SEPTA sales offices, newsstands, or the Independence Visitor Center (see p47). An Independence pass is a day ticket that allows travel on all forms of SEPTA transport in zone 1 and costs $12. A Family pass is similar to an Independence pass but is $29 and vaild for a family of up to five. Tokens are $1.80; they are cheaper than purchasing individual tickets.

Traveling by Bus

SEPTA also operates bus routes throughout the city. Fares are the same as for subways (see Traveling by Subway), and schedules are posted on the SEPTA website. Tickets and tokens can be bought on board, from newsstands, or from SEPTA sales booths.

Useful routes include bus 38, which runs from Independence Mall to the Philadelphia Museum of Art and beyond. Bus 21 travels passed Penn's Landing to the University of Pennsylvania. Bus 42 circles neighborhoods in Society Hill along Spruce Street before heading west along Walnut Street to the University of Pennsylvania campus, returning via Chestnut Street.

Seats at the front are prioritized for elderly or disabled riders, who can board via elevators. Buses also have bike racks.

Bicycles

Central Philadelphia has designated bike lanes on Spruce Street heading east and Pine Street heading west. Cycling is also permitted on Benjamin Franklin Parkway, which leads to the Philadelphia Museum of Art. This track continues onto the city's most popular cycling route that runs along Kelly Drive and West River Drive. Bicycles can be rented along here during the summer (see p168).

Children under 12 years old must wear a helmet when riding a bike. Cyclists are required to obey all traffic signals and stay off sidewalks.

Bicycling – an enjoyable way to get out and see some sights

Colorful Philly Phlash tourist bus

RiverLink Ferry

Operating from Memorial Day weekend in May through to the Labor Day weekend in September, **RiverLink Ferry** provides a scenic 12-minute ride across the Delaware River to the Adventure Aquarium and the *Battleship New Jersey*.

The ferry departs every 30 minutes from both the Camden Waterfront and Penn's Landing in Philadelphia. Visitors can buy tickets at dockside terminals outside the Independence Seaport Museum for the outbound trip from Philadelphia.

Landlubbers can cross the river via the Waterfront Connection bus service ($2.25), every 30 minutes from the Independence Visitor Center. Like the RiverLink Ferry, it operates only during the summer months.

Guided Tours

Most city tours, ranging from guided walks to trips by horse-drawn carriage, are centered around the Independence National Historical Park district. The **Big Bus Company** offers tours on double-decker, open-roof buses with hop-ons and hop-offs at 20 sights. The **Constitutional Walking Tour of Philadelphia** provides several historic district guide options, including by audio player. **Ghost Tours of Philadelphia** includes a candlelit walk with haunting tales through Old City and Society Hill. The nighttime **Lights of Liberty Show** winds through Historic Philadelphia with narrators recounting America's struggle for independence. Between

May and October (with limited service in November and December), the **Philly Phlash** bus loops from Penn's Landing to Fairmount Park, making stops at more than 25 attractions. Buses depart every 15 minutes and cost $2 per ride ($5 for an all-day pass). Children four and under and seniors ride free.

Taxis

Taxis can be hailed in the street, though the best place to find one is at a hotel. Several cab companies serve the city, and if you must reserve a taxi for a specific time, call at least 30 minutes in advance *(see Useful Numbers on Sheet map)*. Fares vary, with at least a $2.70 base fare and $2.30 for each additional mile. All taxis accept credit card payments.

Driving in Central Philadelphia

Except during rush hour, driving in town is not particularly difficult. The main Center City thoroughfares, Broad and Market Streets, have two-way traffic, while most other streets have one-way traffic. Vehicles are driven on the right side, and right-hand turns can be made at a red light after a full stop, unless a sign prohibits it. Seatbelts are required by law and using cell phones while driving is prohibited. Violators will be fined. With some exceptions, overseas visitors can drive with a valid driver's license issued by their home country. If the license is not in English, an international driving permit is required.

Parking

Street parking is usually hard to find. It costs $2 per hour, payable by cash, credit card, or SmartCards (available from convenience stores) at green parking kiosks throughout Center City and Independence Mall. Put your receipt inside the windshield and keep track of the time; enforcement officers will write a ticket for expired receipts.

Parking on residential streets is often permitted for nonpermit holders but read the signs carefully. Parking lots are numerous; rates can run from $15 to $30 plus per day.

Traveling Outside Philadelphia

Philadelphia has an excellent regional rail service with SEPTA trains running from Center City to far western suburbs, parts of nearby New Jersey, and northern Delaware. Amtrak provides a daily train service to Lancaster, Harrisburg, and towns west of Philadelphia. New Jersey Transit takes passengers to Atlantic City and other areas along the Jersey shore. However, it is advisable and more practical to rent a car when traveling to remote sights in the Pennsylvania Dutch Country and Gettysburg.

SEPTA train – an ideal way to go beyond Philadelphia

Main Train Stations

Amtrak's **30th Street Station** is a hub for train services along the East Coast with frequent transits to New York, Boston, and Washington, D.C. as well as daily departures to Lancaster, Harrisburg, and towns west of Philadelphia. "Red cap" staff offer free baggage assistance, but be sure to accept assistance only from uniformed staff, and request a claim ticket for each bag. Other facilities include free

Interior of 30th Street Station, one of the biggest in Pennsylvania

Wi-Fi and a selection of shops. **Suburban Station** at 16th Street in Center City is a central point for regional rail service with connections to SEPTA's Market-Frankford Line. Here, dozens of underground shops offer a variety of wares.

Jefferson Station, is adjacent to the Fashion Outlets Philadelphia and also intersects with the Market-Frankford Line.

Regional Rail Service

SEPTA provides outstanding rail services to many of Philadelphia's outermost suburbs to the north, south, and west of the city. Trips to the outermost stops sometimes take over an hour.

SEPTA's Airport Line connects the city and outer suburbs with Philadelphia International Airport (see p182). The Wilmington–Newark Line travels south, with a stop in Wilmington, Delaware. The Paoli–Throndale Line travels west and north from Center City, with Doylestown (see p127) as the last stop. The Manayunk–Norristown Line runs through Manayunk (see pp99), while the

Chestnut Hill East and Chestnut Hill West Lines end their routes in Chestnut Hill, stopping along the way in Germantown (see p98).

Trains are comfortable, air-conditioned, and have lots of seats. However, they fill up quickly during the morning and afternoon rush hour.

Tickets can be purchased at the three Center City stations, at suburban stations, and on board.

Services to New Jersey

New Jersey is a short drive or train ride from Center City, Philadelphia. In summer the best way to reach the Camden Waterfront, just across the Delaware River from Penn's Landing, is by RiverLink Ferry (see p187). You can also take the **PATCO** High Speedline over the Benjamin Franklin Bridge and get off at the Broadway stop for waterfront attractions. Collingswood and Westmont stops are also well placed for exploration on foot.

To reach New Jersey beach resort towns, you can take a 1 hour and 30 minute journey on **New Jersey Transit's Atlantic City Rail Line** departing from 30th Street Station.

Services to Pennsylvania Dutch Country and Gettysburg

Renting a car is the best way to explore most of the towns and villages that lie beyond Philadelphia, but it is also possible to take organized bus tours or public transportation.

Amtrak provides train services from Philadelphia's bustling 30th Street Station to towns west of Philadelphia, including Lancaster and Harrisburg.

In Lancaster, the **Red Rose Transit Authority (RRTA)** operates bus schedules in the city and for surrounding towns, including Pennsylvania Dutch communities. These buses have busy timetables and tend to have limited services to the outlying smaller communities, including Paradise, Lititz,

Toll booths on Interstate 76, Philadelphia

Intercourse, Bird-in-Hand, and Ephrata. Buses to these areas usually stop after the afternoon rush hour. On weekends, service is reduced.

To reach Gettysburg, you will need to rent a car, as no public transport travels there.

Roads and Tolls

Turnpikes are interstate highways that charge tolls. The Pennsylvania Turnpike and the New Jersey Turnpike both require motorists to pick up a toll ticket before entering the highway, and then pay the toll when exiting.

The Pennsylvania Turnpike (I-76/276) is the fastest route from Philadelphia to Harrisburg, and a one-way toll costs approximately $15. Although not an interstate, the Atlantic City Expressway is also a toll road. Some expressways have both numbers and names, such as the Vine Street Expressway (I-676/30).

Some toll booths accept only cash or exact change while others use an electronic system known as "E-Z Pass" which scans vehicles and deducts the toll from the driver's account.

Car Rentals

To rent a car, US and Canadian residents must have a valid driver's license, while foreign visitors need an international driver's license and valid passport. The minimum rental age is usually 25, and a major credit card in your name is required.

Personal auto insurance often covers rental cars, but check the limitations of coverage with your insurance company. If

you're not covered, it is a good idea to purchase liability and collision insurance.

ZipCar *(see p186)* offers by-the-hour car rental. Fees include a modest membership, and hourly rates can start from $7 per hour. A valid driver's license is required and, depending on country of origin, additional documentation might be requested.

Gasoline

Most gas stations in Philadelphia have self-service pumps. However, in New Jersey, state law mandates that attendants pump the gas. Rented cars should be returned with a full tank to avoid extra charges.

Rules of the Road

The speed limit on interstates is usually 65 mph (105 km/h), and 55 mph (88 km/h) on highways in and around Philadelphia. City streets usually have a 25 to 35 mph (40 to 56 km/h) limit. It's wise to heed speed limits, since a speeding ticket can result in a hefty fine. In Philadelphia it is illegal to drive while talking on a cell phone.

Unless otherwise noted by a sign, making a right turn is permitted at a red light. Watch for pedestrians, since they have the right of way.

Drive carefully during bad weather, as semi-trucks often spew mist during heavy rainstorms, resulting in poor visibility. Also, bridges and overpasses can become ice-slicked during winter.

Wearing a seatbelt is required by law. It is also a good idea to keep all doors locked, stay on

main roads, avoid unfamiliar neighborhoods, and abstain from drinking alcohol. Be aware that drink-driving offenses are vigorously prosecuted in the US.

Members of affiliated international automobile clubs are entitled to take advantage of reciprocal benefits offered by the **American Automobile Association** (AAA).

DIRECTORY

Main Train Stations

30th Street Station
2955 Market St.
Map 1 B3.
Tel (800) 872-7433.
W amtrak.com

Jefferson Station
1170 Market St. & 12th Sts.
Map 1 B3.
Tel (215) 580-6500,
(215) 580-7428.

Suburban Station
34 N 16th St & JFK Blvd.
Map 2 E4.
Tel (215) 580-5739.

Services to New Jersey

Atlantic City Rail Line
Tel (800) 772-2287.

New Jersey Transit
Tel (800) 772-2287.
W njtransit.com

PATCO
Tel (856) 772-6900.
W ridepatco.org

Services to Pennsylvania Dutch Country and Gettysburg

Red Rose Transit Authority (RRTA)
45 Erick Rd., Lancaster
(Lancaster County).
Tel (717) 397-4246.
W redrosetransit.com

Rules of the Road

American Automobile Association
24-hour emergency road service.
Tel (800) 763-9900.
W aaa.com

PHILADELPHIA STREET FINDER

Map references given in this guide for sights, hotels, restaurants, shops, and entertainment venues refer to the Street Finder maps on the following pages *(see How the Map References Work)*. Map references are also given for Philadelphia's hotels *(see pp136–9)* and restaurants *(see pp143–53)*. A complete index of the street names and places of interest marked on the maps can be found on the following pages. The map below shows the area of Philadelphia covered by the four Street Finder maps. This includes the sightseeing areas (which are color-coded) as well as the rest of central Philadelphia. The symbols used to represent sights and useful information on the Street Finder maps are listed in the key below.

Key

▨	Major sight
▨	Place of interest
▢	Other building
Ⓡ	SEPTA regional rail station
Ⓟ	PATCO rail station
Ⓢ	SEPTA subway stop
🚋	SEPTA trolley stop
🚌	Greyhound bus terminal
⛴	Ferry boarding point
🅸	Visitor information
➕	Hospital
🏛	Police station
✝	Church
✡	Synagogue
☪	Mosque
═	Railroad line
═	Expressway
	Pedestrianized street

Scale of Map Pages 1–4

0 meters   250
0 yards   250

0 meters   500
0 yards   500

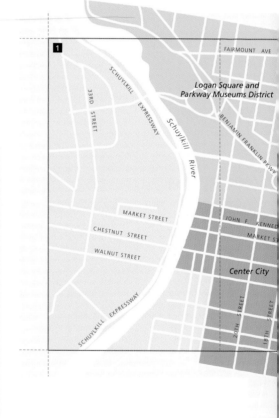

FAIRMOUNT AVE

Logan Square and Parkway Museums District

33RD STREET

SCHUYLKILL EXPRESSWAY

Schuylkill River

BENJAMIN FRANKLIN PKWY

MARKET STREET

CHESTNUT STREET

WALNUT STREET

JOHN F. KENNEDY

MARKET ST

Center City

SCHUYLKILL EXPRESSWAY

20TH STREET

18TH STREET

How the Map References Work

The **first figure** tells you which Street Finder map to turn to.

❽ The Oval

Benjamin Franklin Parkway. **Map 1** C1
🚉 30th St Station. 🚇 Spring Garden.
🚌 38, Philly Phlash.

The **letters and numbers** form the map coordinates. Letters are along the top of the map, while numbers are along the sides.

Street Finder Index

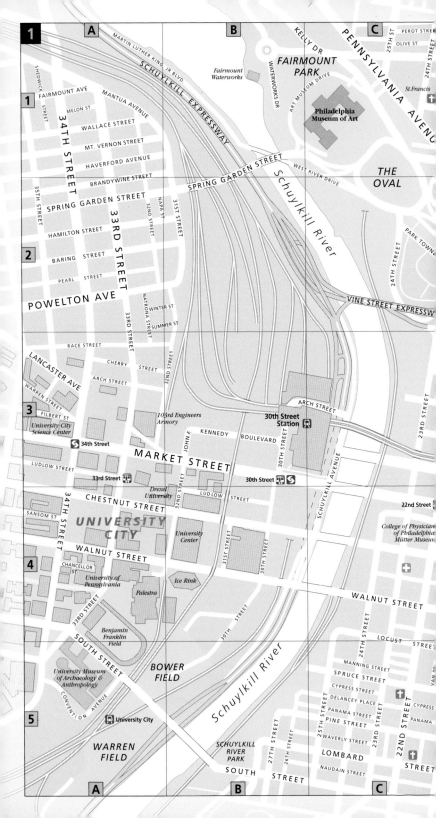

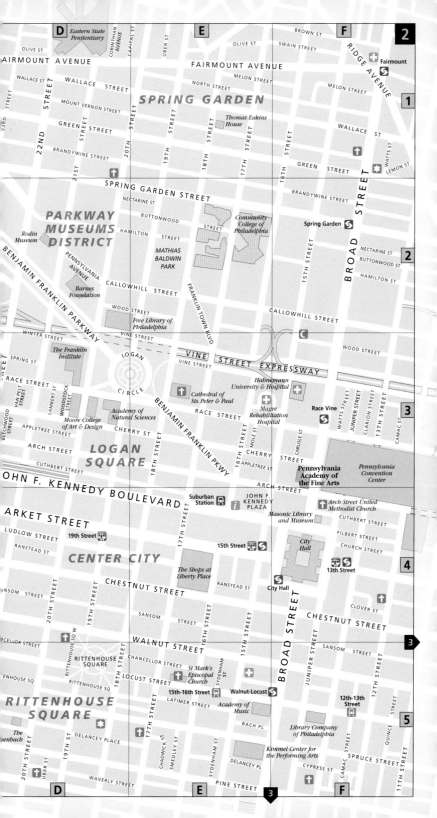

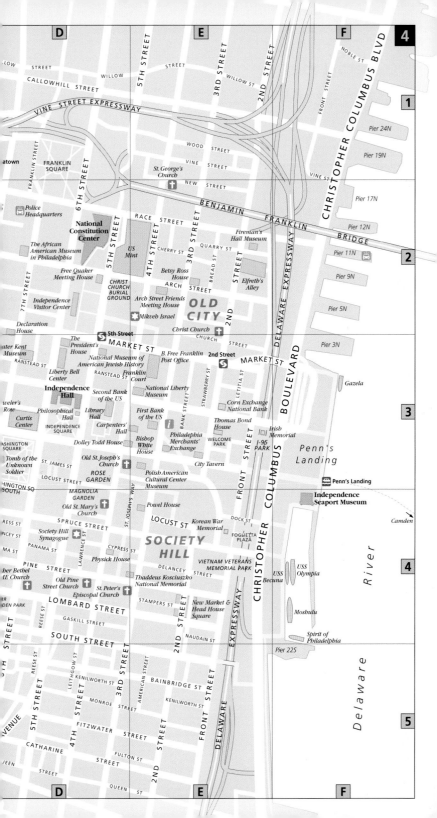

4

D · E · F

1

5TH STREET
WILLOW STREET
3RD STREET
WILLOW ST
2ND STREET
FRONT STREET
CHRISTOPHER COLUMBUS BLVD
NOBLE ST

LOW STREET
CALLOWHILL STREET

VINE STREET EXPRESSWAY

Pier 24N
Pier 19N

WOOD STREET
VINE STREET

atown
FRANKLIN STREET
FRANKLIN SQUARE
6TH STREET
St. George's Church ✝
NEW STREET

Pier 17N

BENJAMIN FRANKLIN BRIDGE

Pier 12N

2

Police Headquarters 🅿

National Constitution Center
The African American Museum in Philadelphia
US Mint
Free Quaker Meeting House
RACE STREET
4TH STREET
CHERRY ST
3RD STREET
QUARRY ST
Fireman's Hall Museum
BREAD ST
Elfreth's Alley

Pier 11N
DELAWARE EXPRESSWAY
Pier 9N

7TH STREET
Independence Visitor Center
5TH STREET
Betsy Ross House
CHRIST CHURCH BURIAL GROUND
ARCH STREET
2ND STREET
Arch Street Friends Meeting House
Pier 5N

Declaration House
✡ Mikveh Israel
OLD CITY
Christ Church ✝
CHURCH STREET
Pier 3N

water Kent Museum
◼ 5th Street
MARKET ST
STREET
MARKET ST

RANSTEAD ST
The President's House
National Museum of American Jewish History
B. Free Franklin Post Office
◼ 2nd Street
Gazela

3

weler's Row
Liberty Bell Center
RANSTEAD ST
Franklin Court
National Liberty Museum
STRAWBERRY STREET
BANK STREET
LETITIA ST
Corn Exchange National Bank
BOULEVARD

Independence Hall
Second Bank of the US
First Bank of the US
Thomas Bond House
Irish Memorial
Penn's Landing

ASHINGTON SQUARE
Curtis Center
Philosophical Hall
Library Hall
Carpenters' Hall
ℹ
Bishop White House
Philadelphia Merchants' Exchange
WELCOME PARK
I-96

Tomb of the Unknown Soldier
Dolley Todd House
ST. JAMES ST
Old St. Joseph's Church ✝
City Tavern
FRONT STREET

HINGTON SQ SOUTH
LOCUST STREET
ROSE GARDEN
Polish American Cultural Center Museum
Penn's Landing 🚢

MAGNOLIA GARDEN
Old St. Mary's Church ✝
Powel House
Independence Seaport Museum

ST. JOSEPH'S WAY
LOCUST ST
Korean War Memorial
Camden

RESS ST
NCEY ST
SPRUCE STREET
Society Hill Synagogue ✡
CYPRESS ST
DOCK ST
FOGLIETTA PLAZA

MA ST
Physick House
SOCIETY HILL
VIETNAM VETERANS MEMORIAL PARK
USS Becuna
USS Olympia

River

4

ber Bethel IE Church ✝
PINE STREET
LAWRENCE STREET
Old Pine Street Church ✝
St. Peter's Episcopal Church ✝
DELANCEY STREET
Mosbulu

DEN PARK
Thaddeus Kosciuszko National Memorial
CHRISTOPHER COLUMBUS

LOMBARD STREET
STAMPERS ST
New Market & Head House Square
Spirit of Philadelphia

GASKILL STREET
2ND STREET
NAUDAIN ST
EXPRESSWAY
Pier 22S

SOUTH STREET

STREET
REESE ST
3RD STREET
AMERICAN STREET
FRONT STREET

STREET
LEITHGOW ST
KENILWORTH ST
BAINBRIDGE ST
DELAWARE
Delaware

AVENUE
5TH STREET
4TH STREET
MONROE STREET
KENILWORTH ST

5

FITZWATER STREET

CATHARINE STREET
FULTON ST
2ND STREET
QUEEN ST

D · E · F

General Index

Acknowledgments

Main Contributor
Richard Varr spent a part of his childhood in Philadelphia and returned to the area in 1999. A former television and newspaper reporter, he now writes for newspapers, magazines, and websites, including Porthole Cruise Magazine and onboard publications of several cruise lines.

Factchecker
Scott Walker

Proofreader
Word-by-Word

Indexer
Jyoti Dhar

DK London
Publisher Douglas Amrine
Publishing Manager Lucinda Cooke
Managing Art Editor Kate Poole
Senior Designer Tessa Bindloss
Senior Cartographic Editor Casper Morris
Senior DTP Designer Jason Little
Dk Picture Library Martin Copeland, Romaine Werblow
Production Controller Louise Daly

Revisions and Relaunch Team
Ashwin Adimari, Beverley Ager, Emma Anacootee, Shruti Bahl, Stuti Tiwari Bhatia, Julie Bond, Andi Coyle, Dipika Dasgupta, Nick Edwards, Emer FitzGerald, Anna Freiberger, Rhiannon Furbear, Camilla Gersh, Vinod Harish, Phil Hunt, Sumita Khatwani, Hayley Maher, Sonal Modha, Helen Peters, Marianne Petrou, Jeanette Pierce, Arun Pottirayil, Rada Radojicic, Ellen Root, Sands Publishing Solutions, Azeem A. Siddiqui, Beverly Smart, Jeanette Tallant, Rachel Thompson, Jeffrey Towne, Helen Townsend, Nikky Twyman, Vinita Venugopal, Ajay Verma, Ros Walford, Tanveer Zaidi.

Additional Photography
Shaen Adey, Paul Bricknell, Geoff Dann, Steve Gorton, Dave King, Andrew Leyerle, Tim Mann,Ray Moller, Stephen Oliver, Ian O'Leary, William Reavell, Tim Ridley, Clive Streeter, Scott Suchman, Matthew Ward,Jerry Young.

Dorling Kindersley would like to thank the following people whose contributions and assistance have made the preparation of this book possible.

Cartography
Back Endpaper reproduced with permission from SEPTA.

Special Assistance
The Barnes Foundation: Henry Butler; Independence National Historical Park: Superintendent; Gettysburg Convention & Visitors Bureau: Stacey Fox; Greater Philadelphia Tourism Marketing Corporation: Paula Butler, Kristen Ciappa, Meryl Levitz, Cara Schneider, Donna Schorr; National Liberty Museum: Amanda Hall; Pennsylvania Convention Center Authority: Patti Spaniak; Pennsylvania Dutch Convention & Visitors Bureau: Cara O'Donnell; Philadelphia Academy of the Fine Arts: Laura Blumenthal, Gene Castellano, Robert Cozzolino, Barbara Katus,Michelle McCaffrey; Philadelphia Convention & Visitors Bureau: Ellen Kornfield, Marissa Phillip; Philadelphia Museum of Art: Holly Frisbee, Rachel Udell; Philadelphia Water Department: Ed Grusheski; Rodin Museum: John Zarobell.

Photography Permissions
Dorling Kindersley would like to thank the following for their assistance and permission to photograph at their establishments:

Academy of Natural Sciences, Atwater Kent Museum, Bishop White House, City Tavern, College of Physicians of Philadelphia/Mütter Museum, Civil War & Underground Railroad Museum of Philadelphia, Eastern State Penitentiary, Ebenezer Maxwell House, Confederate Memorial Hall, New Orleans, Gettysburg National Military Park Visitor Center and Cyclorama Center, Independence Hall, Independence Seaport Museum, Landis Valley Museum, National Constitutional Center, Pennyslvania Academy of the Fine Arts, People's Place Quilt Museum, Reading Terminal Market as well as all the state and national parks, churches, hotels, restaurants, shops, museums, galleries, and other sights too numerous to thank individually.

Picture Credits
a – above; b – below/bottom; c – center; f – far; l – left; r – right; t – top

Works of art have been reproduced with the permission of the following copyright holders:

© ARS, NY and DACS, London 2011 86b, *Irish Memorial* by Glenna Goodacre 106cr, *Frank Rizzo* by Diane Keller 101br, *Horticulture Mural* by David McShane 91bc, *L'Ouverture* by Ulrick Jean Pierre 53tc, Cover of *The Saturday Evening Post* (June 28, 1958) by Norman Rockwell 29ca.

The publishers would like to thank the following individuals, companies, and picture libraries for their kind permission to reproduce their photographs:

4Corners: SIME / Anna Serrano 132-133.
Alamy Images: Susan Candelario 172-173; Jeff Greenberg 117bc; Sophie James 104; Andre Jenny 102br; Russell Kord 38-39; LOOK Die Bildagentur der Fotografen GmbH 96; Dennis MacDonald 142cla; Mira 183br; Donald Nausbaum 58; SuperStock / RGB Ventures 85br; vario images GmbH & Co. KG/Hady Khandani 177cl. **Alamy Stock Photo:** Granger Historical Picture Archive 155tc. **Alma de Cuba:** Courtesy of Starr Restaurants 147tr.
Photograph ©2010 reproduced with the Permisson of **The Barnes Foundation:** 27cra, Tom Crane 28cb, 88clb, 88tr, 89bc, 89tl. **Bridgeman Art Library:** © The Barnes Foundation, Merion, Pennsylvania, USA *Postman* 1889 (oil on canvas) by Vincent van Gogh (1853–90) 88tr; *Gardanne* 1885–86 (oil on canvas) by Paul Cezanne (1839–1906) 88cl; *After the Concert* 1877 (oil on canvas) by Pierre-Auguste Renoir (1841–1919) 89cra; *Card Players and Girl* 1890–92 (oil on canvas) by Paul Cezanne (1839–1906) 89crb.
Center City District: 187tl; Cliveden (A National Trust Property): 23cra, 109br. Chris's Jazz Café: 166bl; **Char's at Tracy Mansion:** 152bc; **City Tavern Restaurant:** Concepts By Staib, ltd. 143bc; **Corbis:**17tl, 20t, 22tr, 23cr, 24crb, 25tc, 85cra; The Barnes Foundation, Merion Station, Pennsylvania 85c; Dave Bartuff 42tr; Bettmann 8–9, 19ca, 19bl, 21ca, 21crb, 21bc, 23tl, 23br, 24t, 24bl, 24bc, 25bl, 42cla, 55br; Rose Hartman 63br; Kelly-Mooney Photography 129crb; Bob Krist 188bl; Loop Images / John Greim 149bl; William

Manning 82; Francis G. Mayer 18, 22-3c, 65br, Mary Ann McDonald 117cb; Richard T. Nowitz 26; Charles O'Rear 48bl; Philadelphia Museum of Art: *Peaceable Kingdom* by Edward Hicks (1780–1849) 20crb, 92tr, *Sunflowers* by Vincent van Gogh (1853–90) 92cl, *Dormition of the Virgin* (1427) by Fra Angelico (1387-1455) 94cl, *Jester Vase* (1894) by Marc-Louis-Emmanuel Solon (1835-1913) Joseph E. Temple Fund 94bc, *The Staircase Group* (1795) by Charles Willson Peale (1741-1827) The George W. Elkins Collection 94br; 95tl, *Bird Tree* (1800–1830) Bequest of Lisa Norris Elkins (Mrs. William M. Elkins) 95c, *Gala Ensemble* Italy (late 19th to early 20th century) Bequest of Helen P. McMullen 95bc; PictureNet 115 tr; Poodles-Rock 22cl, 22br; Bill Ross 129t; Joseph Sohm: Visions of America 23crb, 44bl, 50c; Joseph Sohm-ChromoSohm Inc. 45cla. **CORBIS SABA:** CVS/pharmacy: 176br. **Cornerstone Bed & Breakfast:** Jumping Rocks 138tl. **Dreamstime.com:** Americanspirit 12tc, 170cla; Aviahuismanphotography 5tr; Jon Bilous 112-113; Dibrova 2-3; Cezary Dulniak 169tr; F11photo 12br; Richard Guinon 125br; Jhernan124 4tc; Robert Mullan 75tl; David M. Sacerdote 4crb. **Fairmount Waterworks & Interpretive Center:** 171bl. **Fleischman gerber and associates:** Esto/Peter Aaron 79 br. **The Food Trust:** 175bc; **Free Library of Philadelphia:** 20bl, 21br, 23bc. **Getty Images:** Bruce Yuanyue Bi 13br; Gilbert Carrasquillo 137tr; Tom Gralish 70; John Greim 40; UniversalImagesGroup 13tr; Alex Wong 25crb. **Gettysburg Convention & Visitors Bureau:** Paul Witt 125cl. **Greater Philadelphia Tourism Marketing Corporation:** R.Kennedy 46cra; **Greyhound Lines, Inc.:** 185tl. **ING Direct – Philadelphia Café:** 180bl. **Jim's Steaks:** 145br. **Kling House Restaurant:** 153tr. **Lacroix at the Rittenhouse:** 148tl. **Landis Valley Museum:** Cindy Kirby-Reedy 119tc. **Leonardo media ltd.:** 135tl. **Morris House Hotel:** 136br. **National Constitution Center:** 50tr. **National Museum of American Jewish History:** 29cr, 43tc. **La Peg:** Peggy Woolse 144tl. **Pennsylvania Academy of the Fine Arts:** Images courtesy of Pennsylvania Academy of the Fine Arts 76tl, 77tc. 29tl, 76tr, 77cra, 77crb, *The Fox Hunt* by Winslow Homer Oil on canvas. 38 x 68 1/2 inches. Accession no: 1894.4. Joseph E. Temple Fund 76br. **Pennsylvania Dutch Convention & Visitors Bureau:** 36cla, 114bl, 120br; K. Baum 115bl. **The Pennsylvania Turnpike Commission:** 189tl. **Percy Street Barbeque:** 141tl. **Philadelphia Convention & Visitors Bureau:** ©Alma de Cuba PR 166c; ©Barnes Foundation 27cra; ©Bob Krist 16tr; ©Cuba Libre Restaurant & Rum Bar/Mimi Janosy 140br; Melvin Epps 60cl; © Independence Seaport Museum/Rusty Kennedy 67cr; ©The Inn at the Union League of Philadelphia 72tr; ©National Constitution Center/Scott Frances Ltd. 27cb, 42cl, 50bl, 51tc, 51cr; Jim McWilliams 34cla, 36br, 168bl, 170bl, 184t; ©Pennyslavania Ballet/Steve Belkowitz 164c; ©Pennyslavania Horticultural Society/Rob Ikeler 34br; Jon Perlmutter 32cl; ©Philadelphia International Airport/Richard McMullin 184bl; ©Philadelphia Office of the City Representative 35cra; ©Philadelphia Orchestra/Eric Sellen 162br; ©The Plaza and The Court at King of Prussia 155bl; ©Ritz Carlton, Philadelphia 134bl; Edward Savaria Jr. 27bl, 37cla, 37br, 48c, 72cl, 72bl, 73crb, 103b, 140cl, 158tr, 160cl, 163tl; Anthony Sinagoga 43crb, 46cl, 158bl. Philadelphia Museum of Art, Pennsylvania: 93cra, Portrait of Dr. Samuel D. Gross (The Gross Clinic) (1875) by Thomas Eakins. Gift of the Alumni Association to Jefferson Medical College in 1878 and purchased by the Pennsylvania Academy of the Fine Arts and The Philadelphia Museum of Art in 2007 with the generous support of some 3,600 donors 93bl; Noah's Ark (1846) by Edward Hicks, Bequest of Lisa Norris Elkins, 1950 93crb. **Philadelphia Police Department Office of Media Relations:** 177cla, 177tl. **Philadelphia Record Exchange:** 161tc. **Photolibrary:** Mark & Audrey Gibson 186br. **PNC Financial Services Group:** 178cla; **Philly Beer Week:** Kristine Kennedy 35bc. **Pod:** 151br **Pure:** 167tr. **Queen Victoria:** Jumping Rocks Photography 139br. **Spasso Italian Grill:** 141br. **STA Travel Group:** 175clb. **Standard Tap:** George Widman for GPTMC 150tr. **The Inn at Westwynd Farm:** 135bl. **Richard Varr:** 45cr. **White Dog Café:** 150bl. **Wyk House and Garden:** 109tl. **Zahav:** 146bl. **Front endpaper:** Alamy Images: LOOK Die Bildagentur der Fotografen GmbH tl(R); Donald Nausbaum tr(R). **Corbis:** William Manning tr(L). Dreamstime.com: Jon Bilous cl(L). **Getty Images:** Tom Gralish bl(L); John Greim ca(R).

Cover images: Front and Spine - Alamy Stock Photo: incamerstock. Back - Dreamstime.com: Mandritoiu.

Map Cover - Alamy Stock Photo: incamerastock.

All other images © Dorling Kindersley. For more information see www.dkimages.com

SEPTA Regional Rail & Rail Transit

Amtrak to:
New York
Boston

NJ Transit to:
New York
New Jersey Points

Trenton — Trenton Transit Center

River Line to Camden

West Trenton

Delaware River

Levittown
Bristol
Croydon
Eddington
Cornwells Heights

Torresdale
Holmesburg Jct
Tacony
Bridesburg

Frankford Trans. Ctr.

Arrott Trans. Ctr.
Church
Erie-Torresdale

Tioga

Fox Chase
Ryers
Cheltenham
Lawndale
Olney

Yardley
Woodbourne
Langhorne
Neshaminy Falls
Trevose
Somerton
Forest Hills
Philmont
Bethayres
Meadowbrook
Rydal
Noble

Elkins Park
Melrose Park
Fern Rock T.C.

Wyoming
Hunting Park
Erie
Allegheny

Doylestown

Delaware Valley University
New Britain
Chalfont
Link Belt
Colmar
Fortuna
9th Street
Lansdale

Warminster

Hatboro
Willow Grove
Crestmont
Roslyn
Ardsley

Glenside
Jenkintown-Wyncote

Fern Rock Trans. Ctr.

Olney T.C.
Logan

Pennbrook
North Wales
Gwynedd Valley
Penllyn
Ambler
Fort Washington
Oreland
North Hills

Washington Lane
Sedgwick
Stenton
Germantown
Wister

Wayne Jct.

N. Phila (CHW)

Chestnut Hill East

Gravers
Wyndmoor
Mt Airy

Highland
St. Martins
Allen Lane
Upsal
Carpenter
Tulpehocken
Chelten Ave
Queen Lane

Chestnut Hill West

Norristown
(Elm St)

Norristown Trans. Ctr.

Main St
Norristown

Norristown Trans. Ctr.

Conshohocken
Spring Mill
Miquon
Ivy Ridge
Manayunk
Wissahickon
East Falls

Schuylkill Riv

Bridgeport
DeKalb St
Hughes Park
Gulph Mills
Matsonford
County Line
Villanova

Thorndale

Downingtown
Whitford
Exton
Malvern

Paoli
Daylesford
Berwyn
Devon
Strafford
Wayne
St. Davids
Radnor

Amtrak to:
Harrisburg
Pittsburgh